Contents

FOREWORD

Few historical events drew the attention among international observers and social scientists like "Chavismo" in Venezuela. Some reasons that explain this boom become relevant because, precisely after the cold war, when Francis Fukujana proclaimed the advent of world democracy, the appearance of antidemocratic regimes contradicted this thesis (The Hegelian analysis). Socialism of the twenty-first century—one of the most champions of this trend was Hugo Chavez—signified for many people on the left, the resurrection of socialism under new conditions, forms, and above all under a new period.

Fukujana's utopia needs to be relegated to the waiting room. Kant's idea of the emergence of a republican order, where there would be no wars and contradictions, is very far from being fulfilled. Democracy is being questioned and challenged by the enemies of socialism of the twenty-first century; it emerged as a new antidemocratic alternative of our times. The leader of this process was Hugo Chavez, the commander that, according to his admirers, was able to establish a perfect alliance between the theoretical legacy of Bolivar and the scientific socialism of Marx. This absurd combination was only the simple surface of a more profound process; this is one of the merits of authors like Ari Chaplin, who in his book, *Chavez's Legacy: The Transformation from Democracy to a Mafia State*, demonstrated the radical, antidemocratic character of Chavism.

Relying on the excellent designation of a mafia state, put forward by Moises Naim, Chaplin demonstrated, combining historical narration with sociological analysis, the ideological facade of Chavism. The process of destroying the values and political institutions, that in spite of some deficiencies, were part of preceding governments in Venezuela, is being concealed. In other words, according to Chaplin, the fundamental contradiction in Venezuela is not between democracy and totalitarianism, but between democracy and the mafia state.

In Central and Eastern Europe, the construction of mafia states was the fate of diverse countries in the post-communist period. In Latin America, the ALBA countries adopted characteristics of mafia states inspired by the Venezuelan model.

What the mafia states share in common is the appearance of a "new state class," the "Bolibourgeisie," is similar to the emergence of a similar strata in the Soviet Union. However, there are important differences between these groups. While in the Soviet Union the construction of socialism was based on force ("dictatorship of the proletariat"), the mafia states lack a coherent ideological line.

Chavez's Venezuela, Ortega's Nicaragua, and Correa's Ecuador represent a type of domination based on "ad hoc" ideology, which unites vernacular ideas of the post-colonial Latin America traditions: such as charismatic caudillo, militarism , anti-Western bias, and nationalism. Under Chavism in Venezuela the above characteristics appear to be more clearly manifested than in the other countries mentioned. The reason is that Chavism has in its possession a principal mode of production—oil.

Venezuela under Chavez destroyed national industries and social organizations, such as trade unions. Chavism was converted into a national religion, a corrupt state party, or to put it in other words a mafia organization supported by the oil income. Chavism, to some extent, is a political sub product of oil.

The strong opposition that emerged in Venezuela could not destroy Chavez's mafia state. Chavez was able to establish nearly total control of the mass media and the judicial branch which functioned to prosecute and terrorize those people that were viewed by the mafia as enemies.

Ari Chaplin's book, without any doubt, is an important theoretical contribution that allows us to better understand, not only the morphology of Chavism, but furthermore the reasons why regimes that adopted electoral democratic forms reproduce military dictatorial political systems similar to the communist world.

In countries with democratic traditions, such as Venezuela, the mafia came to power lacking a historical project and a clear ideology and are condemned to survive as long as the leader is in power. While after the death of Stalin, "bureaucratic socialism" appeared in the Soviet orbit, there does not exist the possibility for the emergence of a "bureaucratic Chavism." On the contrary, the death of the caudillo brought into the existence mafia sects whose main objective is not to administer "Chavez's legacy," but rather to distribute the country's loot. Nothing more.

One question remains open in Chaplin's book: Are the mafia states of our times the last residue of totalitarism of the twentieth century, or are we dealing with a new political formation, unprecedented historically, destined to reproduce and multiply? It is too early to give a definite answer to this question.

However, in any case, the comprehension of the historical narration of the internal structure and the logic behind the mafia states of the twenty-first century, Ari Chaplin's book is an indispensable tool; a book that surpasses its academic value, acquiring political connotations of enormous importance for all who worry about the danger of new contradictions represented by the emergence of mafia states, completely opposed to the ascending march of the universal democratic process.

FERNANDO MIRES
Author of Democracy and Barbarism, *2009, and numerous*
other books and articles.

Preface

As a young child in Romania, I witnessed firsthand the horror of communism when all my parents' possessions were confiscated by the new government. My friend Frank Barrio shared a similar experience when Fidel Castro took power in Cuba.

Chávez's regime in Venezuela attempted to revise communism as it had been applied in the Soviet Union. Following the Italian Marxist scholar, Antonio Gramsci, an attempt was made to gradually transform the country's economic system into communism. However, this change does not erase the shortcomings of communism. Venezuela has suffered from the same problems as the Communist Soviet Union did.

While my first book, *Terror: The New Theater of War* (www.univpress. com), dealt with the imperilment that the international community faces as a result of increase employment of terrorism; my current book emphasizes another important challenge initiated by the enemies of capitalism. It is my intention to demonstrate that economic development and the reduction of poverty can only occur by the employment of free market policies. Economies dominated by governments will further deteriorate the country's economy.

The events of 9/11 demonstrated that terrorism has become the primary enemy of United States and the Western countries. Chávez's involvement in international terrorism and drug trafficking should become a major concern for the United States.

This book is intended not only for people interested in Latin America, but for people with a general interested in current affairs, economics, and foreign affairs. It should be of particular interest to students, who mainly are exposed to different sets of ideas.

Introduction

The collapse of the Soviet Union and its satellites produced important changes in the international system. Francis Fukuyama predicted that the cessation of the Cold War would foster the "end of mankind's ideological evolution and the universalization of democracy as the final form of human government."[1] However, the examples of Chávez's Venezuela, the rise of Islamic states (Iran and Turkey) and the ideology of Islamic Fundamentalism have demonstrated the incorrectness of Fukuyama's ideas.

The death of President Chávez on March 5, 2013 offers us the opportunity to evaluate the Venezuelan leader era. An important lesson from the 14 years of Chávez's reign is that one needs to beware of charismatic demagogues who follow socialist policies at home and revolution abroad.[2] Chávez's body will be embalmed similar to Lenin and Mao. Maduro who was sworn as president on March 8, 2013, before the National Assembly, asserted that the purpose of this act is that "people can have him forever in a glass urn."[3] However, due to technical problems Maduro's plan could not be implemented. The cult of personality is a common characteristic of authoritarian/totalitarian regimes.

Marx's ideas, as implemented in the Soviet Union, demonstrated an inability to achieve positive change. Several scholars believed that this failure should be interpreted as a negation of Marxism, but others claim that it was caused by inability of the Soviet Union to implement Marx's ideas correctly. There were also Marxist scholars who found fault in Marx's writings and claimed that they needed to be revised.[4]

The Italian Marxist scholar Antonio Gramsci, Lenin's contemporary, believed that a Communist revolution in the Soviet Union could not be imitated in Europe.[5] Gramsci was arrested by Mussolini's guards and wrote his political philosophy while in jail. He claimed that in order for a Communist revolution to succeed, a long period of education was necessary in order to transform the prevailing consciousness and values of the population. This would be a long process that would take more than one generation; but it was the only way of introducing Communism to a country.

The Venezuelan president gradually transformed the country's democratic institutions into an authoritarian/totalitarian political system.

Corruption, the mismanagement of funds, especially from oil revenues, and the huge expenses required to export his ideology forced Chávez's regime to seek new sources of income. Enabling the drug cartels and organized crime to operate freely in Venezuela brought billions of dollars to the country. These funds were distributed to those persons close to the Venezuelan president. In this respect Moisés Naim's reference to Venezuela as a mafia state is an important contribution to understanding the country's political evolution.[6] Naim's thesis is confirmed by Otto Reich, a former United States ambassador to Venezuela, who declared in March 2013 that Chavistas functionaries are Mafioso.[7]

A crucial finding of this research is that transformation to a mafia state is an inevitable process that Venezuela and its puppet states, Bolivia, Ecuador, and Nicaragua, have been undergoing. As Naim correctly asserts, organized crime cartels are not taking over these governments, but have become an integral part of their political units. An important by-product of this process is that narco-traffic and acts of terror have become indistinguishable from each other. The cooperation between Venezuela and Ecuador and the Colombian terrorist group Revolutionary Armed Forces (FARC) constitutes evidence of this link. In addition, Hezbollah, an Iranian proxy, is also involved.

Heinz Dietrich, one of the principal organizers of this movement, considered the Venezuelan President Hugo Chávez to be the "new Lenin of Latin America."[8] Chávez' twenty-first century Socialism is thought to be a model to be closely observed and analyzed. Dietrich urged Chávez to take drastic steps in order to transform the country's political system, and the Venezuelan president listened to his mentor. In the last several years there has been a concerted effort to alter the democratic character of this country.

The purpose of this research is to critically analyze the efforts of this movement, and to observe how twenty-first century Socialism (the Chávez regime) sheds a light on the possibility of altering other political systems. Dietrich and his associates claim that learning from the errors committed during the Soviet Union's rule, can prevent these mistakes from recurring.

This research demonstrates that in spite of changes introduced in the twenty-first century Socialism in Venezuela, its similarities to Soviet Communism are too great to be ignored. An important issue is that party affiliation, as was the case in twentieth-century Communism, is the most important criterion for career advancement. The lack of efficiency was an important factor that prevented Marx's ideas from being implemented correctly in both the Soviet Union and Venezuela.

José Guerra, a former head of economic analysis at the Venezuela's Central Bank (BCV), claimed that the main issue of the 2012 presidential elections should be a choice between two opposing philosophical outlooks:[9] the state, as the principal source of the means of production, or private property and initiatives as the principal tool of government. Chávez's victory in the October 7, 2012, elections demonstrated the advantages of a regime that controls the mass media and uses fear and dependency to control people's voting behavior. As the editorial in the *Wall Street Journal* correctly asserted, Chávez reelection illustrated that democracy can be hijacked more easily than many Americans choose to admit.[10]

Venezuelan democracy was replaced by a new class headed by Chávez. The new order primarily includes the military, member of the Venezuela United Socialist Party (PSUV), and some businessmen (bolibourgeoisie). This privileged group that emerged under Chávez corresponds to Yugoslavian scholar Milivan Djilas' *The New Class*, written during the Cold War.[11] Djilas asserts that Communist governments that tend to abolish social classes, in accordance to their ideology, in reality create a new privilege stratum, which benefits from the Communist regime.

This book begins with the liberator Simón Bolívar, who is used as a symbol intended to raise the regime's legitimacy. It analyzes both Spanish and English writings on Bolívar's life and his contributions to Latin America's independence.[12] My view, supported by other Latin American scholars is that Bolívar's teachings, similar to Marx's writings, should be divided into two periods. During the last two years of his life (1828-1830), the liberator altered many of his views and adopted authoritarian-dictatorial tendencies.[13] It becomes clear, therefore, that Chávez's socialism of the twenty-first century is strongly influenced by the last two years of the Bolívar's life.

The first chapter analyzes Chávez's attempts to indoctrinate the Venezuelan people in Marxist principles, through mass media and education. It demonstrates Chávez's adherence to Antonio Gramsci's ideas on how to initiate the radical transformation of a society. The mass media hegemony and control of the educational process are important ingredients that Chávez needs in order to achieve his goal.

A former Cuban official commenting on Chávez's decision to embark on Twitter, (April 27, 2010), declared that it should be compared to the date of the Russian Communist Revolution of 1917.[14] Paraphrasing Karl Marx's famous 1848 declaration "Proletarians of all countries unites," the former Cuban official asserted, "Revolutionary Twitter of all countries unites."

On December 9, 2010, more than seven months after Matos's official publication described above, the National Assembly amended the Law of Social Responsibility for Radio and Television (also known as RESORTE law) to include the Internet as a network being under government control.[15] This law further increases censorship and control of free expression of ideas.[16]

The educational law passed by the National Assembly in August 2009 must be viewed as an additional step in the indoctrination of the people in Marxist ideology. The date of this law's passage (August 13, 2009) is important because it was a present given by the National Assembly to Fidel Castro on his eighty-third birthday.[17] This law corresponds to Gramsci's idea for the need to indoctrinate the people in Communist ideology.

The first chapter attempts to explain what Bolívarism is. It includes analyses from the work numerous Latin American scholars about the nature of the Venezuelan regime under Chávez. Although some characterize Chávez's government as authoritarian-totalitarian, others consider it to be Communist.

There are also those scholars who view the Venezuelan president as a fascist.[18] J. R. López Padrino asserts that the Chávez regime intends to transform the country into a "military state," where discipline and obedience are the norm. The armed forces are assigned a primary role; they must defend against an attack by external forces and at the same time maintain enough oppression to be able to crush the internal enemy. Chávez's government is also characterized by compulsory purchase of war materials, disregarding vital aspects of national life, such as health, education, housing, and workers' social security.[19] As a result of inconsistencies in Chávez's policies, his altered views fit all the political philosophical outlooks described above.

It is important to mention that as a professional military person, without a distinguished educational record, Chávez does not always follow an ideologically clear line. Like Fidel Castro he affirmed his belief in Marxist-Leninist principles. But unlike Castro, (a lawyer) who is well versed in

Marxism, Chávez never read Marx's *Capital*. He follows policies that some scholars consider Communistic and others fascistic.

The first chapter analyzes sources from both the government and the opposition. Following the legislative elections of September 26, 2010, which reduced the parliamentary majority that Chávez enjoyed, the Venezuelan president declared that he intends to arm the Bolívarian militias.[20] The editorial asks who will be in charge of these arms and what assurances exist that these weapons will not fall into terrorist hands. Such a habit, the article contends, was a practice of the twentieth-century criminal dictators, such as Hitler (Germany), Mussolini (Italy), Stalin (the Soviet Union) and Franco (Spain).

The first chapter also includes a comparison between President Rómulo Betancourt's democratic revolution and the Socialist revolution of Chávez.[21] After a decade of dictatorial rule, Betancourt (1959-1963) attempted to restore democracy in Venezuela. The most important change introduced by his administration was agrarian reform. Land was distributed to poor peasants; however, full compensation was given to the land owners. The 1961 Venezuelan constitution, similar to its Mexican counterpart, incorporated agrarian reform. This can be contrasted with Chávez's land reform which employs force to seize land without compensation.[22]

This chapter also presents an analysis of state-church relations in Chávez's Venezuela. The disagreements between Chávez's government and the church started from the time he came to power in 1999. However, from 2007 to 2010 the relations deteriorated, reaching its nadir in 2010. The Bishop conference (2010) in Venezuela expressed its discontent with the antireligious spirit exhibited by the current Marxist-atheist regime. A Vatican newspaper reported that a hostile war of words erupted between President Chávez and Cardinal Jorge Urosa Savino.[23]

In the last days of 2010, the Cardinal harshly criticized the Venezuelan National Assembly laws passed in its last session and asserted that these laws contradict democratic principles and run against the will of the people. [24] He further claimed that Venezuela is heading towards dictatorship.

An important part of the first chapter deals with civil-military relations in Venezuela.[25] Relying on Latin American scholars, I contend that Chávez aimed to convert the armed forces from professional to revolutionary entities. He intended to transform the military into an ideologically politicized organization that serves the party in power exclusively. Such a transformation would have assured Chávez the right to absolute rule.

Cuba's experiences in economics, security, and other pertinent issues are an important inspiration for Chávez's regime. Many analysts, however, wonder why Chávez would imitate a failing system. One scholar analyzes a 1967 Castro speech in which he emphasized the superiority of the Communist utopia over capitalism. In this speech the Cuban leader predicted that in the near future his system of government would produce an abundance and happiness for everyone. This prediction was clearly false and ironically in 2001, when an American ship delivered food supplies to Cuba, the failure of Cuba's Communist system was demonstrated.[26] However, whereas Cuba may follow the Chinese model, allowing accommodation with the public sector,[27] Chávez is imitating Fidel Castro's pre-reform regime.

The first chapter also deals with the application of Lewis Coser's book: *The Functions of Social Conflict* as regards Chávez's policies and politics. Coser showed how group hostility toward others may be used as a way to increase social cohesion.[28] His observations and findings are especially important in analyzing authoritarian/totalitarian regimes. Leaders of such countries lack legitimacy and will employ the denigration of the enemy to strengthen their rule.

The second chapter deals with Chávez's economic policies, emphasizing his efforts gradually to abolish the capitalist system and replace it with Socialism. Under the title the New Socialist Institutions (*Las Nuevas Instituciones Socialistas*), Miguel González Marregot claims that new measures adopted by the Chávez's regime make Venezuela similar to the twentieth-century Soviet Union.[29] The new law assures that the state, the main component of centralized planning, is the forerunner of decision making in the economic field. Oil income becomes the main source of government revenues and a strong restriction is imposed on private property.

This chapter also concentrates on the writings of various economic experts mentioned in the Venezuelan opposition press: Niall Ferguson, *The Ascent of Money*[30]; Arnold Kling and Nick Schulz, *From Poverty to Prosperity*[31]; Milton Friedman, *Capitalism and Freedom*[32]; and others. These books attempt to demonstrate the advantages of a free market in a country's development, as contrasted to a controlled (centrally planned) economy. These books were analyzed in the Venezuelan opposition press in order to demonstrate the shortcomings of Chávez's economic policies.

Kling and Schulz emphasized the crucial role entrepreneurs play in a country's economic progress. Dan Senor and Saul Singer demonstrated that Israel has developed an entrepreneurial culture that explains the country's economic miracle.[33] It is based on private initiatives and basic skills that young people acquire while serving compulsory military service. This book is also analyzed by a Venezuelan writer who emphasizes the importance of the Israeli economic model as an exemplary system that should be imitated by others.[34] In this respect, it would be interesting to compare Venezuelan and Israeli economic systems. Israel initially embarked on Socialism; it later embraced capitalism. Venezuela, on the other hand, went in the opposite direction. Starting with Chávez's coming to power in 1999, it abandoned capitalism and gradually embraced Socialism.

Criticizing those who claim that Socialism increases the role of the state and offers the best remedy for poverty, Kling and Schulz assert that only a free market can result in eliminating deprivation.[35] The solution lies in giving jobs to the poor, which can be accomplished by the creation of entrepreneurships that will create work. Innovation is a vital key for improving the country's economics and decreasing the level of poverty.

Nationalization of private companies is an ongoing process in Venezuela and the nationalized businesses are losing value. The government doesn't know how to manage these companies. Expropriation and dismantling of Venezuela's private enterprises has resulted in massive economic losses. Nationalization of private companies, in the last several years, has cost $25.22 billion.[36]

On January 8, 2010, the Chávez's regime devaluated the Bolívar (Venezuela's currency), a fact many analysts contend contributed to the country's inflation.[37] This date also known as "Red Friday," established different rates of exchange for the Bolívar. The decline in value of Venezuela's currency epitomizes the failures of Chávez's economic policies. The last decade of his government witnessed the dismantling of industries and the paralyzing of investments. Similar devaluation against the dollar was introduced on February 8, 2013, a move that will further increase inflation and deteriorate the economy.[38]

Those who are engaged in Venezuela's economic policies are not economists. Chávez is a military man, the president of Venezuela's Central Bank (BCV) is a mathematician, and the finance minister is a lawyer. No one can expect these people to stop inflation. Chile's economy is one of the best developed in Latin America largely because of the qualifications, both theoretical and practical, and experiences of President Sebastián Piñera, who has a Ph.D. degree in economics from Harvard University.

Inflation may also be attributed to Chávez's attempt to subordinate the monetary and financial policies of the Venezuelan Central Bank (BCV).[39] This was done contrary to the constitution which explicitly states that the Central Bank is independent and not subject to regulations from the executive branch. It specifically mentions that it cannot receive or finance fiscal deficit policies.

Chávez's policy toward the Central Bank is similar to Domingo Perón's course. In 1946 Perón embarked on a policy to utilize the Argentinian Central Bank funds to finance his fiscal deficits.[40] Similar to the case of Perón's Argentina, the Venezuelan Central Bank was converted into a government tool in charge of printing money according to the dictates of the executive branch.

The Law of Fair Costs and Prices, which was published in the official Gazette on July 18, 2011, constitutes a new phase in enlarging the state's control of the private economic market.[41] This law reflects what may happen when a country loses the fight against inflation, as has occurred in Venezuela. The government revives an absurd doctrine aimed at blaming others for its errors.[42] According to this law, each product sold to the public needs to be registered with the National Superintendent of Costs and Prices. This increases shortages and also increases the role of the state in the economy. This law is the practical application of a central Communist planning economy, which mandates that a group of people decide what is produced, how much and what the price of the product will be.[43]

Rafael Rivera Muñoz claims that Chávez's expropriations should be considered as an act of state terrorism.[44] He begins his article by quoting Pope Juan Pablo II, who asserted that terrorism is born of hatred and contempt of human life and constitutes a grave crime against humanity. Directors of Fedecamaras (Federation of Trade and Industry Chambers) strongly criticized the beating of four managers in a private company expropriate by the Chavez's regime. The writer states that the government has full control of all armed groups; they act only upon receiving instructions from Chávez's administration.

Chávez's expropriation of large estates is reminiscent of Stalin's extermination of the Kulaks (owners of large farms) in the 1930s in the Soviet

Union. Unlike the Soviet dictator who destroyed his enemies, Chávez only took away their land. However, collectivization efforts in the Soviet Union and Chávez's land expropriation were complete failures and resulted in food shortages. Unlike Stalin, however, President Chávez was able to avert hunger by using oil income to import subsistence items.

Following Gramsci's ideas, Chávez was gradually suffocating the private sector. He had declared that he had the authority "granted by the people" and the constitution to expropriate any company. He declared: "I have been granted authority to expropriate companies."[45] Government officials are using such terms as *excessive earning, speculative earning, fair prices,* and others in order to weaken the private sector.

Emphasis will be given in this chapter to the state oil company, Petróleos de Venezuela (PDSVA), which provides the major income for Venezuela's government. Nationalization of this industry in 1976 contributed to both the decline of free markets and the rule of democracy.[46]

In an open letter to Ali Araque Rodríguez, who serves both as president of the state oil company Petróleos de Venezuela, (PDVSA) and the minister of mines and energy, Gustavo Coronel blames the Chávez regime for mismanaging the industry.[47] This accusation involves the dual loyalties of Rodríguez, who is both a cabinet member in Chávez's government and the president of PDVSA. His duality has destroyed the separation between monitoring and monitored agents, which are now the same. It makes it difficult, or impossible, to evaluate the company's performance.

Lack of transparency becomes a major issue; it inevitably leads to corruption and waste estimated to be a trillion dollars during the first twelve years of the Chávez regime.[48] The subordination of oil policies to political and ideological considerations is no doubt responsible for most of the problems of this industry. During the protest and strike of the oil industry in 2002-2003, thousands of competent technical staff were dismissed. They were replaced by 100,000 unqualified persons, hired solely because they were ideologically loyal to Chávez. As a result, work accidents in the oil industry multiplied; there have been other consequences as well, such as reduction in both work efficiency and oil production.

PDVSA was converted into a state monopoly in the service of the political, antidemocratic project. It should concentrate on its efforts to improve commercial objectives and not ideological ones. The company needs to be replaced with a private open industry that follows financial regulations.[49]

Chávez's government praised Che Guevara's economic ideas, especially his desire to get rid of money as a medium of exchange.[50] Ferguson, on the other hand, contends that money and credit are essential elements for a country's economic development. Like Kling and Schulz, Ferguson claims that a country's economic success depends on people who own property and feel a sense of ownership in their future.[51]

Venezuela's capital flight is a result of Chávez's distrust of the private sector.[52] The government envisioned that by applying a policy of exchange control, it would regulate the flight of capital and safeguard international reserves. However, the policy implemented since February 2003 has had the opposite effect.[53]

Alex Vallenilla makes an interesting comparison between Venezuela's and Japan's capital flights.[54] As a result of the March 2011 tsunami and nuclear disaster in Japan, a major part of capital invested abroad was channeled to Japan. The comparison between investment patterns in Venezuela and Japan illustrates how different ideologies affect nationalism and decisions about where money should be infused. Disappointed with Chávez's economic policies, many Venezuelans preferred to move their wealth outside the country. In Japan, on the other hand, the opposite occurred during a period of crisis, and investments were redirected into the home country.

In dealing with the syndicate movement, Chávez government produces neglect and a lack of attention to labor's demands. Robin Rodríguez employs the term *labor terrorism* to indicate how workers have been treated and dealt with in the oil industry.[55] In a meeting with PDVSA's workers, the labor union representatives expressed their determination to resist and fight for their rights. The PDVSA's management postponed elections for the union's representatives. The syndicate's leaders urged management to allow observers, both national and international, to supervise the election process; it should be a secret vote and management should not interfere in this course.

Corruption is characteristic of many countries. When it occurs, the allocation of resources to the people becomes problematic. Alberto Rodríguez Barrera, analyzing corruption in Venezuela, claims that it is an integral part of the country's history. However, during forty years of democracy (1958-1998) it was reduced by 80%.[56] On the other hand, under Chávez's regime, corruption increased to levels that have never before been seen. A commission that supports democracy in Venezuela declared that for 100 Bolívares (Venezuela's currency) that were robbed by past administrations, such as Carlos Andrés Pérez and Rafael Caldera for example, the Chávez administration increased this amount of stolen money, during the period 1999-2003 by 3000% in relations to previous governments.[57]

Venezuela's controlled government press downgrades Chile's economic achievements, emphasizing the inequalities of its economic system.[58] Although this is confirmed by Chilean publications, the solution to the unequal distribution of wealth cannot become solely the responsibility of the government, but must involve the private sector. Two private sector organizations, The Foundation Microfinance (Microfinanzas) and the Hope Fund (Fondo Esperanza), which operate in several Latin American countries, are projecting to help 25% of the Chilean poor, who represent 15% of the country's population.[59]

An important reason Chile is considered to be one of the richest states in Latin America, is that unlike the Chávez regime, which constantly increases the state's payroll, Chile has gone in the opposite direction. A report issued by the nongovernmental organization of Transparency International ranked Chile as the least corrupt country in Latin America (ranked number 21 out of 178 countries). Venezuela on the other hand ranked as the most corrupt.[60]

A comparison between the two countries' economic systems further demonstrates the weakness of Chávez's economic policies and leaves no doubt that the free market initiatives followed by Chile are far superior to policies followed by Venezuelan counterpart. It contrasts the Chilean route to economic development with that pursued by the Chávez regime.

Analyzing the Chilean route, Venezuelan journalist Antonio Muller claims that the implementation of a market economy brought Chile social stability with economic growth, reduction in poverty, and low levels of both inflation and unemployment.[61] In the last twenty-five years, the Chilean model achieved important goals such as diversification of the economy, creation of a pension system and promotion of the well-beings with fiscal equilibrium.

Piñera's business background was evident in a speech given in November 2010, in which he outlined fifty initiatives that aims at increasing economic growth, investments, and productivity in the country.[62] One of the president's main objectives is to erase poverty. Therefore, improving the quality education becomes an important task; increasing work opportunities for everyone and strengthening family bonds are also significant component in the attempt to reduce poverty. Unlike Chávez's regime which relies on the Venezuelan leader's military experience, where decisions are made from the top and the rest have to follow, the Chilean president stated his intention to meet with the opposition and discuss alternate ways to improve the country's well-being.

Venezuela's economic policies contributed to the Gross Domestic Product (GDP) declining to near zero in the third quarter of 2010.[63] The Minister of Planning and Finance, Jorge Giordani, claimed that in the last three quarters of 2010, the GDP fell 5.2%, 1.9%, and 0.4%. He blamed the fall of on the global financial crisis. In contrast Chile's economy, also affected by the international economic crisis, grew by 7% in the third quarter of 2010.[64]

Chávez could have learned a great deal from the Israeli kibbutz experience. These communal settlements (Kibbutzim) in Israel, which may be characterized as the closest social experiment resembling Karl Marx's ideas, are going through a process of radical social and economic transformation. This came about because of heavy economic losses; they needed to adapt to market policies and privatization, in order to continue their existence. Chávez should conclude from the Israeli kibbutz experience that he needs urgently to reverse his policies and embark on a process of privatization and market economy.

Venezuela's communal system and the Israeli kibbutz (communal settlement) are compared in order to highlight the major differences between the two political and economic systems. González Maregot analyzed Venezuela's communal system, which is based on central planning, social property, and barter directed and ruled by the central government.[65] This is in contrast to the Israeli communal system (kibbutz) which was based on individual initiative and not state enterprise.

Whereas the Chávez regime attempts to increase political control by the establishment of communal systems, the Israeli counterpart (kibbutz) has gone in the opposite direction. This transformation from collective to individualistic values is considered by Professor Alberto Montaner to be a real revolution.[66]

The Kibbutzim embraced market principles, selling parts of their land to city dwellers to build private homes, on land that was previously used for agriculture. A noted example was Kibbutz Afikim, which successfully transformed itself from a collective settlement, a failed socialist venture, to a place dominated by private enterprises.[67]

It is important to note that in Chile and Israel, starting from about May 2011, important protest movements emerged. To some extend, they represent the price of economic success and the rising expectations of people. As both countries became richer, wealth, as is the case in every capitalist society was not distributed equally. While some became richer others struggled to maintain their livelihood.

The publication *The Power of Pull* is instrumental in explaining the global protest movement in general and the mass demonstrations in Chile and Israel in particular.[68] The authors claim that technological innovations and the new digital infrastructure are transforming the business and social landscape and have begun to reshape the twenty-first century's institutions.

An important distinction must be made between previous and current technological revolutions. In the past technological innovations experienced a rapid renewal for a short time and then began the flattening of improvements. This pattern enabled business to stabilize quickly following the initial disruption of the innovation. At present and for the first time, the new technological inventions show no sign of stabilization in term of price/performance ratio improvement.

Israeli economist, Tamar Almor, was asked how Israel was able to prevent the 2008 economic crisis. Almor pointed to Stanley Fischer, the Israeli central bank governor, and his decision to ensure that the government did not bail out any companies experiencing economic problems.[69] During the year 2008, foreign direct investment in Israel increased by 11%, unemployment declined by 1.2%, and the GDP increased by 4.1%.

As the result of the economic crisis in Europe and the United States, Chile, Israel, and many other countries attempted to increase their economic cooperation with China. The plan to build a train link between Israel's Red Sea and the Mediterranean ports could spur increased trade with China. It could serve as an alternative to the Suez Canal.[70] The victory of Islamic parties in the Egyptian parliamentary and presidential elections of 2011 and 2012 may increase the country's political instability and endanger the ability of all nations, especially Israel, to use the canal. The Jewish state has not forgotten the closing of the canal to Israeli ships by President Abdul Nasser in 1956.

The third chapter attempts to analyze Chávez's behavior in the international arena. Octavio Paz's remark that ideological blindness impedes thinking is an important reflection on the Venezuelan president's foreign policy, which runs counter to the country's national interest.[71] Animosity toward the United States is a central theme of Chávez's foreign policy.

The Venezuelan president emphasizes his desire to create a multipolar world. According to Chávez,Venezuela has been able to create an alternative to capitalism that should be adopted by the entire world. Chávez employs oil revenues to influence elections throughout Latin America, aiming at the establishment of regimes with similar philosophical underpinnings. There is a lot of validity to the claim that Chávez's international behavior is solely directed by the objective of world revolution against capitalism.[72]

The Bolívarian Alliance of the People of our America (ALBA) was created by Chávez's initiative in 2004. The purpose of this treaty was Chávez's attempt to spread his ideology by offering economic incentives or bribery. These countries, which include Bolivia, Ecuador, Nicaragua, and others, are considered to be Chávez's puppet states; they have been following in Chávez's path by gradually abandoning democratic rules and replacing them with authoritarian political systems. The Bolivian president Evo Morales declared, following Chávez's electoral victory of October 7, 2012, that more countries would follow the Venezuela president path and adopt anti-capitalist forms of government.[73] However, Chávez' death will weaken ALBA, because there are no leaders who are capable of replacing the Venezuelan leader.[74]

ALBA's countries find it of utmost importance to discuss the creation of a common communication project, in order to withstand the media's attacks on certain power centers.[75] It calls for the creation of a common agency, radio, television, publications, and information network. A special effort would be made to produce reliable reporters. This means that journalists would need to be trained to view the world from their political perspective.

A former minister of the Bolivian government, Carlos Sánchez Berzain, described how Evo Morales's regime has transformed Bolivia into an authoritarian and tyrannical state.[76] His analysis is also applicable to other ALBA countries, such as Ecuador, Nicaragua, and Venezuela. Bolivia, according to Berzain, violated Montesquieu's separation of powers. In all these countries the judicial and legislative branches of government are controlled by the executive.

Bolivian President Evo Morales, speaking in front of 5,000 members gathered for the eighth Socialist Movement Congress (*el Movimiento al Socialismo*, MAS), declared that he would like to stay in power forever.[77] Anti-imperialist, anti-capitalist and anti-neoliberal leaders, when coming to power, do not relinquish their positions. The Bolivian president added that the congress can debate this issue. Morales's position is shared by Chávez and the leaders of other ALBA countries.

The most important priority of the Chávez regime and those of the other ALBA countries are to maintain power. Bolivia's 2011 budget allocation is an illustration of this trend. A little more than 50% of the ministerial budget was spent on matters related to the state's repressive apparatus (defense and security) and only 11.2% on health and education.[78] This statistic demonstrates the true character of the Bolivian government.

Similar to other ALBA states, Bolivia is engaged in narcotic traffic. This became obvious after the expulsion of the United States' Drug Enforcement Agency (DEA) in 2008. It is important to note that chewing coca leaves constitutes part of the indigenous culture. The attempt, however, to differentiate between coca leaves and cocaine is problematic. The leaves constitute the basic production of cocaine. Bolivia did not sign the 1961 convention related to narcotic traffic.[79]

The former Bolivian defense minister, Ernesto Justinián claimed that narcotic traffic is caused by the inequality of conditions, lack of control, and the absence of real government policy to combat this trend.[80] During the period of Morales's administration, cocaine production increased by 50%. This becomes evident when one views the construction of luxurious apartments and expensive cars belonging to cocaine mafia, who enjoy free movements in the country.

When the United States' DEA was present in Bolivia, it paid $50,000 to informers. It ceased operation in Bolivia after Morales ordered the American agency to leave. The United States identified twenty countries as producers or places of transit of narcotic trafficking in 2010. Both Venezuela and Bolivia are included in this list.[81] Bolivia should be added to the list of countries Naim labeled as mafia states.

In Ecuador, similar to Venezuela and Bolivia, transformations have taken place that turned the country into an authoritarian political system. Rafael Correa's administration is following Chávez's style of a state dominated by Socialism and dictatorship.[82] Following his mentor Chávez,

Correa launched a referendum in which the people were asked to express their opinions on various proposal issues. Many human rights activists viewed the referendum of May 7, 2011, as an attempt by the Ecuadorian president to grab power and weaken democratic institutions.

Scholars and opposition members viewed the referendum's approval as converting Ecuador into an authoritarian state. Freedom of expression is prosecuted and those who protest are considered enemies of the state.[83] The state becomes the dominant institution resembling North Korea and following the path of both Evo Morales's Bolivia and Hugo Chávez's Venezuela.

The control of the mass media is an important characteristic of the Chávez regime and his proxy states. The sanctions imposed by Correa's administration on the Ecuadorian television station Teleamazonas in 2009 was a warning that the authoritarian process had started.[84] The reason for shutting down the station was that it reported that PDVSA drilling natural gas in Ecuador is harmful to the environment and causes the death of fish. The station was accused of presenting false information, which is considered a violation of citizens' rights to be freely informed.

In spite of the fact that President Correa pardoned the editor and assistants of *El Universo*, he asserted that the "abuse press has been defeated."[85] His change of mind is attributed to the strong pressure by human rights and press freedom groups in Ecuador and around the world. In spite of this pardons, freedom of expression would remain a problem in Correa's Ecuador.

Ecuador is a volatile state with fragile institutions. Since Correa assumed power, the bond market and direct foreign investments have been continuously declining. The 2010 failed coup in Ecuador was a result of the failures of the country's social and economic policies, which reduced the president's popularity. Ecuador ceased to have access to external finance, from the 2008 stoppage of payments on global bonds worth $3.2 billion. Ecuador's problem is lack of business pressure groups, capable of functioning as a political counterbalance.[86]

Similar to Venezuela and Bolivia, Ecuador may also be considered a narcotic state. There is a strong partnership between the Colombia terrorist group FARC and Correa's regime. Several of the Ecuadorian president's assistants had direct links with FARC. The International Institute for Strategic Studies (London) reported that during the 2006 campaign,

President Correa received the sum of $100,000 as a financial contribution from FARC.[87] This information was gained as a result of 8,382 electronic documents found in the computer of Raúl Reyes, a top FARC's commander who was killed in March 2008 by the Colombian army across the border in Ecuador.

An expert on security, Fernando Carrión Mena claimed that Ecuador has been converted into an important center of narcotic traffic.[88] According to information from the U.S. Department of State, Ecuador became an important place for international criminal organizations, including drug cartels from FARC's Colombia, Mexico, Russia, and China.[89] There are several important reasons narcotic traffic flourished in Ecuador. The country's geographical location among producing and consuming drug countries, the official currency, the American dollar, are all factors contributing to the increase in narcotic traffic. The weakness of Ecuador's institutions, the debility of the judicial branch, and the lack of police are also contributing factors.

The Ecuadorian opposition press highlighted the diplomatic suitcase scandal viewing it as a government abuse of power. It is another illustration of Ecuador's path toward becoming a narcotic (mafia) state. The diplomatic suitcase belonged to Ecuadorian foreign minister, Ricardo Patiño, and was discovered on its way to Ecuador's general consulate in Milan, Italy.[90] A foreign minister spokesman claimed that the suitcase was opened en route to Italy. This view was disputed by diplomacy and security experts, who asserted that shipments of diplomatic suitcases have been rigorously protected.[91]

Similar to Venezuela, Bolivia, and Ecuador, Nicaragua followed policies that gradually transformed the country into an authoritarian/totalitarian political system. Independent mass media were weakened and the regime took control of half of the country's television stations. The former United States' ambassador to Nicaragua, Robert J. Callahan, compared Daniel Ortega's influence in the country to the former Nicaraguan dictator Anastasia Somoza, who employed nepotism to control the country.[92] Ortega's Sandinista party overthrew his dictatorship in 1979. Callahan mentioned that Nicaraguans employ the term "Somocismo without Somoza." It refers to Somoza's style of ruling through favoritism. Non-Sandinista reporters are threatened. One journalist, Silvia González, fled the country because she received threats, after reporting that soldiers had killed a person opposed to Ortega's reelection.[93]

Similar to Venezuela, Ortega's regime is creating a new class of rich people who are in close relationships with the Nicaraguan president. Chávez's oil money is not directed toward improving people's standard of living, but is channeled toward Ortega, his family and supporters.[94] Ortega's extended families are in charge of funds derived from a Venezuelan oil accord, communication media and oil distributions.

Ortega has followed in Chávez's footsteps in strengthening relations with drug cartels.[95] Under Ortega, Nicaragua may turn into another narcotic state, providing key transit routes to narcotic traffic and hence increasing anarchy and chaos in the region.

My research strongly emphasized Venezuela and Iran's cooperation in international terrorism. The views of Hugo Chávez and his Iranian counterpart Mahmud Ahmadinejad are not similar in their attempt to create a new international system. However, they share a common attribute, the requirement to weaken the United States as an important player in the international arena, a precondition for their ability to form a new international system. In order to reach this goal, strong cooperation between the two countries and terrorist organizations such as, FARC, Hezbollah, Islamic Jihad, Hamas, ETA, and others has been established.

Chávez would like to create a new international order where Socialism of the twenty-first century would become the dominant force among nations. Ahmadinejad, on the other hand, would like to create a world theocracy ruled by his version of the Koran. These two models of a future international system, if implemented, would clash with each other. Relating to this contradiction Pilar Rahola asks, "How can one reconcile Karl Marx's writings with those of the fundamental version of the Koran?"[96] Referring to the January 2012 visit of the Iranian president to Venezuela, Rahola claims that applauding in Caracas, a regime that stones females is absurd.

FARC is a Marxist group that originated in the 1970s with the aim of taking over the government in Colombia by violence. FARC supported Chávez before his election in 1999 and contributed money to his campaign.[97] Chávez's relations with FARC are an illustration of his populist tendencies, without clear guiding principles. Ideologically, there exist a great affinity between the Venezuelan president and FARC. Political interests were the primary factor that determined these relations.

Moisés Naim, a well-known journalist whose articles have been published in many countries, said in 2007, "Wherever the narcotic traffic economy flourishes it produces political consequences. The huge sums of money involved in this trade affect high levels of corruption and complicity in the highest echelons."[98] In May 2012 Naim further elaborated on this idea and coined the term of *mafia states* to identify an important concept.[99] Mafia states are not states that criminal networks take over, but inversely the government takes control of drug cartels and other illegal groups in order to promote and defend its national interests, especially those of the ruling elite. The criminal networks are put in the state's service. Venezuela is among the states mentioned by Naim that belong to this category.

The Makled affair is a classic example of Venezuela's being characterized as a mafia state. Walid Makled, a Syrian-Venezuelan narcotic terrorist was arrested in August 2010 in Colombia. United Sates authorities have visited Makled at least three times in a Colombian jail. Both the United States and Venezuela demanded his extradition for crimes such as cocaine trade, extortion, kidnapping, terrorism training, and cooperation with FARC, Hezbollah, and Iran's search for nuclear weapons.[100]

The official Venezuela view was that Makled is a criminal engaged in narcotic traffic who needs to be investigated and brought to justice by the country's judicial system. In reality, as Luis Egana correctly stated, Makled is a good illustration of how the Chávez regime operates. Makled's crimes have implicated high officials such as generals, admirals, members of the legislative branch, the police department, and judges, including those who serve on the Supreme Court; in summary, a representative sample of the highest echelons, and the elite of civil and military strata.[101]

Makled's extradition to the United States could have shed light on the Venezuelan narcotic traffic links to Hezbollah. A Venezuelan diplomat of Syrian origin, Ghazi Atef Nassereddine Salame, the second in command of the Venezuelan embassy in Syria, was in charge of directing the growing numbers of Hezbollah networks in South America. The United States accused four enterprises directed by Makled of dealing with narcotic traffic.[102]

An important question under consideration is why Colombian president Juan Manuel Santos decided to extradite Makled to Venezuela and not to the United States. Santos claimed that U.S. President Barack Obama did not object to the decision to extradite Makled to Venezuela.[103] Prior to Makled's extradition, the Colombian president visited Venezuela and bilateral trade agreements were signed that increased economic cooperation in the amount of $6 billion.[104] Chávez also delivered Joaquín

Pérez Becerra, a FARC member, to Colombia in appreciation for Makled's extradition.[105]

An important idea in the conclusion of my book is that Gramsci's ideas of transformation to Communism did not occur as he predicted. The gradual transformation to authoritarian regimes, the disappearance of independent branches of government, the attack on independent mass media, and the emergence of a strong unchallenged leader have led to the creation of a mafia state; the criminal networks become an integral part of the government. Venezuela and Bolivia have already reached this stage; Ecuador and Nicaragua are on their way to becoming mafia states. As a result of his electoral victory of October 7, 2012, Chávez will increase his influence and the socialist revolution may become further radicalized.[106] The death of Chávez, the failure of his political model, Venezuela's economic crisis, will weaken the attractiveness of this type of government being imitated by others. The elections of a new Pope from Latin America in March 2013, with his emphasis on helping the poor, may further contribute to the weakening of Chávezism.

In the post 9/11 period, a great deal of attention must be given to Venezuela, its puppet states, and their close relations with Iran. Hezbollah, an Iranian proxy operating freely in these countries and its terror networks are awaiting orders from Teheran to commit a terrorist act on American soil. Hezbollah, which also deals with narco-traffic, makes it impossible to distinguish between drug dealers and terrorists.

United States' dependency on OPEC oil (especially Venezuela) is detrimental to the country's security. The same can be said about illegal drugs brought to the United States; the mafia states (Venezuela and its partners) play an important role in this process. These funds are used to foster terrorism against the United States. Venezuela therefore should be immediately placed on the list of countries that sponsor terrorism. It is too early to predict if the death of Chávez will bring changes in these policies.

Notes

1   Francis Fukyama, The End of History and the Last Man, New York (Avon Books 1992) see also Izar As, Pahad Elohim, Yediot Ahronot, (Israel) July 22, 2010
2   Editorial, Hugo Chávez, The Wall Street Journal, March 6, 2013
3   Chávez's body will be embalmed for "eternal" display, Eluniversal.com, March 8, 2013

4   W. Paul Cockshott and Allin Cottrel. Towards a New Socialism, (Nottingham, Eng-land, Spokesman Bertrand Russel House, 1973)

5   Fernando Martínez Heredia, Gramsci entre nosotros, Analitica.com, Noviembre 3, 2009

6   Moisés NaimMoises , Estados mafiosos, Analitica.com, Mayo 7, 2012

7   Reich llama mafiosos a funcionarios chavistas, Hoy.com.ec, Marzo 20, 2013

8   Heinz Dietrich, Bolívar, Lenin y Hugo Chávez en la revolución Bolívariana, Anal-itica.com, Noviembre 8, 2009

9   José Guerra, Ideas para Venezuela, economía y petróleo, Analitica.com, Marzo 10, 2011

10 Editorial, The Misery of Venezuela, The Wall Street Journal, October 8, 2012

11 Milovan Djilas, The New Class, (New York, Frederick A. Praeger Publisher) 1957

12 John Lynch, Simón Bolívar, A Life, (New Haven, Yale University Press, 2006)

13 Heinz R. Sonntag, Contradicciones, Analitica.com, Septiembre 19, 2009

14 Eliades Acosta Matos, Con Chávez y la revolución Twitter, Cubadebate, Mayo 3, 2010, it also appeared in Agencia Bolívariana de Noticias, Mayo 8, 2010

15 Venezuelan government seeks media law to regulate the Internet, Eluniversal.com December 10, 2010

16 Freddy Lepage Scribani, Luchas internas del PSUV (II), Analitica.com, Diciembre 11, 2010

17 Fernando Luis Egana, El lío de la LOE, Analitica.com, Augusto 16, 2009

18 José Rafael López Padrino, La Barbarie Socialfascista, Analitica.com, Enero 18, 2010

19 José Rafael López Padrino, Militarización socialfascista Bolívariana, Analitica.com, Octubre 20, 2010

20 EDITORIAL, Milicias y amargura, Analitica.com, Octubre 6, 2010

21 Robert Alexander, The Venezuelan Democratic Revolution–A Profile of the Regime of Rómulo Betancourt, (New Brunswick, New Jersey, Rutgers University Press, 1963)

22 Simón Romero, A Cash of Hope and Fear As Venezuela Seizes Land, The New York Times, May 17, 2007

23 Venezuela Cardinal target of 'Verbal Aggression' Says Vatican Paper, Catholicnews.com, July 8, 2010

24 Cardinal Urosa Savino: Enabling law threatens the country peace, Eluniversal.com, December 30, 2010

25 Fernando Ochoa Antich, Crisis Militar en la Fuerza Armada Bolívariana, Analitica.com, Abril 7, 2010

26 Baldomera Vásquez, La revolución Cubana murió de fracas, Analitica.com, Marzo 9, 2010

27 Cuba se abre por primera vez a los anuncios del sector privado, Elmundo.es, Mayo 31, 2012

28 Book summary of the functions of social conflict, beyongintractability.com, Decem-ber 4, 2009

29 Miguel González Marregot, La nueva institucionalidad socialista, Analitica.com, Diciembre 15, 2010

30 Niall Ferguson, The Ascent of Money, (New York, Penguin Book, 2008)

31 Arnold Kling and Nick Schulz, From Poverty to Prosperity, (New York, Encounter Book, 2009)

32 Milton Friedman, Capitalism and Freedom, (Chicago, The University of Chicago Press, 2002)

33 Dan Senor and Saul Singer, Start-Up Nation, (New York, Hachette Book Group) 2009

34 Pablo Pardo, El 'modelo Israel' derrota al de Dubai, Analitica.com, Diciembre 11, 2009

35 Arnold Kling and Nick Schulz, From Poverty to Prosperity, Op-cit p. 174

36   Expropriations Dismantle Venezuela production model, Eluniversal.com, October 12, 2010
37   Eduardo Mayobre, Bolívar, Fuerte? Analitica.com, Enero 29, 2010
38   Ezequiel Minay and Kejal Vyas, Venezuela Slashes Currency Value, The Wall Street Journal, February 8, 2013
39   Orlando Ochoa P, Breve análisis del proyecto de ley de reforma a la ley del BCV, Analitica.com, Octubre 30, 2009
40   José Guerra, El BCV al margen de la ley, Analitica.com, Febrero 24, 2010
41   Cost law ends with economic rights, Eluniversal.com, July 21, 2011
42   José Guerra, Ley de costos y precios justos, Analitica.com, Julio 21, 2011
43   José Guerra, Derrotados por la inflación, Analitica.com, Agosto 11, 2011
44   Rafael Rivera Muñoz, El terrorismo de estado y sus variantes, Analitica.com, Noviembre 4, 2010
45   María de Lourdes Vásquez, Chávez, I have been granted authority to expropriate companies, Eluniversal.com, October 27, 2009
46   Michael Rowan, A Sick Country, Eluniversal.com, December 15, 2009
47   Gustavo Coronel, The petroleum policy of Hugo Chávez government, Eluniversal.com, February 21, 2011
48   Ibid.
49   Gustavo Coronel, Un post chavismo sin PDVSA y sin ejército, Analitica.com, Noviembre 26, 2009
50   El pensamiento económico del Che sigue vigente a 42 años de su muerte, Agencia Bolívariana de Noticias, Octubre 9, 2009
51   Niall Ferguson, The Ascent of Monet, op-cit, p. 269
52   Capital Flight Amounts to USD 8.11 Billion in Six Month, Eluniversal.com, August 28, 2009
53   Jesús Casique, Fuga de capitales Enero-septiembre año 2009, 13.333 millones de dólares, Analitica.com, Noviembre 25, 2009
54   Alex Vallenilla, Con $39 de divisas fugadas del país se estabiliza la economía venezolana, Analitica.com, Marzo 29, 2011
55   Robin Rodríguez, Trabajadores petroleros derrotan el terrorismo laboral, Analitica.com, Septiembre 4, 2009
56   Alberto Rodríguez Barrera, Algunas raíces de la corrupción chavista, Analitica.com, Diciembre 15, 2009
57   Ibid.
58   Gissel Molina, Chile es el país de mayor desigualdad social de América Latina, Agencia Bolivariana de Noticias, Julio 25, 2010
59   Entidad de microcréditos prevé ayudar a 1 de cada 4 pobres en Chile, Lanacion.cl, Enero 13, 2011
60   Chile es el mejor Latino Americano en el índice de corrupción, La Nacional.cl Octubre 25, 2010
61   Juan Antonio Muller, La Ruta Chilena, Analitica.com, Marzo 13, 2010
62   Nicolas Westermeyer, Piñera traza agenda para que Chile sea desarrollado en 2018, La Nacion.cl, Noviembre 9, 2010
63   Venezuela's GDP decline is almost zero, says Planning Minister, Eluniversal.com, November 17, 2010
64   Economía Chilena creció 7% en el tercer trimestre, Nacion.cl, Noviembre 18, 2010
65   Miguel González Marregot, Sobre el estado comunal, Analitica.com, Febrero 28, 2011
66   Carlos Alberto Montaner, ¿Qué significa Israel para el occidente?, Analitica.com, Julio 26, 2011

67   Tali Heruti Sober and Hila Weisberg Iozma lo shitufit: Cah leebha atnua akibutzit lehamemet pratit. Themarker.com, June 8, 2011

68   John Hagel III, John Seely Brown, and Lang Davison, The Power of Pull (New York, Perseus Books Group) 2010

69   Tamar Snyder, Israel economy nimble, but education investment needed, The Jewish Week, September 16, 2011

70   Calev Ben-David, Netanyahu Sees Red Sea-Negev Rail Spurring China Trade Freight, Bloomberg.com, March 6, 2012

71   Sadio Garavini di Turno, Chávez y su política exterior, Analitica.com, Septiembre 15, 2009

72   Emilio Nouel, Un negocio chueco llamado ALBA, Analitica.com, Febrero 25, 2011

73   Evo Morales: Triunfo de Chávez consolida un modelo antiimperialista, Agencia Bolivariana de Noticias, Octubre 9, 2012

74   Gloria Picon y Tania Sirias, Autoritarismo Huerfano, Laprensa.com.ni, Marzo 6, 2013

75   ALBA se propone crear red de medios de comunicación para fortalecer integración, Agencia Bolivariana de Noticias, Febrero 3, 2012

76   Carlos Sánchez Berzain, Gobierno de Evo Morales tiene un exceso de tiranía, Hoybolivia.com, Febrero 23, 2012

77   Morales dice que se quedará en el poder para siempre, Hoybolivia.com, Marzo 25, 2012

78   Jimmy Ortiz Saucedo, La salud, otro embuste plurinacional, Analitica.com, Febrero 4, 2012

79   El presidente de Bolivia anima a masticar la coca, Elmundo.es, Febrero21, 2012

80   Maibot Petit, Gobierno de Evo Morales penetrado por el narcotráfico, Analitica.com, Abril 1, 2011

81   Ibid.

82   Daniel Sayani, Ecuadorian Socialist President Rafael Correa's Power Grab, thenewamerica.com, June13, 2011

83   Gustavo Coronel, Ecuador: en camino a ser una Correa del Norte, Analitica.com, Enero 2, 2012

84   Directivo de Teleamazonas teme que la democracia esté llegada a su fin en Ecuador, Analitica.com, Diciembre 23, 2009

85   William Newman, President of Ecuador to Pardon Four in Libel Case, The New York Times, February 27, 2012

86   Crisis Ecuador expone "doble vida" de economía A. Latina, Analitica.com, Octubre 3, 2010

87   Ecuador President May Have Sought Money from FARC for Elections, Says Report, Latino.Foxnews.com, May 11, 2011

88   Fernando Carrión Mena, Ecuador exporta unas 270 toneladas de cocaína al año, Hoy.com.ec, Abril 6, 2012

89   Andrea Espinoza, La industria del narcotráfico se expande en Ecuador, elpais.com.es, Mayo 31, 2012

90   La oposición inicia acciones para indagar origen de valija con droga, Eluniversal.com, Marzo 1, 2012

91   Alijo de droga en valija diplomática de Ecuador, Hoy.com.ec, Febrero 10, 2012

92   Blake Schmidt, Nicaragua President Rules Airways to Control Image, The New York Times, November 28, 2011

93   Ibid.

94   Impacto Alba sólosolo en la fortuna de Ortega, Laprensa.com.ni, Enero 17, 2012

95   Luis Fleishman and Nancy Menges, Silence on Fraudulent Rule in Nicaragua Detrimental to Latin America and U.S. Interests, The American Report, December 1, 2011

96   Pilar Rahola, La alianza del mal, Analitica.com, Enero 15, 2012
97   IISS: The FARC financed Chávez before 1999, Eluniversal.com, May 13, 2011
98   Rafael Rivera Muñoz, Walid Makled García confirmado y silenciado, Analitica.com, Mayo 26, 2011
99   Moisés Naim, Estados mafiosos, Op-cit
100   Michael Rowan, The US $6 billion man, Eluniversal.com, November 30, 2010
101   Fernando Luis Egana, Los caceleros de Makled, Analitica.com, Mayo 14, 2011
102   Roger Noriega, ¿Noriega, Existe una red terrorista de Chávez a las puertas de Estados Unidos? Analitica.com, Marzo 23, 2011
103   Milos Alcalay, Makled y el crimen de Lesa Humanidad, Analitica.com, Abril 24, 2012
104   Michael Rowan, The US $6 billion man, Op-cit
105   Lus Mely Reyes, La deportación express de Pérez Becerra, Analitica.com, Mayo 2, 2011
106   Valentina Lares Martz, La revolución socialista se va radicalizar en Venezuela, Analitica.com, Octubre 10, 2012

Chapter 1

What Is Bolivarism?

Simón Bolívar—A Legend Intended to Legitimize Chávez's Regime
An editorial in *Analitica.com* quotes George Orwell: "Whoever controls
the past controls the future; whoever controls the present controls the
past."[1] Each political regime, especially authoritarian or totalitarian,
needs to alter the country's history in order to legitimize and achieve
support for its government.[2]

In Germany the fabrication of superior Arian race was employed in
order to increase the country's nationalism. In Italy fascism used the eter-
nity of the Roman Empire to increase its support and legitimacy. Bolshevik's Russia employed the utopia of the commune ("all the power in the
Soviets"). In Venezuela Bolivarism is idealized as being an integral part of
"Marxism." This, in spite of the fact, that Marxists viewed Simón Bolívar's
accomplishments negatively. The liberator of Latin America was able to obtain independence from Spain with British support. Later Bolívar handed
over the region, which was exploited by English capitalists.

The purpose of Bolívar's legend is to erase the past before the installa-
tion of the Chávez regime, similar to the Nazi's who constantly attacking
the Weimar Republic's achievements; Chávezicism negates the accomplishments of the democratic period, 1959-1998 (the Fourth Republic). Chávez
views everything that occurred during this period negatively. Obviously
some of his criticism may be valid, but there were also many achievements.
Sonntag concludes his article by asserting that Chávez's regime should concentrate on its problems and not be allowed to persist on his neototalitarian
legends that threatened the democratic coexistence in Venezuela.

Chaffardet claims that there is another reason for changing the name
of the country to the Bolivarian Republic.[3] Besides satisfying Chávez,
the change intends to divide the population between "Bolivarian" and
"anti-Bolivarian," patriots and antipatriots, revolutionary and antirevo-
lutionary. This denomination forms an integral part of the psychological
warfare that commenced with the Chávez regime. Those who are not

Bolivarian are fearful to reveal it. In the 1999 constitution inaugurated under Chávez, Bolívar is mentioned as a symbol of national unity, justice and the well-being of the people. However, the writer of this article is quick to note that Bolívar's political thought is a product of the nineteenth century and, therefore, it has little to do with the requirements of the twenty-first century in fields such as education, science, technology, productivity, and globalization.

The Chávez regime is employing Bolívar's fame and victories in order to increase the government's legitimacy. The official government press repeatedly links current government policies to Bolívar's ideas. An official in the Chávez regime claimed that the formation of communal councils was inspired by Bolívar's thought.

John Lynch presents a classical bibliography of Bolívar's life that is considered to be the first liberator's narration in English for the last fifty years.[4] Lynch mentions that the cult of Bolívar had been used as a convenient ideology by many military dictators. From his mentor, Simón Rodríguez, Bolívar received an excellent background in the ideas of the enlightenment. However, his interest was more empirical and not metaphysical. Bolívar's ideas were also strongly influenced by Jeremy Bentham (1748-1832), considered to be the father of modern utilitarianism. Bentham's ideas, however, were rejected by the majority of thinkers. Chávez, relying on Bentham, claims that the most perfect government (his own) is the one which grants citizens the greatest amount of happiness.[5]

According to Lynch, Bolívar's life should be divided into three stages: revolution, independence, and state building. The first phase 1810-1818, Bolívar was a revolutionary leader; in the second phase, 1819-1826, he was a universal liberator; in the third phase, 1827-1830, he was a statesman. Lynch claims that in spite of some changes in Bolívar's thought his principles remained unchanged throughout is entire life. His insistence on liberty and equality was always accompanied by a search of a strong government. Lynch also correctly contradicts Chávez's view that Bolívar promoted social revolutions. However, he was a reformist who promoted land distribution, racial equality, and abolition of slavery and pro-Indians decrees.

Lynch is also correct in asserting that Chávez's and Castro's regimes exploited the authoritarian tendencies in Bolívar's thoughts and actions to justify their policies, distorting Bolívar's views in the process. The liberator's views on liberty and equality were twisted by Marxist regimes, which do not hold these values in high esteem, but needs a substitute for a failed Soviet model.

While I hold that Lynch made an important contribution to the understanding of Bolívar's life, it is my contention, shared by others, that in the last stage of Bolívar's life important changes occurred in his political philosophy. The Venezuelan scholar Sonntag claims that it appears that there is more than one Bolívar.[6] Changes in Bolívar's thought can be traced in his altering ideas from the Angostura address (1819) to his writing of the Bolivian constitution (1826). Bolívar declared in 1819, "The continuation of authority in the same individual has frequently meant the end of democratic government." However, the Bolivian constitution that Bolívar proposed called upon the president to be appointed by the legislature for life and had the right to appoint his successor.[7] Lynch claims that this change of opinion is due to disillusion; my contention, however, is that Bolívar altered his ideas as a result of changing circumstances. It is obvious that Chávez intended to imitate Bolívar's proposal about being president for life.

Sonntag claims that the last two years of Bolívar's life, which were characterized by personal decline, health problems, and especially the failure of his political project, caused the liberator to amend his ideas and degenerate into one-person dictatorship. This scholar claims that Bolívar reversed his ideas and believed that the military tribunals should be superior to civilian courts. Previously Bolívar declared that there should be a separation between the armed forces and those who administer justice. It is less dangerous if there are two jurisdictions than one. Bolívar's views changed drastically and he took draconian steps, which made a mockery of his previous liberal views.[8]

This last period in the liberator's life is completely different from the one presented in Angostura address (1819), in which he defended political liberties. In this speech he shows himself to be an admirer of Britain's parliamentary system and a strong supporter of Montesquieu's ideas. Bolívar also claimed in the Jamaica letter (1815) that the fighting for Latin America's independence is a continuation of the revolutionary movement that commenced with the United States in 1776 and culminated with the French Revolution in 1789. In order to justify the revolution in Latin America, he brings forward Enlightenment scholars such as Rousseau, Montesquieu, and Lock, to justify the rebellion.[9]

Sonntag correctly asserts that similarly to Bolívar, Chávez's ideas and political philosophy amended the ideas that Bolívar presented in Angostura address (1819), shared many similarities with Chávez when he assumed his presidency. At that time he defended political and civil liberties and proclaimed his respect for democratic institutions and the separation of powers. Therefore, Chávez's ideas in his first three years of governing are similar to Bolívar's liberal period.

After three years in power, Chávez pulled out of his original project and became radicalized in economics, social issues, politics, and culture. He insisted in combining the terms Bolivarism-Marxism-Leninism; it is Bolivarism if we think about Bolívar the dictator (the last two years of his life) and the term *Marxist-Leninist* is equally a falsification of the intellectual political history of Venezuela. Sonntag own and other investigations concerning Latin American independence confirm the shift that had occurred in the last two years of Bolivar's life. Therefore Chávez's socialism of the twenty-first century is strongly influenced by the last two years of Bolivar's life (1828-1830).

The new official version in Venezuela is that Simón Bolívar is alive and continues to live.[10] It is not meant to be a metaphor that "Bolívar continues to live in the heart of the Venezuelan people." The liberator continues to live; it is affirmed by officials. This idea is not new and is shared by many collective authoritarian regimes. Chávez's death produced similar results, the workers of Venezuela's oil company(PDVSA) chanted: Chávez lives.[11]

Stalinism did not accept the idea of Lenin's death. His body was embalmed so it can be exhibited to the public. Similar things were done to the corpse of Mao-Tse-Tung in China and Kim II Sung in North Korea. Similar to other dictators, after Chávez's death, his body was embalmed in a glass urn, so that people can see him forever.[12] The cult of personality is a common characteristic of authoritarian/totalitarian regimes. Elevating Chávez status as the second liberator intends to raise Maduro's legitimacy to rule. The former vice-president was personally picked by Chávez to replace him. However, due to technical problems Maduro's plan could not be implemented.

The War for People's Minds: Mass Media and Education in Chávez's Venezuela

Chávez's Bolivarian Revolution follows the ideas promulgated by the Italian Communist scholar, Antonio Gramsci, who claimed that there is a need for slow and gradual transformation of the society as a precondition for the arrival of Communism. The mass media and education, therefore, need to be altered radically to enable the sweeping changes of society. The "media hegemony" is an important objective that Chávez would like to achieve in order to maintain and enlarge socialism of the twenty-first century.

According to Teodoro Petkoff, the media hegemony has two aspects.[13] One is the demonstration that the Chávez regime has full control of the state's media under his supervision. The other is to crush the communication networks under private control. In spite of many radio and television stations controlled by the state, it receives a very low rating (about 4%). The state's newspapers have a reduced circulation. The ideological orientation of the state's newspapers may account for their reduced distribution. This factor explains why the Chávez regime prioritizes pushing aside and eliminating the independent mass media, where dissident voices are predominantly heard.

Chávez's administration terminated the license of thirty-four radio stations and numerous television stations. On May 27, 2007, the television station RCTV was obliged to transmit only on cable. Chávez was hoping that this act would reduce the number of listeners. However, many people made financial sacrifices in order to continue watching its programs, which included news, opinion, and educational and other issues. RCTV was transformed into a bastion of opposing the regime. The Chávez regime decided to terminate RCTV's license, justifying its decision by claiming that the signal is needed to set up a public channel.

The Law of Culture that was initiated in 2005 and edited in November 2009 constitutes another attempt by the government to control the mass media.[14] It contains fifty-seven articles; article thirty obliges the media to transmit programs that intend to preserve of Venezuelan cultural heritage. However, another article stipulates that the executive or the legislative branches will have to approve the type of cultural programs that are needed to be broadcasted. Christopher Jiménez, a national assembly deputy, claimed that this law goes hand in hand with article ten of the Law of Social Responsibilities of Radio and Television, which obliges the media to transmit freely programs that the ministry of communication has called upon.

The National Assembly proposed in October 2009 that the National Commission of Telecommunication will have the authority to terminate the work of national and international radio and television channels operating in the country.[15] It will also have the authority to revoke and supervise cable operations. Chávez claimed that the private mass media are the country's enemies.[16] RCTV is the oldest television channel in Venezuela. It operated for the last fifty years. It was shut down by Venezuelan authorities for allegedly lying and manipulating news. The Venezuelan minister of communication William Lara claimed that Globovision and the American channel CNN incite and magnify lies and manipulate news. Chávez accused the private media of attempting to overthrow his regime. He called Globovision a virus and renamed it Globovirus claiming that its programs constitute a danger to the people.[17]

The Chávez regime's justification in controlling the mass media is based on their understanding of the concept of democracy. In their view, information and communication must assure the democratic process of increasing popular participation.[18] It is, therefore, necessary to convert social communication into an instrument of integration, a facilitator for the process of uniting Latin America and Caribbean.

A former minster of communication and information, Blanca Eckout, presented a similar view, emphasizing that the socialist model of communication is necessary in order to construct a new Venezuelan society.[19] It is important to comprehend, Eckout claimed, that the media as an instrument of communication is solely for the people. Communication must be an integral part of the political process. The changes that have been introduced into Venezuelan society must be accompanied by a cultural alteration and the communication media must play an important role in this process.

The opposition press reported that the Chávez regime has in its disposal 238 radio stations, 28 television stations, and 340 daily newspapers and weekly journals. It also possesses 125 Web pages. In total Chávez has in his disposal 731 media outlets of communication which permits him and his regime to consolidate the communication hegemony, thereby enabling him to spread his Communist ideology.[20]

Another attempt by the Chávez regime to control and justify the government's rein of the communication media is the designation of the term *media guerrilla,* for high school students who will become "activists for truth" and retain some characteristics of subversive movements that will fight the private media.[21] This revolutionary message attempts to guarantee future loyalty to the Chávez regime and at the same time threatening the opposition. The announcement confirms the fact that ideological conviction of Venezuelan people is of utmost priority to Chávez's government;

using all the state's powers to achieve their objectives. The decision to use this concept was criticized by educators who claimed that young people should not be exposed to experiences or events that relate to war.

The media guerrilla system reminds Moreno Arrache of the recruitment of youngsters in order to integrate them in the Hitler's youth movement, established by the German National Socialist Party in 1926 in order to precipitate the creation of a new political system; the purpose was enabling them to join military training and develop obedience to the Nazi ideology.[22] It also reminds him of the constant kidnapping of children in Colombia in order to convert them into Revolutionary Armed Forces of Colombia (Fuerzas Armadas Revolucionarias de Colombia (FARC) guerrilla fighters. The media guerrilla constitutes an imminent danger to the educational process because it promotes subversive guerrilla and is in contrast to the educational law which advances education for peace; it also contradicts family values.

The fear instilled by authorities restricts what you can write about, therefore hindering one's ability to criticize the government. The Chávez regime contributed in creating a climate of fear. This has been achieved by using his authority to give or negate television and radio licenses. Media's outlets have been forced to change their programs concentrating on nonpolitical broadcasting. One example was the program called *Run Runners*, directed by Nelson Bocaranda, transmitted by Union Radio. In this program Bocaranda constantly criticized the government by revealing its violations and corruptions. This information was never denied. The government offered to change his program to a nonpolitical one in order to be able to continue broadcasting.

Alexi de Tocqueville's writing on American democracy is used by various Venezuelan scholars as an example to criticize Chávez's autocratic regime. Alberto Consalavi attempts to demonstrate that Tocqueville witnessed freedom of the press as an important characteristic of the United States democracy.[23] The French traveler, arriving in the United States in 1831, observed that in the Vicenne's journal, President Andrew Jackson policies were being criticized. He realized that this fact constitutes an important characteristic of North American democracy. The episode gave Tocqueville an understanding of the complex relations between democracy and the communication media. He realized that abuse of the right of free press leads to despotism.

The French writer couldn't foresee the twenty-first century's information revolution. If liberty of expression is the basis of democracy, it is incompatible with dictatorship. Information is the most important feature of the twenty-first century. Tocqueville's writing will be further analyzed at a later stage in this chapter.

The "Internet war" created strong debates between those in the opposition who claimed that it should remain free and those in the government who demanded control of this medium. The American journalist Gordon Crovitz claimed correctly that this type of technology helps dissidents around the world to share information.[24] However, at the same time Crovitz asserts such a technology enables authoritarian regimes to possess a new power monitoring and punishing critics.

One can discern four stages in the Chávez regime's dealing with the Internet. In the first, the government attempted to control this medium. In the second, the National Assembly decided that further consultations with ordinary people are needed to enable them to render a decision. In the third stage, the Chávez regime's ruling was to use the Internet as a tool for spreading the Bolivarian revolution. The fourth stage was a return to the first one.

President Chávez declared (first stage) that the Internet cannot be free.[25] The Venezuelan president claimed that there exists the need to regulate this network. People should not be allowed to transmit whatever they wish and poison the people's mind. Chávez referred to Digital News, which broadcast false news about the death of an official in Chávez's government. It also called, according to Chávez, for a coup d'état against his regime. It claimed that the Chávez regime supports drug traffic and trains terrorists, such as ETA and FARC. Such false accusations, Chávez asserted, cannot be permitted and the people who are responsible should be accused of committing a crime. As usual in the president's announcements, he blamed the Yankee Empire for spreading these false rumors. Chávez reiterated his view that the Venezuelan people are ready to defend themselves against any possible aggressor.

"The Internet cannot be a space without law," declared the Attorney General, Luisa Ortega Díaz.[26] The National Assembly needs legislation on this issue. The parliament designated a special commission on March 26, 2010, to investigate the administration of Web pages. It called for the exploration of employing improper and unethical language on the Internet.[27]

The National Assembly declared that while article 58 of the constitution stipulates liberty of expression, article 108 establishes that the communication media must strive for the formation of a good citizen and public peace. The state must assure that the mass media doesn't threaten peace and tranquility of the Venezuelan people.

Conversely, the deputy Juan José Molina defined the Internet as a mechanism of divulging information. Therefore there cannot be any legislation to regulate it.[28] Only authoritarian countries such as Iran, Cuba, and China control the Internet.

In their attempt to regulate the Internet, Chávez's supporters claimed that this practice is also used in the United States.[29] This country pioneered the inspection and punishment of those who employ the Internet. After 9/11, the Bush administration approved the "Patriot Act" which authorized the interception of any exchange of information that is taking place in the communicational network. The aim of this legislation was to regulate any type of communication, under the presumption that "terrorists" are planning an attack. The cybernetic command that was created in 2006 by the U.S. Air Force aimed at assisting in this task. The Obama administration extended the Patriot Act without any modification.

Numerous articles in the opposition press denounced the Chávez regime's attempt to control the Internet.[30] Gerver Torres claims that only authoritarian regimes, such as Cuba, North Korea, and China, control this network. This is done in order to restrict people's freedom and be able to control them. Socialism wants to regulate Internet use, negating liberty, which is the essence of this network. The Internet is employed as a foundation in the irreversible globalization process.[31] Any attempt to control the Internet will be considered a step in oppressing the Venezuelan people.

Another opposition newspaper claimed that the arrival of Cuba's Vice President Ramiro Valdez known as the "strong Internet censor" raised the possibility that the Cuban official would advise Chávez on how to control this network.[32] The Law of Telecommunication was approved in 2008 by a ministry council, but it somehow disappeared mysteriously when it arrived at the legislative branch.

My impression was that there were strong debates among the Chávez regime's cadres on the subject of controlling the Internet. First, the government denied its intention to control this network. The Chávez regime responded to the criticism by claiming that it promoted the democratization of this network.[33] It rejected as false the idea that it intends to regulate this medium. Chávez claimed that his government installed the Internet in school networks around the country. However, Chávez reiterated his position that the Internet cannot be used to circulate news that is against peace, tranquility, and public institutions. It should be employed with responsibility.

The president of the National Assembly's permanent commission on science, technology, and mass media, Manuel Villaba claimed that the decision to control the Internet will be taken after a "popular consultation" with ordinary people on this topic.[34] This announcement should be considered the second stage in the process of determining the Internet's status. The puzzle about the fate of the Internet was solved by an article in the official Venezuelan government press and *Cubadebate* (Cuban publication) written by Eliades Acosta Matos, a former official of the Cuban Communist party.

Matos resigned as the cultural secretary of the Cuban Communist Party on July 2008.[35] However, he continues to represent Cuban views in the journal *Cubadebate*, dedicated to fight "media terrorism"; the abuse of the bourgeoisie capitalist mass media. He is currently employed as a staff member of the leftist *Progresso Weekly* (*Progreso Semanal*). Matos views correspond to Fidel Castro's ideas such as what he declared in September of 2010: "The Cuban model doesn't even work for us anymore."[36] In spite of the fact that Fidel Castro attempted to retract his statement, it becomes clear that the firing of over half a million state employees in Cuba indicates that important changes will take place in this country.

The former Cuban official commences his article by mentioning that Twitter has been used by counterrevolutionaries as an instrument to maintain their political interests.[37] Therefore, Hugo Chávez decision to utilize this network should be viewed as an important contribution to world revolutions, refuting the stigma that socialism and new technologies are incompatible.

Chávez embarked on Twitter on April 27, 2010, and received 175,990 messages. The former Cuban official claims that it is estimated the a million users followed Chávez on Twitter; most of these people are antiglobalization supporters. This activity, according to Matos, represents a new stage in the world's culture. With this move by the Venezuelan President, socialism takes a Leninist path, cyber-delinquency, by its ability to increase and enlarge its supporters. Chávez demonstrated creativity by employing the Internet to organize production and the collectivization of property.

In Cuba, Matos adds, the electronic media is employed by the state to divulge articles, especially Fidel Castro's reflections. This ideology represents a new stage in the ideological, cultural war. It enables the oppressed people to listen and organize themselves in order to initiate radical changes in their lives. While in the past it was mainly employed for the support of United States' policies, Chávez enabled the network to be used for revolutionary causes.

The former Cuban official claims that Chávez on Twitter should be compared to the attack on the Winter Palace (the Russian Revolution). Revolutionaries from all countries that love justice and equality can unite on Chávez's Twitter. Today, Matos concludes, internationalism is digital and global is the enemy. This media can be used to win the cultural war. Paraphrasing Karl Marx's famous 1848 declaration, "Proletarian of all countries unite," the former Cuban official asserts, "Twitter revolutionaries of all countries unite".[38]

Michael Rowan presents a different a different view on Chávez's joining Twitter.[39] Unlike Chávez's appearance on the television program *Alo Presidente*, which is only one way, the digital network includes two ways. Rowan claims that people may respond to Chávez's inquiries by telling him that the country is not doing well. There are shortages of water, electricity, food, jobs, and money. The president will be told that there exists more poverty today than had existed when he took power. Chávez wasted a trillion dollars and more than a decade of people's time. Other questions that the people may ask the Venezuelan president are if he is helping Iran to build a nuclear bomb and how many Cuban there are in Venezuela.

On December 9, 2010, more than seven months after Matos's publication, in which he claimed that a free Internet would benefit Chávez's regime, the National Assembly amended the Law of Social Responsibility for Radio and Television (also known as RESORTE Law) to include the Internet as a network under government control.[40] This law further increased censorship and control of the free expression of ideas. As indicated before, it shows that Chávez's United Socialist Party of Venezuela (PSUV) is composed of various groups, persons with different objectives, reasons, and political thought, bonded together by the caudillo leader.[41] Scribini claims that it is possible to divide Chávez's supporters into two camps. One part includes moderate Chavist, also known as "the endogenic right" and the radical Chavist, also known as the "left Chavist."

Penaloza claims that the above law aims at impeding critical thinking and introducing Stalinist methods of controlling people's minds. This is done, according to the writer, to assure Chávez's victory in the 2012 presidential elections by silencing the opposition. The communication media (including the Internet) is the biggest enemy of a totalitarian project.[42] Penazola reminds everyone that there exists a difference between the fates of Carthage and Venezuela. Carthage was destroyed and its habitants were sold as slaves. However, unlike Carthage, Venezuela was not defeated and therefore does not have any interest in becoming slaves to Castro's Cuba.

The Law of Organic Education approved by the Venezuelan National Assembly in August 2009 constitutes another attempt by the Chávez regime to increase its power and influence and enhance the country's direction toward socialism of the twenty-first century. The date of this law's passage, August 13, 2009, is important because it was a present given by the National Assembly to Fidel Castro on his eighty-third birthday.[43] As was the case in discussing the role of the mass media, it follows the outline given by the Italian Communist scholar Antonio Gramsci. The point could be made that what Chávez calls socialism of the twenty-first century may also be labeled *Gramsci's socialism* (Communism). The Italian Communist scholar felt that Marxism should be gradually established after a prolonged period of education, drastically altering the society's norms.

The educational law must be viewed, as Carlos Aptiz correctly affirmed, as an additional step in the creation of a new political system.[44] The law constitutes an integral part of the social and economic development plan approved by the National Assembly that aims at the construction of socialism of the twenty-first century. It aims at perpetuating the Chávez regime and introducing socialist ideology in all levels of the educational system's levels. This law precipitated a strong debate between supporters and opponents, who employed historical evidence to justify their positions.

Chávez's control of the mass media played a crucial role in the election victory of October 7, 2012. Unlike the United States, where presidential debates take place, Chávez refuses to be engaged in a similar process. The last time a political debate took place in Venezuela was in 1998, when Chávez aspired to become president. The fear of debating an opponent leads to the creation of a climate of polarization, in which attacks and insults of the opposition dominate the political campaign. The sharp differentiation between "us" and "them" (the enemy) is an intelligent political strategy for those who govern without the need to give account on their actions.

In order to sustain a continuous attack on the opposition a strong propaganda apparatus is needed. Therefore, the Chávez regime created governmental communication media, which are used to promote the Venezuelan president's views. The media aim to inform the population through its channels without being challenged. Private mass media which attempts to criticize the government are discriminated against and prosecuted.[45]

The opposition claimed that Chávez's reforms in the educational area show his lack of understanding. The changes that his administration introduced in education will further deteriorate the teaching of youngsters in Venezuela. García Larrada correctly shows the correlation between income and education. Poverty will increase with those with fewer years in the educational system.[46]

Andrés Borges expands on this idea by asking what the main theme of the educational debate should be.[47] He points to basic structural problems that the educational system faces in Venezuela. 40% of preschool children (ages three to five) are excluded from receiving any instruction. Out of ten youngsters, six start the ninth grade and only three graduate from high school. Multiple causes may explain this problem, including economics and personal problems. These factors may be significant, but lack of available schools should also be considered as meaningful.

The Venezuela's average educational attainment is 7.8 years, a lot below the 10 years considered internationally to be necessary in order to avoid poverty. In the urban setting, where there are higher opportunities and conditions for education, the average years of schooling for Venezuelans between the ages of twenty-five and fifty-nine is 8.6, inferior to many other Latin American countries;: Argentina, 10.5; Bolivia, 9.2; Chile, 10.8; Colombia, 9.3; Costa Rica, 9.4; Ecuador, 10.1; Mexico, 9.1; Peru, 10.2; and Uruguay, 9.7.[48]

According to the Venezuelan Federation of Teachers, many children repeat an educational year. Sixty percent of schools are not suited to receive children. The budget for public schools as a percent of GNP in 2008 was 4.6% compared with 7.4% in 1983 (before Chávez came to power).

The Chávez regime emphasizes ideology and political indoctrination in education. It discourages critical thinking, an important ingredient for society's improvement.

A strong criticism of the educational law is directed by the opposition toward its dealing with the higher institutions of learning. It limits the university's autonomy and discourages critical and independent thinking.[49] It constitutes a barrier to the country's economic development. It excludes academic merit as an important criterion in electing academics and rescind upon the university populist tendencies. As a result of the educational law the universities have been transformed into institutions controlled by the government.

The politicization of the university makes it difficult to keep up with scientific and technological knowledge, a fact that will increase isolation, misery, and backwardness; it will make Venezuela look more like Cuba. The institutes of higher learning are in the process of becoming tools in the construction of the socialism of the twenty-first century.[50] The major consequence of the educational law will be an increase of subdevelopment and poverty in the country.

Chávez's views on the role of the universities are in sharp contrast to those enunciated by President Rómulo Betancourt (1959-1963) who viewed the higher institutions of learning as a vehicle of exchange of opinions and an important tool for the country's development. President Betancourt asserted that the universities need to promote the development of scientific investigation, especially oriented toward the country's economic development.[51] He stressed the importance of practical education and combined the schools of Sea Life (fishing) and Agriculture to a regular institution of higher learning (Orient University).

Garavini di Turno claims that the educational law is a drift toward a totalitarian regime.[52] Chávez's policies correspond, according to di Turno, to the classical studies written by Hanna Ardent, *Origins of Totalitarianism*, and Carl J. Friedrich and Zbibniew Brezeninski, *Totalitarian Dictatorship and Autocracy*, which emphasize the total control of society by the state. Such a state will have hegemonic ideology, which will indoctrinate the entire population, starting with the youth; an ideology that projects a perfect and rosy future society; a unique mass party, headed by a charismatic caudillo; a system of physical and psychological terror, a party, police paramilitary, and civilian armed organizations.

Venezuela under Chávez possesses all these characteristics and has many similarities with Nazism (Germany), Fascism (Italy), and the defense committee of the revolution in Cuba. The caudillo controls all the state's power, institutions, especially the judicial branch. The regime controls the mass media and the economy. The writer concludes his article by claiming that in Venezuela we are not yet in a totalitarian state; however, it is becoming self-evident that a drift toward such a regime has been occurring.

On December 10, 1948, the General Assembly of the United Nations adopted the Universal Declaration of Human Rights. Article 26 states that "parents have a prior right to choose the kind of education that shall be given to their children." Rivas Leone mentions this right, demonstrating that the educational law contradicts this declaration.[53]

The educational law gave parents the ability to express their opinion and participate in their children's education. In 2007, the Parents Association rejected the joint resolution of the ministry of education and industry stating that private educational institutions need to maintain the monthly payments as it was in 2006.[54]

The Venezuelan Supreme Court on October 8, 2009, rejected the Parents Association's decision to uphold the ministry's decision. Judge Yolanda Jaimes Guerrero observed in her decision that the government has the legal and constitutional right to decree what private colleges should charge. The justification for this decision lies in the fact that education is a "public service" and the state assumes full responsibility to convert it as an instrument of obtaining social transformation. The judge reiterated her view that the Parents Association has the right to express its opinion about the cost of education. However, this privilege is not absolute but is subjected to limits established by the government. The national executive needs to inspect and keep an eye on all people's educational activities, both private and public.

Is Bolivarism a Totalitarian/Authoritarian Movement?

In her book, *The Heritage of the Tribe* (*La Herencia de la Tribu*), Anna Teresa Torres claims that the historical memory of Venezuela passes through warlike scenarios, where the military power plays a crucial role.[55] The militarism of past and present impedes the construction of civil democratic institutions. The author of this book claims that the Independence war

(1810-1811) was forced on the Venezuelan people. However, years of war destroyed the economy and for more than a century prevented the chance to create republican institutions, with opportunities for all. The bishop's conference in Venezuela held on January 12, 2010, called for a stronger emphasis on human and Christian values.[56]

An interesting perspective on the major differences between the emergence of political philosophies in North and South America is presented by Mires.[57] The writer commenced by mentioning Aristotle, who claimed that the political power in the polis (city state) was held among all citizens. Sovereignty of the law means that power must be given to the multitudes of citizens. Aristotle anticipated that political power in the polis might fall in the hands of tyrants. The ancient Greek philosophers considered tyranny as corruption of politics, the appearance of barbarism, and the emergence of nonpolitical conditions.

In order to understand the continued existence of dictatorships in Latin America the writer refers to Alexis de Tocqueville's book, *Democracy in America* (1805-1859), as a monumental work that sheds light on the development of governments in both North and South America. This book was written for Europeans and not for people of the United States.

In North America Tocqueville encountered a democracy that was unlike the one that existed in Europe, after the French revolution. Europe's democracy was established after many years of absolute monarchy and into hostile environment. A rigid class or caste system that existed in Europe and lasted for a long period of time cannot be changed dramatically in a short time. North America did not have the experience of assassinating kings, the Reign of Terror, or Napoleon. The twentieth century witnessed the rise of antidemocratic movements, Nazism and Communism.

The French Revolution, according to Tocqueville, had two lasting results, antimonarchy or antiabsolutism; on the other hand, it was centralist, authoritarian, and despotic. These two concepts dominated Latin America's revolutionary wars of independence. These radical changes did not come from the people, but were initiated by the armies. Whatever Tocqueville said about France is also true about Latin American countries. The French revolution was against royalty and a provincial form of government. Any institution that preceded the French revolution became an object of animosity. This double character of the French revolution influenced those who favored absolute power. By defending centralization, despotism was introduced. In the name of the French Revolution, Tocqueville claimed, the guillotine, holocaust, gulag, and tyranny were reintroduced.

In Latin America, almost all the dictators justified their mandates in the name of the revolution. From the time of the tyranny of Juan Manuel Ortiz De Rosas, through populist military dictators of the Perón's type until the arrival of Fidel Castro, Augosto Pinochet, and later Hugo Chávez, the revolution was the religion preferred by all these dictators. Each tyrant justified his mandate in the name of the revolution.

This was in sharp contrast with North America that considered the constitution as being above everything. The European and Latin America's dictators viewed the revolution as being above any constitution. "The right is only what the revolution needs." This famous phrase by Robespierre will be accepted by most tyrants and especially by Chávez's Bolivarian revolution.

The United States War of Independence emerged as a real revolution and lacked the antidemocratic tenants that characterized the French counterpart. While Hitlerism and Stalinism were part of the French revolution, the American counterpart did not give rise to such antidemocratic movements. The totalitarian movements had their roots in the revolutionary and absolution's forms of government. Therefore it was not a surprise that the European revolutions brought with it the restoration of absolutism (Napoleon) and later absolute radicalization (Stalin).

Without democratic institutions, Tocqueville asserted, democracy cannot exist; however, without exercising democratic norms, the institutions are an empty entity. The sovereignty of the people is the base of democracy. In order for a democracy to function properly it needs to fulfill two conditions: The first is the separation of public powers as outlined by Montesquieu. If the executive branch becomes dominant it tends to become a tyranny. The second important requirement of democracy is decentralization. What Tocqueville admired about United States is not the administrative decentralization but the political one.

Tocqueville strongly stressed the point that only if these two conditions are met (separation of powers and decentralization) other rights, such as liberty of association and press can be materialized. Freedom of the press, as previously mentioned, is labeled by Tocqueville as an "essential liberty," as the most important liberty: "Without freedom of the press there cannot be other liberties."[58]

In Latin America the army initiated the state. Social communities were not formed, like in North America that influenced the emergence of the nation-state. The regimes were forged between wars of independence and caudillos. Castro and Chávez constitute the antidemocratic center of Latin America. The ALBA countries (Bolivia, Ecuador, Nicaragua, and others) are satellites of the Chávez regime. Cuba after the revolution became a military state with an ideology that attempted to justify its rule. In Venezuela progressive regression took place that manifested itself in its military dictatorial form. All major Venezuelan historians agree that there is continuity among the dictatorships of Juan Vicente Gómez (1908-1935), Marcos Pérez Jiménez (1952-1958), and Hugo Chávez (1999-2013). All these dictators repeatedly invoked Bolívar as a mean to legitimize their regimes. Chávez uses the armed forces as a personal instrument.

Mires concluded that in the age of globalization the idea of democracy has become globalized. Therefore, many dictators are forced to accept some forms of democratic representation. Some are employing falsified elections as a mean to get access to power (Nicaragua), while others manipulate elections (Venezuela, Nicaragua). Eduardo Galeano proposed the term *democratura* in referring to weak democracies that emerged after the fall of dictatorships in Latin America. In Venezuela the term *dedocracia* was coined, referring to postmodern dictators. However, one conclusion is certain these are not democracies in the ancient Greek tradition and even less so in terms of Tocqueville ideas.

In another article the same writer classifies Latin America's dictatorships in the following way.[59]

1. Oligarchic dictatorships in the postcolonial period.
2. Military dictatorships during the Cold War (national security dictatorships).
3. Military dictatorships that are national-populist or socialist.

As a result of the independence war, the generals that occupied power, in the majority of cases, represented the armed forces and the landowners' aristocracy. From this derives the Bolivarian myth that casts a shadow on the current Venezuela. Chávez's dictatorship is analyzed in the following way: An alliance between the military, the urban, and agrarian masses.

This alliance is dominated by the military state. The military state nominates itself as being in charge of the popular bases that serve them. The dictator is a caudillo.

Chávez's dictatorship is a combination of two types, populist and militarist. Castro's dictatorship is an example of a populist military regime. Due to its long duration, it acquired special characteristics. It emerged as an antidictatorial democratic revolution and was transformed with the Soviet Union's help to become Stalinist; after the disappearance of the Soviet Union, it inherited the common characteristics of a national-socialist dictatorship. However, Castro's regime may also include characteristics of patriarchal and agrarian dictatorship of the nineteenth century.

The executive branch, similarly to Cuba, was transformed into a closed institution, a place in which only Chávez's affiliates are permitted to participate, including Castro. Cuban functionaries control part of Venezuela's public administration, especially the repressive militia. The legislative branch was handed down to Chávez by the inept, disorganized, and ineffective opposition force. The National Assembly was transformed into a notary office that converts Chávez's wishes into laws and decrees. The judicial power includes immoral judges who are quick to imprison any opponent of the regime.

A Spanish journalist asks an important question which sheds an important light on Chávez's authoritarian/totalitarian regime: what happens to a country where all political power rests on one person's decisions, when this figure disapperars from the public scene?[60] The outcome of Chávez's being hospitalized in Cuba, on December 7, 2012, was that all important political and economic decisions by the Venezuelan government came to an halt. In no time in the country's history, the journalist claimed, a president was able to concentrate such power in his hands. However, a major economic decision was made two month after the Venezuelans had not seen or heard from President Chávez. The devaluation of the local currency (Bolivar) against the dollar is expected to further increase inflation and deteriorate the country's economy.[61]

Chávez paid a price in order to receive the support of the armed forces. The officer's corps. was turned into a new class called *Bolibourgeosie* or *Chavebourgeosie*. This category of people also includes bankers, consortium landowners, administrators, high public officials, and above all directors of Chávez's party, PSUV. Majority of these directors are very corrupt.

Parallel to the armed forces, Chávez created the urban and agricultural militias that fall directly under his command. For the dirty work he created, known as the hooded paramilitary groups that operate in universities and a variety of neighborhoods.

The electoral power was conceived in such a way that for Chávez to lose power it would take nearly a supermajority. This was achieved by modifying the electoral system and rewarding the party that holds power. Chávez controls 70% of the mass media. Similarly to Castro, Chávez built a strong apparatus of domination and repression of the newspapers, television, and radio. The opposition is divided and weak.

Da Costa[62] expands on Aptiz's ideas outlined above. This writer claims that the "Organic Law of Communal Councils" approved by the National Assembly on December 28, 2009, is a duplicate of the Popular Council Law (Number 91) that was promulgated in Cuba in 2000. The National Assembly initiated the Popular Councils Law (Number 56) in 1986. The collapse of the USSR brought a severe economic crisis in Cuba. During this period strict rationing on consumer goods was imposed in order to prevent the destabilization of the Communist regime. As a result of mass discontent, the government decided to deepen its control on the society. One of the measures it imposed was to expand the local Popular Councils, reforming the law in 2000. These councils were an instrument imposed by the Communist dictatorship to defend its rule.

In July 2010 the National Assembly modified the Law of the Communes.[63] Up to then the communes resolved the majority of their problems with their respective mayors. The new law increases the centralization process and calls upon a minister in Caracas to be in charge of the communes. Communes are the Spanish version of what the Russians called Soviets. Lenin said that all power must be held by the Soviets. This declaration was a fraud because in reality all power resided with the Supreme Soviet, the central committee of the Communist party that included only handpicked members.

In the process of establishing Communism in Venezuela, the Cuban law was literally copied. Similarly to Cuba, there was an experimental period of communal councils that corresponded with the period of oil boom. As the oil boom was terminated and the country faced an economic crisis, shortages of basic items led to rationing. Similarly to what happened in Cuba, in order for the government to exercise strict control on society, it decided to expand its control on the people and form the Popular Councils as control from above. These bodies serve as fifth columns of the Communist revolution; it needs to exercise control in each urban or agricultural district to prevent rebellion against the Communist dictatorship and assure its survival.

Following the legislative elections of September 26, 2010, which reduced Chávez's parliamentary majority the Venezuelan president declared that he intended to arm the Bolivarian militias.[64] Half the population expressed their dissatisfaction with the government. The opposition Venezuela *Analitica*'s editorial asked who will be in charge of these weapons and what assurances existed that they would not fall into terrorist hands. The article mentioned that mandating armed militias was a practice of the twentieth century criminal regimes, such as those of Hitler (Germany), Mussolini (Italy), Stalin (Soviet Union), and Franco (Spain).

In this respect, it is interesting to analyze an article that appeared in the government-controlled press under the title, "Venezuela is Ungovernable Without Hugo Chávez" (*Venezuela es Ingobernable sin Hugo Chávez*)[65]. Minister of Education (popular power) Hector Navarro claimed that Venezuela cannot be governed without its leader. This declaration contradicts democratic ideas that emphasized the existence of laws and not leaders. George Washington, the first American president, is associated with this idea, as he decided not to run again for office.

Ávila[66] mentions Luisa Estela Morales, president of the Supreme Court of Justice's declaration on December 2009 that the division of powers is a principle that weakens the government. The Venezuelan people, by approving in a referendum the 1999 constitution and rejecting the proposed 2007 constitutional reform, reaffirmed the republican tradition and the democratic nature of their desired government.

This lamentable declaration by the Supreme Court judge opens the door for an antidemocratic form of government. This will become an absolute state, where power resides in one person and is contrary to popular sovereignty. Sovereignty is given to the state and not to the people. The absolute state terminates individual rights and benefits only the political group that it controls.

The inability of the legislative branch to function as an independent unit of government is a constant complaint of various opposition writers. Canache claims that the National Assembly (the legislative branch) is representing other countries, but not the Venezuelan people.[67] It is not concerned with the country's problems, such as unemployment, insecurity, or corruption, but instead concentrates all efforts to enlarge and maintain Chávez's political project.

The lack of independence of the Judicial System is another complains issued by Chávez's opponents. Human rights attorney Gonzalo Himiob Santomé accused President Hugo Chávez of using the judicial system as "a weapon for persecution and intimidation of the opposition and the political dissidents."[68] The opposition parliamentarian Ismael García uses the term *Judicial Terrorism* to designate the malfunctioning of the judicial system.[69] There are judges who act like Mafia members, whose main role is to persecute political dissenters.

In an article entitled "Chávez's Wall" (*El Muro de Chávez*),[70] the writer compares the Chávez regime to the one in East Germany during the Cold War. The Berlin Wall represented a dividing line between opposing ideologies, such as, Communism and totalitarianism, on one hand, and democracy on the other. It differentiated between liberty as opposed to oppression; democracy as opposed to dictatorship; sovereignty as opposed to external control; wealth creation as opposed to centralized economy; free thinking as opposed to thought control. Therefore the destruction of the wall represented liberty, democracy, sovereignty, wealth's creation, and free thought.

The Chávez regime that came to power in 1999 constructed a wall in order to divide the Venezuelan people. Chávez's wall, similar to the one in Berlin, resulted in an inefficient government of corruption and flattery, justifying its hold on power by past events. The fall of the Berlin's wall demonstrated that socialism is disguised as Communism, which is not a source of improving people's welfare or economy. The centralized economy demonstrated the inefficiency of the bureaucracy. With its fall, it refuted the paradigm of state's property as an advantage in economic development. It violated freedom of speech and the press and liberty was curtailed. The state became an instrument of repression.

Chávez regime is attempting to form new identities and holidays becomes evident when the Venezuelan government decided to remove Christopher Columbus's statue.[71] It's obvious, that the Spanish explorer, who discovered America, is a symbol of the revolutionary government's resentment. The Venezuelan caudillo looks upon the pre-Columbian period in Latin America, as an ideal time when "good wild" people ruled themselves. This view is a myth, antihistoric and an illusion that forms a part of a legendry view that contradicts reality. The fight of the Indians against Columbus indicates a racial dimension, a reverse discrimination against white people. The "lost indigenous paradise" neglects the fact that Bolivar married an oligarchic woman from Spain. Imperialism and war among the Indian's tribes were common.

The disfiguring of Columbus's statue hastened the identity crisis of many Venezuelans. It eliminated their Spanish heritage, an important component of people's identity. It is obvious that the people of Venezuela are the product of a racial mixture during hundreds of years. It is therefore absurd to claim that the Spanish heritage needs to be eradicated. Flores claims that Chávez and his followers need to read Lewis Hanke's book, *Spanish Fight for Justice during the Conquest of America* (*La lucha española por la justicia en la conquista de America*). The writer realized that the revolutionary government only reads materials that correspond to their belief system and therefore will reject his advice.

The display of militancy is an important element in keeping Chávez in power.[72] In order to influence the population at large, the PSUV must emphasize the following lines: integral defense of the country, social control, ideological formation, diffusion of revolutionary ideas, voluntarism, memorial construction, and historical analysis. The final objective is to transform and radically change the society.

Romero analyzes the characteristics of totalitarian regimes relying on the philosophy of the German scholar Hannah Arendt's book, *Origins of Totalitarianism*.[73] According to the writer, Arendt's ideas are implemented in Chávez's daily policies. Essentially totalitarianism is an ideology based on terror, repression, purging, condemning, disqualifying, and destroying the individual human person.

Chávez emphasis on war and militarism is indirectly criticized by a writer who outlines the ideas of the Japanese scholar Daisaku Ikeda's contributions to a peaceful world.[74] The Japanese scholar mentions the fact that the art of war is more popular than the art of peace. Citing the examples of the Islamic Fundamentalists and indirectly Chávez, Ikeda claims that warlike messages may have a wider public appeal. The Japanese scholar claims that peace depends on the individual person who inculcates the importance of peace values. Each individual must transform himself to become appreciative of the importance of peace. The importance of peace values is a message that Dr. Ikeda attempted to contribute to the people of the world. In order to achieve this aim, the Japanese scholar founded cultural, educational, and peace research institutions around the world.

Saucedo claims that it is necessary to put limits on presidential terms. Such a law is important for a real democracy.[75] Mexico is mentioned as an example, where the constitution mandated only one presidential term. The caudillos distort democracies by creating a political party of one person. This writer quotes Aristotle, who said that it is bad when a man and not the laws exercise sovereignty. Men are subject to passions and moods. The institution of one presidential term would bring an end to the practice of caudillos.

Another example of the above is Colombia, whose leaders, unlike those in Venezuela and other Latin American countries, followed the constitution.[76] Colombia's Constitutional Court voted 7-2 in March 2010 to strike down a law that would permit President Álvaro Uribe to run for a third term. The Colombian president responded to the court's decision that he would respect and obey the constitution. Uribe's decision should be considered an important boosting to Colombian confidence in its democratic institutions. When the legislative branch passed a law allowing the Colombian president to run for a third term, the court claimed it was unconstitutional.

Other commentators emphasize the cult of personality as an important characteristic of totalitarian/authoritarian societies. Stalin, Mao, and Castro strongly stressed this idea. In 2009, in Beirut, the capital of Lebanon, a restaurant named Hugo Chávez was opened. The waiters wear red shirts and a beret that resembles the Venezuelan caudillo. The restaurant was inaugurated by the Venezuelan Chávezist ambassador Zoed Karam.[77]

In a 2010 official government press (*Agencia Bolivariana de Noticias*), it was mentioned that the budget for security projects, health, and industry were increased.[78] The Bolivarian National Police (*Policía Nacional Bolivariana*, PNB), whose main function is to protect the current regime in Venezuela, will enjoy an increase in funding and work in conjunction with local communities to be able to fulfill its primary role as the protector of the regime.

Is Chávez the New Lenin of Latin America?
The question of what Bolivarism or socialism of the twenty-first century is is both controversial and complicated. There are many scholars and analysts who view the Chávez regime positively and believe that the Venezuelan leader was able to correct the mistakes previously made by the Communist regimes in the Soviet Union and its satellites. An important idea advanced was that the transition from capitalism to Communism in the Soviet Union and its allies was incorrectly performed. There are other Marxist scholars, however, who believe that Marx was not specific enough in describing what would occur after the revolution.

A special Congress of PSUV in April 2010 declared the principles of building a new model called the "new socialist state."[79] The document claims that the enemies of Bolivarian revolution are imperialism and capitalism—especially the United States government, with its transnational monopolies, and its financial, technological, military, and economic sectors. The enemies also include the "Ecclesiastic Hierarchy." The PSUV declared itself Marxist, anticapitalist, and antiimperialist. Therefore, the need arises for a "new architecture of international alliances," such as the Bolivarian Alliance for the People of Our America (ALBA). The document also calls for the eradication of capitalism and the removing of private ownership.

Heinz Dietrich promoted the idea that Chávez was converted into a new Lenin who will lead the Latin American countries to become Communists.[80] However, the Marxist scholar, after the parliamentary election in Venezuela, on September 26, 2010, claimed that the outcome of the people's voting might indicate the end of the Chávez regime. This idea corresponds to an article that Dietrich wrote in March 2010 in which he asserted that the scientific foundation for the transformation to socialism of the twenty-first century has been established.[81] The only link that is missing is the political will of the people. Therefore, as mentioned above, the result of the elections of September 26, 2010, in which about half of the population voted against Chávez, demonstrated the inexistence of Venezuelans' political will.

In an article entitled "Response to Heinz Dietrich" (*Respuesta a Heinz Dietrich*), Mackenzie attempts to refute Dietrich claims of Chávez's merits in particular and Communism achievements in general.[82] While Dietrich glorifies the Russian Revolution of October 1917, the writer of this article claims that in reality it was a coup d'état executed by a minority that imposed a totalitarian regime. The new regime abolished the liberties that were gained in the "bourgeoisie" revolution of February 1917.

Mackenzie claims that the question should not be if Latin America "needs a Lenin" and a "socialist revolution." Rather the proposition must address the merits of the Bolshevik's regime in Russia and its contributions for Europe and humanity. October 17, 1917, was not as Dietrich says an assault on the modernization process. Communism is not equated with "modernization." It was a restoration of a totalitarian regime, a lot worse than the Czarist government. The regime of the "new man" led to the Nazi-Soviet pact of 1939. The expansionist logic of these two totalitarian states, Soviet Communism and German Nazism triggered the Second World War.

The intention to immerse Venezuela and other Latin American countries into Leninist dictatorships constitutes an example of how difficult it is for humanity to get rid of utopias. Dietrich claims, that Lenin's ingenious work was to give a qualitative boost to the process of Bolshevik's modernization; turning it into a postcapitalist society, against bourgeoisie and imperialism. The writer of this article claims that Dietrich is wrong in characterizing the Leninist dictatorship as a "civilization," ignoring the fact that millions of people perished under the Soviet system.

Mackenzie claims that Lenin didn't understand that there couldn't be political and economic modernization without the bourgeoisie. It requires all the components of society to freely engage in the process that includes all spheres of production, above all in the areas of politics, culture, and intellectual life. "Modernity" for Lenin was to install a minority government, violent in nature, led by one party and leader whose aim is to destroy the "reactionary" classes.

Dietrich blames Stalin, who destroyed the leadership that created the historical project of "socialism of the twentieth century." Lenin showed innocence in front of Stalin, who is characterized as a bad Communist and a terrorist. Dietrich, therefore claim that Stalin should be blamed for all the problems the Soviet Union faced. Mackenzie claims that no serious historical study will confirm this thesis.

In the Bolshevik conference of April 1917, Lenin's comrade Rykov said that only the triumph of socialism in the West can justify the dictatorship of the proletariat in Russia. The Mensheviks claimed that in order for the socialist revolution to be successful there is a need for Russia to achieve a higher amount of economic development. Dietrich claims that the Men-sheviks were mistaken, but Mackenzie disagrees.

Dietrich claims that Chávez, like Lenin, needs to give a "qualitative assault" and dedicate himself to the rapid destruction of all private prop-erty, the "bourgeoisie" parties, and the "dying" social classes. The Marxist scholar also hints that Castro's brothers want Chávez to "pass the Rubi-con" and do what Castro had accomplished in 1960, when he launched Cuba's total rupture with the United States and ordered the confiscation of the American big business in Cuba. Later he received guarantees from the Soviet Union to preserve his regime. The problem is that the world is no longer bipolar, and there is no guarantee that Chávez will be defended by Putin with the same enthusiasm that Khrushchev gave Castro in August 1960 and April 1961.

Mackenzie claims that Dietrich is a good student of Frederick En-gels, the inventor of wiping out entire races, liquidating people, such as Czachs, Basques, Slovaks, Poles, and Scots; these people, according to Engels, "have no future" and play a reactionary role in history. Engels wrote this in January-February 1849 in the new *Renana* newspaper. Karl Marx wrote an article in 1852 (some say that it was written by Engels, but received Marx's signature) in which he proposed the sickening idea of the extinction of the French and Spanish Creoles in Central America. Referring to these texts, George Watson concludes that these brutal frank proclamations constitute the principal heritage of Marx and Engels on Hitler and Stalin.[83]

Alan Woods, a British Marxist, who represents a minority view in the international Communism movement because of his affiliation with Trotskyism, is a new ideological adviser (replacing Dietrich) to President Hugo Chávez.[84] The new political adviser urges Chávez to expand the revolution rapidly; otherwise, he will be defeated in the 2012 presiden-tial elections.

According to Woods, the September 2010 elections demonstrated that the masses are impatience because of the slow pace of the revolution and the only way to win the 2012 elections is to expropriate big capitalists. The people must be convinced that the revolution is invisible. Woods' politi-cal philosophy may be summarized as follows: "While going too fast is dangerous for the revolution, there is no time to loose. There is the need to speed up."[85]

The Italian Marxist scholar, Antonio Gramsci, the last European Marxist theorist of Lenin's time, believed that the Communist revolution in the Soviet Union cannot be imitated in Europe. Gramsci was arrested by Mussolini's guards and wrote his political philosophy while in jail. He claimed that in order for a Communist revolution to succeed, a long period of education was necessary to transform the prevailing consciousness and values of the population.

Gramsci was interested in studying the culture, the spiritual and moral ideas, and the construction of ideal instruments in the formation a new conception of the world. The ability, not only to oppose the dominant culture, but also to reformulate capitalism; this is a long process and may take more than one generation; this is the only way to successfully introduce Communism to a country.

Gramsci had a profound influence on Chávez's ideas. The Venezuelan president, in a speech commemorating Simón Bolívar's victory on August 13, 1813, mentioned the importance of Gramsci's contributions to his political organization.[86] It is vitally important to create a mass party that will generate cadres. However, Chávez complained that it is impossible to obtain cadres with bourgeoisie education that is based on domination. Romero claims that Gramsci abandoned the insurrectional option and opted for an institutional change through political means. Therefore, Gramsci's ideas were distorted by Chávez and his followers.[87]

Socialism of the twenty-first century isn't an analytical ideology, but a sum of slogans and proclamations oriented toward polarizing the population and consolidating central power.[88] This view received indirect support from President Chávez when he declared that the delegates of his party (PSUV) must become the fundamental guides of the militants.[89]

Padrino asks a very important question: why do so many scholars support the Chávez regime?[90] How can such people, who are capable of critical reasoning and able to analyze world affairs, express their admiration of socialism in the twenty-first century without noticing its populist, antiworkers and totalitarian nature. The list of scholars and artists who support the current government in Venezuela includes, among others, Meszaros, Petras, Chomsky, Penn, and Stone. The writer of this article claims that the Chávez regime is repressive and opposed to Marx's ideas. Chávez uses the judicial branch of government to crush and eliminate any political dissent labeled as "internal enemies." Padrino claims that these intellectuals who support Chávez should be considered mafia, who are twisting the events of the postmodern period. The "intellectuals," the writer concludes, were transformed thanks to the Bolivarian oil checks.

The cynicism of Chávezism is unlimited. The energy minister Ali Rodríguez Rafael Ramírez didn't fully explain why Venezuela gives electric plants to Nicaragua and Bolivia, at the same time that the country faces electric shortages. While Chávez spent $70 million dollars on an airbus and thousands more on suits and expensive watches, the people are living in ignorance and witnessing the loss of work. Sandia concludes his article by claiming that Marx lived in poverty while he was writing his failed theory for liberating the poor, his student (Chávez) is surrounded by riches and wealth, causing the people to become poorer.[91]

In spite of the fact that Chávez claims that socialism of the twenty-first century is different from the one that preceded it, many analysts refute this view and claim that the similarities are too great to be ignored. One commentator compares Chávez to Castro, who declared in January 1959 that he was not a Communist. Later Castro reversed his statement and pronounced that he is a Marxist-Leninist. Chávez, gradually shifted his views until it became evident that what the Venezuelan leader calls "socialism of the twenty-first century" is basically Communism. In December 2009, Chávez, Like Castro before him, declared that he is a Communist.

Castillo asserted before Chávez's announcement that he is a Communist on December 2009 that the Chávez regime should be considered Communist for the following reasons:[92] a. Concentration of power is given to one citizen. b. Many media outlets were confiscated. c. Justice does not serve the rights of the citizens. d. Decentralization was weakened and a the central power was increased. e. The educational system was oriented toward indoctrination of the youngsters. f. The government attempted to transform the state so it would become the only producer of services and goods. g. The government proposed to cancel private property. h. The constitution was violated by the will of the dictator. i. Hatred was fomented and the church and its Christian values were condemned. All these factors allowed him to designate the Chávez regime as Communist.

In the dialectic approach to history, Communism is presented as being "liberating," while those groups that are not Communist are considered to be "bourgeoisie," "reactionary," and "fascist." The diffusion of Marxist terms is assisted by employing the following terms: *oppression of the bourgeoisie, alienation, reactionary,* and *exploiters of the people.* Those who use these terms are not always Marxists: nevertheless, they contribute to the spread of Marxist's terminology.

Marxism is also presented as a humanist ideology. There are progressive Christians who encourage a dialogue with Marxists. However, Marxism in its orthodox form is devoid of any spirituality. Marx saw his ideology as being perfect, natural, and identical with humanism. Marxism rejects the role of religion in human behavior and is therefore atheistic. Marx viewed religion as a source of alienation, "the opium of the proletariat." He strongly condemned Christianity for its justification of classical slavery, glorification of the medieval order, and approval the oppression of the proletariat. According to Marx a state that relies on religion is not a real one.

In 1998 Chávez promised to reform the Venezuela's political system. A new constitution was proposed and the Fifth Republic commenced. Chávez, after being in power ten years, confessed that he was a Marxist, in spite of the fact that he had never read Marx's *Capital*. He envisioned Castro's Cuba as a political system to imitate. In the first years of Chávez's Bolivarian revolution, some believed that his ideology was similar to past populist caudillos in Latin America. However, starting in 2006, Chávez's socialism of the twentieth-first century mixed Stalinism with collectivism, as in to Cuba. It employed authoritarian concentration of power, the elimination of decentralized political forces and a strong contempt for the opposition.

Boyd claims that: "Hugo Chávez's twenty-first century socialism is but an oppressive dictatorship, more resembling to authoritarian Communism than to democracy."[93] In similar fashion to Lenin's Soviet Union initiative that was intended to terminate private ownership, the Venezuelan National Assembly discussed the "Labor Organic Law," which aims to "end private property as a form to appropriate the capital gains of producers."[94] The document, which includes many quotations from Karl Marx, calls for the breaking of the capitalist system and its replacement with socialism. In addition, the document stresses the importance of the need to "replace the market as the economic pillar with the life of human beings served by a conscious planning to meet their needs."[95]

It is important to note that the Venezuelan Communist Party (*Partido Comunista de Venezuela*, PCV), in a document published in March 2011, declared that Chávez was a despot.[96] This has been affirmed in spite of the fact that the party is an active participant in the government. The document claimed that Chávez's regime resembled a bourgeoisie government and possessed the less desirable characteristics of a socialist regime. It criticized Chávez's concessions to China and asserted that it amounted toundermining the Venezuelan president's assertion of national sovereignty. It also asserted that Chávez created an agricultural disaster by importing all its food supplies.

Is Bolivarism Similar to Fascism/Nazism?

Aure finds a lot in common between Joséph Goebbels' fundamental principles and Chávez's policies.[97] The founder of Nazi's propaganda machine employed eleven rules that guided the Nazi regime.

1. *The principle of simplification and the mention of the unique enemy.* Adopt a unique idea and symbol; individualize the enemy as unique, ("empire"equals the United States).
2. *The principle of linking enemies.* reunite diverse enemies in one category so they are inseparably viewed (Colombia and the United States).
3. *The principle of transposition, charging enemies with errors or defects.* Respond to each attack with a counter one; if you cannot negate some bad news, invent new ones. The shortages in Venezuela's public sector may constitute a good example to the above idea. Chávez blames the shortages of water on rich people who use extra for the use of their private pools. You may get the impression that the garden of Chávez's dwelling is made of artificial flowers.
4. *The principle of exaggeration.* Chávez's repeated assertion that the Yankees will attack him.
5. *The principle of vulgarity.* All propaganda needs to be popular and adopted to the people's intellectual level. Chávez follows this rule in its extreme form; it is not limited only to his colloquial language; it includes the insults of his enemies and lying with sarcasm.
6. *The principle of orchestrating through coordination among a multitude of performers.* Propaganda must limit itself to a few ideas that constantly repeat themselves and be presented from different

perspectives and points of view, but adhere to the same concept; if one repeatedly lies it is converted into truth. *Examples:* Chávez's repeated assertion that they want to kill him or his repeated saying that "I am the people." If deficiencies against Chávez's government are exposed, this represents a personal threat against him and also against the people that he supposedly represents.

7. *The principle of renovation.* You need to omit information and new arguments constantly; when the adversary responds, the public is interested in other issues; the adversary's answers cannot counteract the level of accusations; when the people view a threat, Chávez's government introduces a distraction to prevent people's concentration on this problem.

8. *The principle of probability.* Using diverse sources and fragmented information and mentioning famous people of the world to support their point of views; in reality the information derives from limited number of sources but gives the impression that it is universally accepted.

9. *The principle of silencing.* Questions or news that favors the adversary that cannot be answered are dismissed. The Venezuelan leader's treatment of the student movement is relevant to this point of view; he silenced the movement without responding to their grievances. Chávez's friendly mass media is recruited to assist him in this endeavor.

10. *The principle of transfusion.* As a rule, propaganda employs national myths, hatred, and prejudices; it must be presented in primitive ways so it can be accepted. Chávez exploited the Bolivarian mystic and the national sentiments in a similar fashion to past dictatorial leaders. The Venezuelan leader is a defender of the country's idiosyncrasy, the poor against the rich, exacerbating the resentment among the social classes.

10. *The principle of unanimity.* Creating a false impression of unanimity. Chávez includes everyone in one category. The Venezuelan leader represents and solves everyone's problem.

The writer concludes that the people must be aware that the Chávez regime is incapable of solving the country's problems. Therefore, the need arises to unify the opposition and create an alternative to the current regime in Venezuela.

The state enterprises established by the government were not transformed to the worker's control, but remain under Chávez. The only change that occurred is that profit doesn't go to the owners of production, but to the state. The state doesn't pay any rent to the property owners. The workers, contrary to what Chávez says, don't gain any benefits. To the contrary, they lost social benefits, collective bargaining, and the right to discuss their contract. The workers are confronting a new, strong patron that employs demagogue, criminalization of social protest, and brute repression.

All these actions taken by the Chávez regime are contrary to Karl Marx, founder of Communism. Marx, in his extensive writings, never mentioned such a form of state control. The opposite may be true, he envisioned that the workers would be the ones who administered the means of production—never the state. Marx, according to the writer, favored federalism and was an enemy of centralized political power. Marx promoted the transformation of the social and economic structure in order to achieve human emancipation.

The Chávez regime cannot be Marxist if workers' rights are abused, the syndicate role is questioned, and if the energy wealth is shared with transnational companies. We are witnessing the emergence of a Bolivarian social fascism political system, a controlled society that needs to obey orders from above, with military discipline. This system is a fraudulent, militarized socialism that falsifies Marxist revolutionary ideas. Instead of creating changes of socialist control, state's capitalist projects are designed utilizing intimidation, exploitation, and political arm twisting. The writer concludes that it is imperative to build a solid impassable wall against Chávez's system of social fascism and its military affiliates who attempt to regress to the worse times of the twentieth century.

Padrino, in one of his articles, claims that Chávez instituted a vulgarized capitalist state system (social fascism) that employs socialist slogans that degenerated into an almighty state that administers everything.[98] This includes, health, education, food distribution, ports, airports, roads, the merchant fleet, transportation services, gas companies, electric, telephone, oil, cement, and an important part of the banking system. It amounts to a militarized system that permitted exploitation, looting, and delivery of capital obtained from oil to the needs of other countries.

During the period 1999-2010, inflation rose 733%, irresponsible indebtedness that led to the devaluation of the monetary system (the Bolívar). Chávez justified the devaluation, claiming that it was intended to stimulate national production. The writer negates this assertion by claiming that it achieved the opposite, destroying national production. The agro-industrial sector was destroyed by the current regime. Poverty hasn't improved, according to data from the national institute of statistics.

The same writer, in an article entitled "The Barbaric Social Fascism" (*La barbarie socialfascista*), claims that the Chávez regime constitutes the biggest fraud of the century.[99] The barbaric social fascism aims at securing state capitalism with the assistance of employing violence. It aims at militarizing the nation, converting the country into a military barrack and the people into soldiers that are obliged to obey caudillo's orders. This military obsession includes the structure of the government's party (PSUV), integrated into patrols, squads, battalions, etc.; converting the party's militants into real soldiers that are not allowed to deliberate or think; only to obey and act accordingly.

The alienated party's militants are also employed as an administrative and electoral instrument, applying Chávez's political line and imposing his will on the Venezuelan society. Given the military character of this project, there is no room for political adversaries, who are considered internal enemies and according to the national security doctrine need to be eliminated.

The militarization of the country includes infantile Bolivarian circles, assigned to indoctrinate preschool children. The formation of "communication guerrillas" integrated into youths aged 13 through 17 for the purpose of guaranteeing the regime's permanency. It also includes the creation of student, peasant, and worker militias destined to liquidate the syndicate and student movements. This regime is also characterized by compulsory purchases of war materials, disregarding vital aspects of the national life, such as health, education, housing, and workers' social security.[100]

In an international social forum in São Paulo, Brazil, the Italian representative Rafaella Bollini criticized Chávez, claiming that the progressive governments in Latin America will not be able to introduce positive changes if human rights and basic democratic principles are violated.[101] She asserted her opposition to the closing of radio and television stations. It is one thing to fight against the economic abuses of neoliberal system, but it doesn't justify accepting fascist ideas.

The Europeans, especially the Italians, didn't forget Benito Mussolini. He started as a Communist and ended up as a fascist. The progressive leaders in Latin America need to be careful not to follow this line. The Chávez era is characterized by police raids, assassinations, and violations of freedom of expression and of other freedoms. If Chávez consider himself a revolutionary, Bollini asks, why does he sell oil to the United States. The Venezuelan leader is engaged in conflict with many countries. He lacks cultural and educated advisers who are well informed. Therefore, the writer concludes that Chávez is his own enemy. If he is overthrown, Chávez will not follow Fujimori route to Japan, but instead will take refuge in Cuba.

In an editorial in the *Venezuela Analitica*, the writer asks if the rich are subhuman. (*¿Los ricos son subhumanos?*)[102] The Venezuela leader claims that the rich people have only a body but lack substance. The editorial proceeds to compare this view to the Nazi's, who also felt that a certain category of people should not be considered as human beings. The Nazis employed the word *untermenschen* to describe such people. In this category were included Jews, homosexuals, mental patients, and gypsies. Such people were considered subhumans. Stalin applied the same idea to the *kulaks* (farmers). This idea was also prevalent during the colonial period in Africa and other parts of the world. South Africa's Apartheid should also be included in this category.

In Venezuela, the writer claims, there exists political apartheid. Some groups are excluded and considered to be subhuman. These include *pitiyankees* (United States sympathizers), counter revolutionaries, and fascists. There doesn't exist a monetary borderline that determines who is rich. Those who became rich as a result of the Chávez regime (Bolibourgeosie) are not included in this category. Hatred is directed toward those who are not revolutionaries.

Padrino claims that an important objective of the Bolivarian social fascist system is to destroy the organized labor.[103] Its aim is to create a new political system with a different method of organizing the society. The current regime, employing totalitarian logic, aims at assembling a corporate structure in order to achieve its aim of destroying the syndicate organizations and replacing them with new paramilitary entities that respond directly to Chávez's orders.

The state's oil revenues (*petroestado*) are employed to crush the syndicate movement. To limit the rights of the workers to organize themselves;

to negate their right of discussing their collective contracts or to refuse recognizing workerss right to strike. Employing military repression and state's terrorism methods, the Bolivarian social fascist regime is frightening workers, jailing their leaders, and weakening their ability to gain economic and social benefits. This is achieved as a result of the imposition of exploitative state's capitalism using its monopoly on power as a means to domesticate and control the country's workers.

The ferocity with which the antigovernment demonstrations were repressed reaffirmed the fascist character of the regime.[104] This new show of force by the government is an illustration of the national security doctrine, conceived years ago by the U.S. Pentagon in order to subjugate the people of Latin America. The current regime in Venezuela attempts to criminalize any type of protest, claiming that it will destabilize the country. This excuse is used in order to crush political dissidents considered to be "internal enemies."

Padrino analyzes Karl Marx's book, *Eighteenth Brumaire of Louis Bonaparte*, in order to compare and contrast the Chávez regime with Napoleon's rule.[105] Marx analyzed the reasons for the defeat of the 1848 revolution in France and what lessons should be drawn from this event. Marx coined the theoretical category known as *Bonapartism*. It refers to a charismatic leader who received his legitimacy from the "people's will." Its main support, however, derives from the military and lumpenproletariat.

The Chávez regime is a good illustration, according to the above writer, of Bonaparte's social fascism. It constitutes a reprint of Marx's theoretical writings of the nineteenth century; in addition to a neoliberal political economy and a wild capitalist system. Chávez is in complete control of all democratic institutions, such as the legislative and judicial branches of government and of moral and electoral powers.

The Chávez regime crushes the opposition, including those of his inner circle; in the event of disagreements, those who express different opinions are viewed as traitors or counterrevolutionaries. Bonaparte's social fascism will sooner or later result in total failure. Those regimes, which employ personal absolute rulers, strangle people's participation and result in perverse elite power. Confusion between personal power and socialism is not a new phenomenon in history. Many other dictators employed socialism to justify their political atrocities. The Bonaparte's project adopted by Chávez has increased resentment and social hatred.

Civil-Military Relations in Chávez's Venezuela

From the time Chávez came to power in 1999, the Venezuelan armed forces have witnessed profound changes in its structure, mode of operations, and values.[106] The Venezuelan leader's objective has been to destroy the professional character of the armed forces, that includes serving the state and transforming it into a politicized organization, ideologically oriented, which serves exclusively the party in power.

Fernando Antich's thesis is validated by President Chávez's signing of a decree on September 3, 2010, converting the Venezuelan Military Academy to the Bolivarian Military University.[107] An institution that would play a key role in the formation and development of future armed forces' officials. It is not mere a change in name. The intention was to create an academy that would educate the cadets to serve with honesty the socialist homeland. It will strongly emphasize anticolonialists, antiimperialist, revolutionary, socialist, popular, and patriotic values.

This process of transformation encountered difficulties as strong resistance surged in important military sectors. The military continued to maintain the thesis that the armed forces, in order to preserve its efficiency, needs to protect certain traditional values, such as discipline, subordination, meritocracy, professional dedication, etc.

Chávez's intention is to stay in power indefinitely. As an acute observer of Latin America's history he is aware that military governments, from both the left and right (of popular origin or those that employ force), are always toppled by their own armed forces. The historical lesson is very clear; the armed forces don't serve to sustain political regimes of personal style. Hugo Chávez desires, therefore, to transform the armed forces from a professional organization to a revolutionary one becomes evident. Revolutionary armed forces will enable Chávez to remain in power for life. Professional armed forces, on the other hand, are loyal to governments that have legal origin, as long as the leaders don't lose their legitimacy. A good illustration of the above is the forty years of uninterrupted democratic rule in Venezuela (1959-1999).

A remark by a high ranking officer confirms Chávez's intention to stay in power indefinitely. General Rangel Silva, who was promoted by Chávez to become general-in-chief, the top military rank in Venezuela, declared in a November 7, 2010, interview with major newspapers that the army was "married" to President Chávez's project.[108] The general asserted that the armed forces would not accept an eventual triumph of the opposition in the presidential elections scheduled for 2012. Chávez defended the remarks given by Major General Silva and added that if the opposition defeated him in the 2012 elections its government would be overthrown in a short time.[109]

Reacting to Rangel Silva's statement, Barrera Tyszka claimed that the general can only be accused of plagiarism.[110] He repeated what Chávez said in his television program; that if the opposition would take over power, they would be removed by the military. Those who oppose Chávez's rule are described as "confused," "deceived," or "manipulated." The official line is unable to recognize an alternative way of thought. Blanco Muñoz, on the other hand, views the general's statement as being typical of authoritarian-totalitarian regimes, which employ intimidation-fear-distress-terror as a fundamental arm to maintain their rule.[111]

Ochoa Antich claimed that Chávez was attempting to intimidate people to abstain from voting in the next elections (October 2012) by using a military threat.[112] In a speech before soldiers and the presence of President Chávez and other important dignitaries, Commander Emil Rafael Ramos Rodríguez declared, contrary to the constitution and the essential values of military professionalism, that the armed forces embraced a new revolutionary conscience and sincere patriotic feelings providing the setting of socialism. Such a speech, Antich concludes demoralize the opposition, increase abstentions and ensures Chávez's victory.

The failed coup d'état against the president by Carlos Andrés Pérez on February 4, 1992, enabled those who participated in the rebellion to establish links with civilians. This was an important wish of Chávez, who was able to form connections with extreme left elements in the country. However, Chávez proceeded secretly to link himself with these groups. The majority of the armed forces were anti-Communist. Therefore, Chávez employed the image of Simón Bolívar, who was strongly admired by the military and could be used as a unifying force. Chávez was also aware that the armed forces admire military regimes who replaced civilian ones.

Chávez should be considered a political activist more than an ideologue. After the failure of the coup, as he secretly kept his ideas of supporting Communism, he outwardly displayed nationalistic and antiimperialistic views. This enabled him to bind with civilians and military personal who did not believe in Communism.

From the time Chávez came to power he attempted to destroy the traditional military values. Initially he was very cautious in is dealing with the military. Firstly, similarly to Betancourt (the president of Venezuela from 1959 to 1963), he increased the military budget. Many of the military garrison commanders committed fraudulent acts and weren't able to account for the money they received. Chávez's attempt to indoctrinate the armed forces becomes evident in a speech he gave before military officers commemorating 199 years of Venezuela's independence.[113] The Venezuela leader declared that no soldier, regardless of his military rank, can avoid the war of ideas. Capitalism represents the dictatorship of the elites and only socialism is a real democracy, reiterated Chávez.

Second, he initiated policies that utilized the military as an integral part of his public administration. This policy forced him to fire many civilian officials who previously performed this role. Chávez was very cautious when he commenced his rule. The constitution of 1999 maintained for the armed forces a democratic, pluralistic, and professional vision. He started to purge military commanders whom he felt weren't in agreement with his views; a strong effort was directed to mold the military as a base of his power. He commenced a strong campaign to "educate" and penetrate ideological Marxist ideas among the military personal. This factor contributed to the April 11, 2002, coup d'état. The failure of the coup enabled Chávez to nominate high-ranking officials in the military, who shared his political views.

Chávez, through the National Assembly, introduced important changes in the military, such as the 2005 "Organic Law," which revolutionized the armed forces' doctrine by copying the Cuban model in this area. This law attempted to dismantle the professional military structure, diminish the role of the military commanders and increase the role of the president in military affairs. It creates a paramilitary organization, the territorial guards; the new military doctrine was oriented to strengthen the "popular defense" in order to be able to confront through an asymmetric (guerrilla) war the possible invasion of a major superpower (the United States).

Chávez strongly increased the Cuban influence in the Venezuelan armed forces, especially in the field of military intelligence. Being unsatisfied with the changes introduced by the military, Chávez attempted to bring constitutional reforms that would repeal articles 328 and 329 of the 1999 constitution. These articles called upon the armed forces to be an apolitical institution in the state's service. Chávez wanted to convert the military so that it will be ideologically committed to his ideas. The rejection of the constitutional reform impeded his ability to achieve this aim.

The new Organic Law approved by the National Assembly on July 31, 2008, further attempted to break the professional spirit of the armed forces. It completely changed the organizational structure of the armed forces; minimized and transformed the ministry of defense and the role of high commanders, who were assigned exclusively administrative functions; increased the role of central strategic operations and those of the Bolivarian militants; increased the concept of share responsibility for defense among the various components of the armed forces, both regular and irregular (militants). Maximized the discretionary of the administration's finances; was able to strengthen influence on the military's ideological education, fracture the military's professional process, and weakened its logistics. Chávez's intention was solely to create a nonprofessional military organization, with revolutionary tendencies to serve as a power base for the Chávez's totalitarian project.

It is important to report in this context that the ambassador appointed by Washington for Caracas, Larry Palmer, testified that low morale exist among Venezuelan militaries.[114] The American ambassador added that that the Venezuelan armed forces are particularly upset about Cuba's meddling in their internal affairs.

Colonel José Machillada, professor at Simón Bolívar University in Venezuela, wrote a 2010 book entitled, *From Military Professionalism to the Militia*. This author confirms the ideas previously presented and further emphasizes the fact that Chávez implemented the Cuban recipe to solve the issue of loyalty of the armed forces to the current regime.[115] The Venezuelan president inherited a professional military organization where the study of military science received precedent over civilian-military relations. Machillanda distinguishes three periods in Chávez's attempt to transform the armed forces.

1. 1999-2002: Military officers joined government positions. The army began to be viewed as the "vanguard of the revolution."
2. 2002-2007: After the failed coup of April 11, 2002, a purge began in the armed forces and a new doctrine of a Cuban "people's war" was adopted.

3. 2007-2010: This period produced aggressive unconstitutional changes. The Bolivarian national militia was added, representing "people in arms." Chávez increased his control over some military upper echelons. The military would be seen everywhere in the government's daily work. The intended result was to create a new model which is "pro-Chávez" military."[116]

Padrino's article entitled, "Populist Neomilitarism of the Twenty-First Century" (*El neomilitarismo populista del siglo XXI*) sheds an important light on civil-military relations in contemporary Venezuela.[117] Although Nazism and fascism were defeated in 1945, they resurged, by way of military coups d'état in the second half of the twentieth century in Latin America. Different types of dictatorships were established by the armed forces.

With the arrival of Chávez in power, a revival occurred of the neo-populist militarist type of government. The new distinct characteristic of Chávezism is social militarization, proposed originally by the fascist Norberto Ceresole, an Argentinean sociologist. His ideas called for combining plebiscite Bonapartism, a messianic authoritarian leader who derives his "legitimacy" from the electoral process that is usually fraudulent; and a mystical bond between the masses and the charismatic leader. This process constitutes a perversion of representative politics. It is controlled by a caudillo's (Chávez) cynicism which manipulates the needs of people suffering from poverty and hopelessness.

Ceresole claimed that militarization of politics is a consequence of a gradual loss of people's rights. Chávez replaced the strong involvement of the political parties in government's affairs with his "general will," with the full support of the armed forces. The militarization of politics meant that the military, its affiliates, the paramilitary and the security services gained political control in Venezuela. A 40% raise in the military's salaries in April 2010 is indicative of this policy.[118] Padrino concludes that the Chávez regime employs perverse socialist rhetoric that increases poverty, corruption, and crisis in the delivery of basic services.

The militarization of politics became obvious when the defense minister declared, after the death of Chávez in March 2013, that the armed forces will support Nicolas Maduro as the next president. The opposition deputy, Abelardo Diaz, strongly criticized the above speech, claiming that it violates the constitution. The military should remain apolitical and not interfere in government's affairs. As a private citizen the defense minister has the right to express his political views. However, as a man in uniform, he has no right or authority to do so. The deputy called upon the defense minister to resign.[119]

The Russian Prime Minister Vladimir Putin completed his visit to Venezuela in April 2010 by signing a contract for selling military weapons to the Chávez regime with an estimated at a worth of $5 billion.[120] The opposition Venezuelan press, *Analitica.com* prominently displayed a letter sent by the Costa Rican president, Oscar Arias, to his counterpart the president of Uruguay, José Alberto Mujica Cordano.[121] The letter constitutes an indirect criticism of Chávez's policies by asserting that the $5 billion could have been spent for more important purposes, such as improving the lot of the poor people in Venezuela.

In order to emphasize the informal nature of his suggestions the Costa Rican president used the revolutionary identity of the Uruguayan president ("Pepe"). Arias strongly emphasized the fact that he had no intention to disrespect the sovereignty of a brotherly nation. The Costa Rican president claimed that history teaches humanity, throughout history that armed forces are the eternal enemies of development, peace, liberty, and happiness.

In some parts of the world, especially in Latin America, the armies are a source of ungrateful collective memory. Using the forms of violence at their disposal, the armed forces violated human rights in Latin America. It was the hand of a soldier who shot innocent people in the back. The armed forces consume a large part of the national income and constitute a permanent danger to the existence of democracies.

Uruguay, the Costa Rican president claimed, does not need an army. Its internal security can be handled by the police force. Its national security will not gain anything by having an army. Referring to Uruguay geographic location; Arias claimed that this country will never be able to deter such neighboring countries as Brazil, Argentina, Colombia, Chile, and Venezuela. Not having an army should be considered the best policy for Uruguay to pursue. The Costa Rican president concluded his letter by recalling his country's history. It was the first country in the world to abolish the armed forces and declare its trust in a peaceful world.

Coronel claims that it is necessary for Venezuela to follow the Costa Rica's model and eliminate the armed forces.[122] There is no reason or justification for its existence because it is not strong enough to defend against a powerful enemy and is too inflexible to counter internal enemies. The only purpose it serves, according to Coronel, is to maintain dictators in power.

Álvarez Paz claims that one of the fundamental principles of a democratic regime is the superiority of the civilian authorities over the military ones.[123] A law approved on October 7, 2009, the Organic Law of the Bolivarian Armed Forces, reversed the situation and enables the military component to be in sole service to the president. The new law established civilian groups that are loyal to Chávez and their main task is to protect his regime against imperialistic threats and landowning oligarchy. It may include foreign citizens such as Cubans, Iranians, Colombians' FARC members, or any subversive groups, such as Palestinians, Hezbollah, and others.

In reality, the above law for reforming the armed forces resembles similar arrangements in the Soviet Red Army and the revolutionary armed forces of Cuba. There are also similarities with Nicolai Ceausescu's Romania's popular war doctrine (1972) and the Iranian military guards. Ugalde correctly summarized the civil-military relation in Venezuela by claiming that the historical memory of the country passes through a warlike landscape, scenery filled with military power.[124] The militarism, of yesterday and today impede the civil construction of a working democracy.

Church-State Relations: The Case of Chávez's Venezuela

Pope Gregory VII's excommunication of King Henry IV represents one of the last victories of the church over the state. "He went to Canossa" (1077 AD) is an expression added to all Western languages to indicate the pope's victory on one hand and the king's gross indignity on the other. The pope victory was premature.[125] Around 500 years ago the state acquired the right to remove and place bishops. Pope Julio II established the right of the council (*derecho de patronato*), which recognized the monarch's right to give his consent to the appointments of cathedrals and bishops. In Venezuela this practice became evident in the case of Monsignor Ramón Ignacio Méndez, the Archbishop of Caracas, in 1827. He was expelled from Venezuela after refusing to swear loyalty to the new constitution.[126]

In general, relations between Chávez's regime and the Catholic Church may be characterized as confrontational. While conflicts have existed from the time Chávez came to power in 1999, they have intensified especially in the last several years of the Chávez regime. Chávez relations with the Church, especially during the period 1999-2006, may be characterized as absolute ambiguity. The Venezuelan leader knew that the Church can become an obstacle to his socialist-Communist project. Therefore, on certain occasions he threatened it, while at other times he flattered it. On some occasions, he declared himself as a supporter of social and educational programs initiate by the Church; on other occasions, he insulted the Catholic hierarchy, promoting disagreements between secular and religious sectors of society. In the last few years, especially in 2010, the relations deteriorated and verbal war erupted between Chávez and the Catholic Church.

A *New York Times* article revealed that discord between Chávez's government and the Catholic Church started in his first year after coming to power.[127] Chávez branded the head of the National Conference of Bishops as a "pathetic ignoramus."[128] Baltazar Porras, president of the Venezuelan Conference of Bishops, objected to the declaration of the new (1999) constitution of the right to life "from conception" instead of "from birth." He claimed that this might open the door to legalizing abortion. The Church hierarchy had objected to the provision in the constitution that described education as a primary responsibility of the state. This provision might limit or even abolish its own network of schools. The Church also separated itself from Reverend Jesus Gazo a Jesuit priest and a liberation theology advocate described as the president's "spiritual guide."

A Venezuelan scholar, Rodrigo Conde Tudanca, claims that Chávez is irritated by the Church, which reveals the truth; the priests are closer to the poor than the government's officials and the Church has more acceptance and credibility than his own regime.[129] One major discord between the Chávez regime and the Catholic Church was the employment of religious symbols by the government to advance the revolutionary process and legitimize Chávez's Bolivarian ideology. In the center of Caracas, the government placed placards opposing the oligarchic church and supporting the liberation theology branch (Popular Church) affiliated with the priest Camilo Torres. The Catholic Archdiocese of Caracas rejected the use of images of Jesus and Virgin Mary of Coromoto carrying war weapons in a Caracas wall painting. The Archdiocese protested that "Venezuelan religious expression has been turned into a warlike political moral."[130] The Cardinal Jorge Urosa Savino claimed that such an act constitutes disrespect for the religious images and they should not be used in supporting any political ideology.

The members of the Venezuelan clergy strongly opposed Chávez's declaration calling upon the people to raise the sword of justice against those members of the church who don't support his revolution. Some clergy members claimed that the Chávez regime would like to control the church. In the early days of his administration Chávez introduced a program to fight poverty and called it "Christ's Mission." Some church members criticized Chávez's use of words. The Venezuelan president replied to the accusations that he manipulated the people with Christ's name by claiming that "Christ is inside me."[131]

In 2004 the newspaper *El Nacional* gave the results of a poll that showed that 73.2% of the Venezuelan people have confidence in the church, followed by banks, 66%; businessmen, 65.1%, industrialists, 63.8%; and the communication media, 60.9%.[132] However, a government official declared in 2004 that the Catholic Church hierarchy has had a negative contribution in the construction of conciliatory bridges between the government and the people. The animosity between the Venezuelan Catholic Church and the Chávez regime revealed itself when no government official participated in the funeral of Pope John Paul II (Juan Pablo II) in April 2005. A few days, later the mass media announced that Fidel Castro presented his condolences to the Vatican's representative.

The Venezuelan government attempted to give the impression that the appointment of the new Pope Benedict XVI marks a new period of relations between the Chávez regime and the Catholic Church. The government boasted that never in the country's history has there existed a state with its mandate and mission is so close to Christ. It also claimed that in spite of the fact the Chávez's government prioritizes helping the poor; the Catholic Church nevertheless is constantly attacking the government. The result of this church's policy is to take an offensive against the Catholic people.

The mutual distrust between the Catholic Church and the government became eminent in the verbal attacks between Cardinal Castillo Lara and President Chávez. The cardinal declared that Chávez to be a paranoid dictator and a leader of a despotic government. There is no democracy in Venezuela, asserted the cardinal. Chávez responded with a personal attack on the cardinal, claiming that Castillo Lara is hypocritical, a bandit, immoral, and a coup initiator. The cardinal is a church member who represents God, but in reality he possesses a devil inside himself.

In October 2005, a new cardinal to Caracas was appointed. A short time after he commenced his duties, he met with President Chávez, initiating a dialogue that would attempt to improve church-state relations and contribute to a favorable climate of understanding between the political and religious sectors of the country. It seems that their encounter had some success as the year 2006 was characterized as a cease fire in the church-state relations. On May 11, 2006, Chávez was received by the pope, an event that some some Protestant church members to label Chávez the "Big Bishop."[133]

In the last several years of the Chávez's government, the regime attempted to implement Dietrich's advice of intensifying the process of transformation to a Communist-socialist regime. These series of actions reached its peak in January 2010, when the Venezuelan president declared that he is a believer in Marxist-Leninist principles.[134] The Catholic Church hierarchy under the leadership of Cardinal Jorge Urosa Savino strongly criticized Chávez's government policies, especially the regime's abuse of human rights. The Cardinal claimed that the Venezuelan constitution allows the existence of political pluralism, and freedom of thought and opinion.

The conference of the Catholic Church hierarchy in July 2010 rejected the imposition of socialism, inspired by the Cuban model.[135] Cardinal Urosa claimed that Marxist-Socialism is an attack against the people's common good. The conference reiterated their view that people want to live in a democracy, under the rule of law, in a climate of justice and freedom. The Bishops further claimed that this was the decision of the referendum held on December 2, 2007, which rejected Chávez's attempt to become a president for life. The document put forward by the church hierarchy expressed concern about the climate of violence and corruption in the country. Monsignor Diego Padrón, archbishop of Cumaná, asserted that the Catholic hierarchy has the right to express their views. The conference asked the Venezuelan authorities to stop the "silence of dissenters."[136]

The bishop of Caracas, Monsignor Jesús González de Zarate, requested the Venezuelan justice system to act on behalf of liberty and free all those people who were detained in prisons for political reasons.[137] This should be done in order to open the way for a national dialogue. The bishop added that there is the need to open channels of communication so that all sectors of society can express their views and a consensus can be reached. Venezuela needs to emphasize the reconciliation among its people. This criticism of the bishop goes hand in hand with Cardinal Urosa declaration that the Venezuelan justice system is impartial.

Chávez negates the existence of political prisoners in his country and claims that his firm stand against people in opposition is judicially legitimate. The opposition denounced the fact that thirty of its leaders are in jails because of their stand against the Bolivarian revolution. Two hundred years after independence, the bishop claimed the current government failed to fulfill the ideas of the founding fathers.[138]

The Bishops' Conference also expressed its preoccupation with the increase of antireligious spirit exhibited by the current Marxist-atheist regime in Venezuela.[139] The members recalled the church scandals and the Marxist-atheist ideas that aim at weakening religious sentiments. Cardinal Monsignor Jorge Urosa Savino expressed this view when claiming that the church faces a danger to its existence from the increase of secularism and the cult of socialism originated by Karl Marx and Frederick Engels. Although these scholars were atheists, they created a fundamental religion that is based on both the ideas of the Hebrew prophets (Moses) and the Egyptian Christian priests (the new man) of the third century AD. In reality, however, these noble ideas were used by authoritarian-totalitarian governments to suppress their people.

Ugalde commences his article with a criticism of the economic policies pursued by the Chávez regime.[140] He then proceeds with the economic ideas expressed by the Bishops' Conference, held in the occasion of the bicentennial year celebration. The bishops claimed that the policy of militarism and dictatorship in the last decade prevented prosperity and peace to materialize. In spite of the existence of abundance of oil (Venezuela's gold), it became obvious that a "rich" state coexisted with a poor society. Oil is not a necessary condition for prosperity. In spite of oil prices tripling in certain years, the revenues were not channeled to end poverty and the poor felt betrayed.

The mere change of government by Chávez didn't bring any improvement in the country's poverty. This, in spite of the fact that Chávez's government considered the war on poverty an important priority of his administration. In reality, this promise was not fulfilled as the Venezuelan president used the oil revenues to purchase both internal and external support. The increase in centralization hindered the state's ability to fulfill its role. The bishops expressed their firm belief that a republic cannot exist without freedom, liberty, and economic opportunities for all. Without these conditions the state is unable to fulfill its obligations.

Chávez and his cronies were fast to respond to the criticism of the Catholic Church's hierarchy. Venezuelan deputy Juan José Mendoza, the president of the National Assembly's Committee on Security and Defense, asserted that President Hugo Chávez planned to review the concordat with the Vatican and warned the leaders of the Venezuelan Catholic Church members that they are acting as political agents openly involved in the opposition's conspiracy.[141]

The Vatican newspaper reported that a hostile war of words erupted between President Hugo Chávez and Cardinal Jorge Urosa Savino.[142] The Venezuelan president was reported by local media to call the cardinal a pig and added that the church official "talks like a troglodyte and tries to scare people about Communism."[143] The insult to the cardinal came after church officials denounced a government shutdown of many media outlet critical of the Chávez regime. The cardinal reiterated his conviction that the Venezuelan president has been leading the country toward a dictatorship based on Marxist-Socialist principles. Savino added that although the church does not presume to play a political role, it nevertheless has the right to speak about issues that affect the life and future of the Venezuelan people.

As a result of the strong criticism of the Chávez regime by church officials, Cardinal Savino was requested to testify before the National Assembly. The government also recalled its ambassador to Vatican, Iván Rincón Urdaneta. The government's official press analyzed Cardinal Jorge Urosa Savino's testimony before the National Assembly and claimed that the cardinal did not show any proof to support his accusations against the president and other state organs.[144] Although the Cardinal claimed that his views are personal and in no way reflect the church's opinion; the National Assembly expressed their agreement that the church needs to be an institution solely dedicated to spiritual matters and not be involved in political issues.

The National Assembly (reflecting Chávez' view) asked to review the appointment of the cardinal.[145] The legislative branch expressed the view that the cardinal acted as a political party opposed to the Chávez's government. A National Assembly spokesman claimed that article 6 of the 1964 treaty with the Vatican stipulates that Chávez's government has the right to approve/disapprove any appointment.

The cardinal, on the other hand, reiterated his view that he is not part of the opposition; however he retains the right to criticize the current government.[146] After the hearings the National Assembly decided to advise President Chávez to revise the appointment of Cardinal Jorge Urosa Savino because of his stand against the government, which clearly constitutes a violation of the 1964 accord between the Venezuelan government and the Vatican. Archbishop Monsignor Baltazar Porras also responded to the above accusations by claiming that the request to revise the accord has no legal standing. Its only purpose is to divert attention from the real problems that the country faces.

In the "war" between Chávez and the Catholic Church, the Venezuelan president threatened to terminate its television license.[147] Chávez ordered the authorities to review the license. However, a spokesman for the Catholic channel claimed that 90% of the audience comes from the poorest levels of the population and the program plays an important role in their lives.

Miguel Acevedo, an expert of the Catholic Church, claimed that the possibility of breaking diplomatic relations with the Vatican would provoke a tremendous discredit for the regime and lead to the sufferings of Catholic Venezuelans.[148] The Vatican maintains diplomatic relations with 175 countries, more than the United States. Only totalitarian states, such as North Korea and Vietnam, or Islamic nations, such as Saudi Arabia, Oman, and Afghanistan, don't have relations with the Vatican.

Cardinal Urosa Savino, in the last days of 2010, harshly criticized the Venezuelan National Assembly laws passed in its last session and asserted, "This is certainly undemocratic, because it nullifies and dismisses the people's will which was expressed on September 26 and threatens the country peace."[149] The Cardinal added that these laws are intended to make the legislature null and void and concentrate all power in the hands of President Chávez. On December 24, 2010, in an interview with television channel Globovision, Savino declared:,"We are heading towards dictatorship; there is no doubt about it. I urge the nation leaders to bear in mind their enormous responsibility before history and God, if they are to impose totalitarian dictatorship which will surely be something terrible for Venezuela."[150]

Comparing Two Models of Political Development: Democratic Versus Authoritarian

Many Venezuelan scholars considered the Rómulo Betancourt administration (1959-1963) to be an important step in the establishment of democracy and a turning point in the country's political and economic development. Robert Alexander, writing in the 1960s, considered the Betancourt revolution to be a rival to Castroism.[151] He felt that the competition between these two types of radical change would decide the future of Latin America. However, because the Chávez regime resembles that of Castro, it enables us to compare the two types of economic and political developments. Betancourt's administration was preceded by a democratic revolution (1945-1948) that followed ten years of dictatorial rule.

On July 5, 1947, Venezuela had the most democratic constitution in Latin America. In December 1947 the Venezuelan people elected a president democratically. Prior to the democratic revolution, oil revenues helped only the rich. Those who were in charge of the democratic revolution decided to use the oil income to further increase industrialization and raise the people's standard of living. Agrarian reforms were also established. Employing rational debates and civic dialogues, it contributed to the well-being of the majority of people; the politically free institutions generated trust, confidence, and credibility. However, the conservative forces that were opposed to the reforms, encouraged a coup d'état on November 24, 1948, that brought an end to these reforms.[152]

Rómulo Betancourt, after a decade of dictatorial rule, attempted to restore the people's rule. He realized that in order to stay in power he must satisfy all groups that are an integral part of the Venezuelan political system. Attempting to revise the democratic revolution Betancourt attempted to reverse the trend of coup d'état and replace it with representative democracy. He, therefore, raised the military salaries to lessen the chances of force used to gain political power.

Attempting to change the country's political culture, as with the first democratic revolution, Betancourt and his party emphasized the use of oil revenues for the development of other sectors of Venezuela's economy. The party, Democratic Action (*Acción Democrática*), argued that economic development can only be achieved through democratic means; it is the only way to assure the happiness and well-being of the people.

The most important change introduced by the Betancourt regime was agrarian reform. Land was distributed to poor peasants; however, full compensation was given to the land owners. The 1961 Venezuelan constitution, similar to its Mexican counterpart, incorporated agrarian reform. This can be contrasted with Chávez's land reform, which employs force to seize land, without compensation.[153] The only exception was citizens of Spain, whose land was confiscated but who received compensation.

Violence was an integral part of Chávez's agrarian reform. It constitutes the largest forced land redistribution in Venezuelan history.[154] Violence is used by both sides. More than 160 peasants were killed by hired gunmen. The sugarcane grown by the farmers was set on fire by Chávez's cronies. The land seizures are described as paving the stones on "the road of socialism."[155] The landowners call it agrarian terrorism encouraged by the state. The government claims that the land seizures will make Venezuela less dependent on food imports. The result of "forced modernization," as was the case in the Soviet Union, is shortages of agricultural products.

While Chávez organized peasants from above, forcing them to join his organization because otherwise they would suffer penalties; Betancourt, on the other hand, stressed the voluntary aspect of joining community peasant organizations. He encouraged the peasants' leaders to organize themselves and assist each other in a variety of areas.

Betancourt, unlike Chávez, emphasized individual, political, social, and economic rights. Chávez, on the other hand, advocates the abolishing of private property and a substantial increase in the state's power. Chávez, following Gramsci's ideas, attempted to ideologize the educational system. This policy brought opposition from a variety of sectors of the society. The net impact was that the educational system deteriorated as many students and professors opposed this policy.

Betancourt, on the other hand, achieved important progress in the field of education.[156] The government initiated the restructuring the educational system, conforming to the needs of the country's economy. During Betancourt's administration, the number of students in primary schools doubled and college enrollment tripled. A strong emphasis was given to vocational schools to prepare the young people for future employment.

The result of the elections of December 1, 1962, is evidence of the people's support for Betancourt's government.

Barrera attempts to demonstrate the superiority of democratic economic planning and development over the authoritarian one practiced by the Chávez regime.[157] He analyzed a plan written by the Betancourt's government in 1963, which made recommendations to the new administration on how to proceed with the process of economic development. In March 1963 a plan for economic-social development was presented to the national assembly that included the period 1963-1966. Betancourt clearly indicated that the new president would have the liberty to alter and modify the plan, if he so desired.

The essential characteristics of the plan were to accelerate and assure progress in Venezuela's economy. Diversification was stressed; job creation and diminishing unemployment were primary objectives. Increasing internal demand and raising the people's standard of living became important priorities. Increasing internal production and decrease in import received utmost attention.

Attempting to criticize Chávez's forced modernization indirectly, Barrera claimed that Betancourt's regime recognized that increasing the workforce and giving people jobs is a primary responsibility of the government.[158] This, however, cannot be achieved without the acceleration of productivity. Therefore, an important priority of Betancourt's administration was to improve productivity, which would ultimately result in a better standard of living.

Stimulating domestic demand was considered an important priority in conjunction with improving income distribution that would lead to an increase in buying power. These steps would lead to an increase in the people's standard of living. Betancourt's government also strongly emphasized the importance of housing construction for low-income families and training people for work.

The plan submitted to the national assembly included input from a variety of international experts. These experts met with Venezuelan representatives, including businessmen and workers in, order to listen to the observations. Betancourt emphasized that these exchange of opinions enabled his government to leave guidelines for economic development to the next administration. These guidelines strongly emphasized peaceful means and the lack of the use of force.

Betancourt attempted to aggregate interests by listening to all the groups in his county. On foreign affairs, he established good relations with the Kennedy administration in the United States. However, at the same time he increased taxes on foreign companies operating in Venezuela. Unlike Chávez, President Betancourt refused to join the nonaligned bloc, believing that his sympathies were with Western democractic regimes and their struggle against Communism. Chávez, on the other hand, joined forces with all the antidemocratic forces such as Iran, North Korea, Syria, and others.

Ruiz, in an article entitle," The Military Party" (*El partido militar*), makes a sharp differentiation between Chávez and Betancourt administrations.[159] Betancourt fulfilled his promise and terminated his rule when he concluded his constitutional period. Unlike Betancourt's party, the Democratic Action (*La acción democratica*), which has followed democratic principles, Chávez's party (PSUV) has a military structure with an authoritarian network. A clear hierarchical demarcation is obvious in PSUV, where one person (Chávez) orders and others comply.

Ruiz claims that Chávez, through his Sunday show, communicates to his vassals in the National Assembly. There are no discussions or debates. The National Assembly, like an army, has to execute the commander's (Chávez's) orders. PSUV is very different from past political parties in Venezuela. In the past, especially during the fourth republic (1959-1999), the leader of a party was considered to be *primus inter pares* (first among equals) and not, like Chávez, an absolute dictator.

Ruiz concludes his article by mentioning that Chávezism led to the termination of democratic political parties. During the period of the end of the fourth republic, some analysts claimed that Venezuela's problems originated with the political parties. Chávez, some claimed, would be able to solve this problem. Ruiz disagrees with this assertion and claims that political parties are an essential ingredient of democracy.

The Cubanization of Venezuela

The strong influence of Fidel Castro's ideas on Chávez's government is a constant theme in the opposition's writings on this topic. Several ideas are advanced to demonstrate that the powerful alliance between Chávez and the Castro regime doesn't serve the Venezuelan national interest. Others emphasize Cuba's poverty and the failures of the Communist regime.

The opposition newspapers stress the Cuban involvement in Venezuela's domestic affairs and claim that it violates the country's sovereignty; therefore; Chávez should be accused of committing treason.[160] Hellum claimed that Chávez betrayed his country and compared him with Vidkun Quisling, the Norwegian leader who was unfaithful to his country and supported the Nazi regime during the German occupation of his country.[161] Chávez should be accused of treason because he voluntarily surrendered Venezuela's sovereignty to Cuba. This event constitutes the first time in history that a smaller and weaker country took control of a stronger state. The Cubans in Venezuela (estimated as 60,000, both civilians and military personnel) are under the direct control of Raúl Castro.

Hellum further claims that, on a daily basis, 100,000 barrels of oil are given to Cuba, while the country's consumption is only 70,000 barrels daily and the rest (30,000 barrels of oil) is used for export or to enrich the Castro family. Chávez's personal security is under Cuban supervision. The writer concludes his article by claiming that Vidkun Quisling, the Norwegian traitor, was reincarnated by Chávez.

An editorial in the opposition press reinforces the view stated above. The article claims that each visit by Chávez to Cuba raised the question of who really governs Venezuela.[162] The editorial further questioned why Chávez doesn't see the failure of Castro's regime. The presence of Cuban personnel, especially the military, raises questions about Venezuela's sovereignty. Venezuela paid $5.6 billion for Cuban staff in 2008.[163] Cuba saved $2 billion because of preferential cost of oil sold from Venezuela in the same year. According to a Cuban Professor (in exile), "Venezuela's subsidy is higher in nominal terms than any historical subsidy provided by the Soviet Union to Cuba..[164]

Romero claimed that starting in 1959 the Castro's regime endeavored to expand its influence by systematically intervening in the external affairs of other countries.[165] There is a need to distinguish among three stages of Cuban interventions attempts. The first phase was characterized by guerrilla wars in the 1960s. The symbol of the period is Che Guevara and his strategic failure. Venezuela was able to overcome this threat in the 1960s and consolidate its democratic regime. Arria reports that in 1963, before a meeting of Communist parties in Cuba, the secretary general of the Cuban Communist party, Blas Roca, was able to anticipate the importance of Venezuela for the future of Cuba's revolution.[166] He declared that when Venezuela freed itself from imperialism, all the Latin American countries would follow the same path and Cuba would have the support of the continent.

The second phase occurred during the Soviet period, in which the Cuban armed forces were utilized as a global intervention force in the service of Communist Soviet Union's expansionist policies. The main targets for this course of action were African and Latin American countries. They included, among others, Angola, Mozambique, Guinea-Bissau, Eritrea, Granada, and Panama. This stage was unsuccessful and contributed to the notion of Communist neocolonialism. Castro could not triumph following Che's formula of many Vietnam wars.

The third stage may be defined as predatory phase. Castro's intervention in Chávez's Venezuela may be labeled as abuse of authority or confidence. After fifty years of failures, the Castro regime found the right way to interfere in Venezuela's politics. Castro changed his approach and achieved success without firing a bullet. Castro's brothers are managing Venezuela affairs. Cuba exposes the idea that a leader can stay in power for fifty years with unlimited power. This lesson Castro taught his protégé, Chávez, Morales, and Ortega. Chávez, being unsuccessful, allowed the Cubans to take over important posts in the government. Román José concludes his article by mentioning that in the past, in Africa and some Latin American countries, Cuba left without obtaining its goal. Will Venezuela permit the Cuban presence when other countries refused to do so?[167]

People came to realize that the Cuban economic model doesn't guarantee productivity. Cuba imports 70% of the food consumed in the country. People's increased dissatisfaction manifested itself in increase social disintegration, such as a resurgence of prostitution, corruption and the yearning to immigrate, especially among the youth. Many people live in deplorable conditions, minimal space. A bag of cement costs more than a third of monthly wages. Padura concludes his article by asking what expectations a person can have after graduating college.

The Spanish newspaper *El País* reports that Cuba needs to cut one million state employees.[168] The government is unable to pay their salaries. This number represents 25% of the people who work for the government. This is a grave political problem for Raúl Castro, and restructuring becomes a first priority. In the past unemployed workers received prolonged compensation and were offered the possibility to study while they collected their entire salary. This procedure no longer exists. The solution, according to the Spanish article, is to extend private initiative and establish cooperatives, without government intervention. The new enterprises, which will increase efficiency, need to become alternative places of work inspiring Cubans.

Vásquez, in an article emphasizing the failures of the Cuban revolution, warns the Venezuelan people not to pursue a similar course.[169] He thoroughly analyzes Fidel Castro's speech given on May 18, 1967, in which the Cuban leader stressed the superiority of a Communist utopia over capitalism. Castro, in this speech, claimed that in ten to fifteen years Cuba would experience abundance in agricultural products, fruits, vegetables, milk, and coffee which would be freely distributed to the people. Castro claimed the capitalists have problems with markets. Prices would decline in the event of abundance. Castro reiterated the fact that Communist do not share this unsettled question. Cuba doesn't need to question how much coffee to produce. All production would be freely consumed. Cuba could raise all the chickens desired by the people.

Money would have no value and be substituted by for people's voluntarism and their ability to freely satisfy their needs. The existence of abundance, according to Castro would demonstrate the superiority of the Communist system over Capitalism. It would show the Yankees that in spite of the embargo the Communist dream survived.

Vásquez, after analyzing Castro's 1967 speech, proceeds to describe an important event that demonstrated the negation of Castro's utopia Communist dream. As a result of shortages in agricultural products, on December 16, 2001, the first American ship arrived in Cuba. After forty years of embargo, it transported from Mississippi 500 tons of frozen chickens. Castro previously claimed that his country would become self-sufficient. The arrival of the American ship in Cuba demonstrates the failure of the Cuban revolution. In the period 2001-2009 Cuba imported food from the United States totaling $3,170 billion. In 2009 Cuba imported $528 million of nutritional supply, especially chickens.[170]

Vásquez concludes his article by mentioning that Castro claimed that the world is witnessing the final stage of American capitalism. The writer states that he hopes Castro's prophesy is wrong, so Cuba can continue to import agricultural products from the United States and the Cuban people will not starve to death.

Chávez feels secure only when the Cubans are in charge of his country's security. According to one estimate there are over 60,000 Cubans in Venezuela. Half of these are medical doctors. Cuban spies penetrated all spheres of Venezuelan life. Cubans are in control of Chávez's personal security and occupy an important role in the Bolivarian armed forces. Cubans control immigration and are in charge of identification cards. The Bolivarian militia consists of civilians who are loyal to President Chávez. They are organized in a similar fashion to their Cuban counterpart. It follows the idea of militarization of society, a Cuban model.

A 2010 article claims that Raúl Castro's regime ordered the registration of civilians who possess weapons.[171] This unusual measure provoked explanations from prominent experts from inside and outside Cuba. Che Guevara believed that in order for the Cuban revolution to survive, it is necessary to arm the entire population.[172] Cuba's demand that weapons be registered is a rejection of Che's ideas and belief that the people fully support the revolution. Some analysts claim that this act demonstrated increase tension in Cuba and the need of the Communist regime to harden its response. Most of the illegal weapons are domestically produced or are the result of theft.

Cuban ministers visit Venezuela and remain there for months. Ramírez Valdez is number three in Cuban hierarchy (Fidel is number one and his brother Raúl, number two). His arrival in Venezuela in 2010 sparked a series of articles in the opposition press claiming that this visit constitutes a clear violation of Venezuela's sovereignty. As minister of technology, Valdez was sent to Venezuela, ostensibly, to help solve the chronic problem of electricity shortages. In reality, being a henchman, his mission was to revive and save the Chávez regime.[173] Venezuelan Engineers Association (CIV) protested and termed this appointment disrespectful.

An article entitled, "Who is Ramiro Valdez?" (*¿Quién es Ramiro Valdez?*), gives a detailed description of his role in the Cuban revolution and aftermath.[174] It becomes obvious that Valdez has no background or knowledge of electrical energy and is famous for his brutal repression of dissidents in Cuba. Che Guevara, who was in charge of Valdez, recorded that he is cruel and had very little knowledge of guerrilla warfare. Valdez was minister of interior in both periods 1961-1968 and 1978-1985. He held many other important posts in Castro's government. He was in charge of imprisoning 70,000 political prisoners. Valdez established a spy network against Cuban people. He employed merchant marines to spy on Cubans living in exile.

Egana claims that the real reason for Valdez's visit is to enable the Chávez regime to continue its despotic ways and maintain without interruption Venezuela's economic assistance to Cuba.[175] The Cuban's presence in Venezuela attempts to assure the longevity of the Chávez regime. Therefore, the need arises for strong centralization of command; similar to Castro's dictatorship, the sending of the most prominent person qualified for this task. Ramiro Valdez is the most suitable person as a result of having ample experience in spying, intimidation, censuring, psychological war, and coercion. Egana concludes his article by claiming that the innumerable transgressions of the Bolivarian revolution and the appointment of Valdez as a henchman should probably be considered as the most dishonest acts. Valdez will make any effort to assure that this mission is not the last one.

Blanco concludes, after analyzing Cuba's external relations, that the manner in which the United States treated Cuba in the past is similar to the way Cuba treats Venezuela at present.[176] Cubans must depart from Venezuela, not because they are Communist, but rather because are colonialists. It, therefore, becomes evident why an opposition newspaper labels Cuban presence in Venezuela "neocolonization."[177]

The mayor of Caracas metropolitan area, Antonio Ledezma claimed, that during Chávez being hospitalized in Cuba, starting on December 7, 2012, Vice President Nicolas Maduro and the president of the National Assembly, Diosdano Cabello were receiving orders from Cuba. However, it is not clear who gives the instructions. Venezuela is a sovereign state and should not receive order from a foreign country.[178] An opposition leader claimed that the capital of Venezuela has moved to Havana.[179] According to a Nicaraguan opposition source, Cuba considered it of utmost importance to return Chávez to Venezuela (during the president's stay in Decemeber 2012), in order to ensure the appointment of Maduro as his successor and impede any possibility that Cabello (compared by Dietrich to Stalin) may emerge as a president.[180]

Commemorating Venezuela's Independence Day from Spain on July 5, Borges claims that what is needed is a legal holiday separating the country from Cuba.[181] Currently Venezuelans live under Cubans occupation. All important government functions such as port administration, telecommunication, oil and energy, immigration, police, and the armed forces are under Cuban supervision. The absurdity of these relations may be seen in the fact that Cuba is used as an intermediary in buying food from other countries and selling it to Venezuela, earning commission. The writer concludes his article by mentioning the forthcoming elections in the near future which will give people the opportunity to become truly independent. The generosity of Chávez's regime was a lifesaver for nearly bankrupt Cuba after it lost its benefactor the Soviet Union. The death of Chávez may impact the Venezuelan economic assistance, but analysts claim that that it will not affect short term help. It may impact long term aid.[182]

External Enemies and the Domestic Sphere

Lewis Coser, in his classical scholarly work, *The Functions of Social Conflict*, showed how group hostility toward others may be employed as a way to increase group cohesion and unity.[183] He claimed that conflict with outside groups tends to increase internal cohesion. Coser also asserted that groups that are engaged in continual struggles with outside associations tend to become intolerant and are less likely to tolerate dissent.

Coser's observations and findings are important, especially in analyzing authoritarian/totalitarian countries. Leaders of such states lack legitimacy to rule and will employ the idea of the enemy to strengthen their rule. A good illustration of the above is the Assads' (both father and son) rule in Syria. Hafez al-Assad, after ruling for three decades as a tyrant, was succeeded by his son Bashir. Syria is a Sunni-majority country, while Assad is a member of a minority Alawite group. Israel or the "Zionist Entity" as it is referred to by Hafez, is used as the eternal external enemy that is responsible for all Syria's problems. His son Bashir continues the father's policies, and the alliance with Iran signifies the uncompromising approach of this Syria regime. However, using an external enemy as a mean to protect the regime, may not guarantee the dictator's survival. As these words are written, Syria is facing a civil war and the outcome is not yet clear.

It comes not as a surprise that in 2010 visit to Venezuela, President Bashar al-Assad called Chávez an "Arab leader."[184] Chávez reiterated the fact that Israel and the Yankee Empire are common enemies of both Venezuela and Syria. The Syrian leader stressed the fact that both countries have been pressured by world powers. Chávez and Assad know very well how to use external enemies in order to legitimize their rule. An article reviewing Bashar al-Assad's visit to Chávez claims that Venezuela should join the countries that former president Bush labeled as the axis of evil that sponsors terrorism.[185] It included Syria, Iran, and North Korea. Assad, according to the article, should nominate Chávez as the general secretary of this group. It is no surprise therefore, that Assad weighs asylum in Cuba, Ecuador or Venezuela.[186]

Alvarez Paz claims that the Chávez regime is employing the idea of the enemy in order to conceal the many problems facing Venezuela.[187] Chávez projects his regime as a victim, about to be invaded by the United States troops, using Colombia as the staging ground for invasion. This would be done in order to destroy the Bolivarian evolution. Therefore, Venezuela needs to be most prepared for the country's defense. The regular army, militia, students, workers, and police must be ready to fight. These people will be able to use all the new weapons purchased, including tanks.

Garavini claims that the reason why Chávez insists on an American invasion is tied to domestic affairs.[188] Following the examples of his mentor Fidel Castro and the teachings of Joséph Goebbels, Chávez knows that the masses are ignorant and have very little knowledge of foreign affairs. Repeating the same lie thousands of times, as Goebbels affirmed, might transform it to become the truth. The American threat with the complicity of Colombia and Holland provided Chávez with the opportunity to view the political opposition as traitors, spies, and pitiyankees (United States supporters). The opposition cannot be blamed for the rampant corruption in Venezuela, but accusing them of being traitors justifies the strengthening of centralization and the elimination of local government. Some local states were accused of collaborating with Colombia. These acts were taken with complete neglect of constitutional requirements.

Turno, in a second article, further elaborates on the idea that Chávez's speeches and presentations constitute an insult to intelligence.[189] One has to wonder about the psychological and emotional equilibrium of the Venezuelan leader. Chávez declared that the United States possesses a weapon that can produce earthquakes and this is the cause of the Haiti's disaster, where thousands of people perished. The writer claims that the use of simple Aristotelian logic would indicate that if United States had such a weapon it would be used against Iran or North Korea, but not Haiti.

In this respect, Chávez's continuous repetition that if you want peace, prepare for war is relevant to the idea of the uninterrupted existence of an enemy.[190] The Venezuelan leader claimed that the presence of United States soldiers in Colombia might be compared to the British secret agent 007, who is able to kill anybody at anytime. Chávez rejected the proposal of the Brazilian president, Luiz Inacio Lula, to have joint patrols (Colombian and Venezuelan) in the border areas and reiterated his position that he would not allow any foreign troops stationed in this zone.

An article in the opposition press emphasize Chávez use of hatred for others as a tool to increase internal unity, support, and cohesion.[191] Aptiz made it clear that hatred and violence are not legitimate tools for a real democracy. The writer described a graduation speech given by an official in the Chávez's administration; the speaker claimed that Venezuela is divided into two hostile camps, bourgeoisie and its allies and the people. There couldn't be any possibility of reconciliation between these two opposing camps. Workers, revolutionaries, and patriots must be separated from the bourgeoisie. This is a historical war where the winner gets everything.

Such a speech increases hatred and fear. It may be natural to install animosity among soldiers who fight against another country. However, internal animosity among people is unacceptable because it shows state's violence and incitement that further promotes lies and hatred. Such activities might contribute to the rise of crime because it indoctrinates people to exterminate a real or imaginary enemy. Aptiz reminds everyone that all revolutions start with the premise of love for humanity; however, they end up institutionalizing terror. Those who promote revolution invoke illusions and spread hatred and violence against fellow Venezuelans, who believe in liberty and freedom. A new political culture emerges that emphasizes hostility and hatred.

During Chávez's hospitalization in Cuba, starting on December 7, 2012, an opposition member claimed that Maduro and other officials were using the clash with the opposition to promote unity among their followers." They can't live without an enemy; the confrontation with the opposition holds them together."[192]

The tendency to blame others for Venezuela's problems is a constant theme in Chávez's pronouncements. In most cases the "Empire" (United States) is blamed for many of Venezuela's shortcomings. Only the "Empire" is responsible for the killing of 150,000 Venezuelans by the underworld in the period 1999-2009.[193] The United States is also responsible for all the shortcomings in Venezuela: inefficiencies in health, education, and physical infrastructure of the nation. It comes as no surprise that United States Deputy Secretary of Defense for Western Hemisphere Affairs Frank Mora claimed that Venezuela is using the United States to divert attention.[194] The American official added that accusation against the United States aims to distract Venezuelans' attention from real problems at home. In this respect, it is interesting to note that Chávez accused United States of violating the country's air space at the same time that he announced the devaluation of the country's currency.

Nicolas Maduro, Chávez's replacement, imitating his former boss, blamed the United States and its allies for Venezuela's problems just prior to Chávez's death. Attemting to unite his supporters, he claimed that there exist an alleged conspiracy by the United States to destabilize his country. Maduro expelled two United States attaches for allegdly plotting against Venezuela. He also suggested that the country's "historical enemies" (United States and its allies) caused Chávez's cancer. In December 2011, Chávez referred to the possibility that a "technology created by the United States" was the cause of cancer diagnosis among several Latin American leaders.[195] Similar accusation came from the Bolivian president Evo Morales who claimed that the "Empire" (United States) poisoned Hugo Chávez.[196]

Chávez's Marxist philosophy may also explain his strong reliance on the concept of the enemy. The Venezuelan leader claimed that the dichotomy between peaceful and violent methods is false.[197] Chávez declared that he considers the politics of his country to be a war that is divided into phases and the violent stage is very important. Muñoz claims that that the above Chávez declaration represents the real content of the socialist revolution that will guarantee violence, persecution, and repression. The writer concludes that these ideas resemble fascism.

The chapter attempted to demonstrate that the interpretation of Bolivarism depends on the knowledge and expertise of each individual analyst. The Venezuelan president has employed authoritarian elements that can be characterized as Communism, fascism, and in some respects totalitarianism. Embracing Antonio Gramsci's ideas, Chávez gradually introduced changes in the Venezuelan political culture that would abolish the rule of democracy. The educational reforms aimed at creating a new man with ideas that are more attuned to the Venezuelan president. The Chávez regime validates Socrates view that a democracy may turn into a tyranny.

Notes

1   Editorial: Eso no fue el 19 de Abril, Analitica.com, Abril 20, 2010
2   Heinz R. Sonntag, Leyendas fundacionales, Analitica.com, Abril 2, 2010
3   Joaquin Chaffardet, Sabias que somos una república confessional? Opinionynoticias.com
4   John Lynch, Simón Bolívar, A Life,(New Haven, Yale University Press, 2006)
5   A. C. Clark, The Revolutionary Has No Clothes,(New York, Encounter Book, 2009) P. 8
6   Heinz R. Sonntag, Contradicciones, Analitica.com, Septiembre 19, 2009
7   Lynch, Simón Bolívar P. 202
8   Sonntag, Contadicciones, op-cit
9   Alexander Forter, A Failed Independence: Enlightment, Rhetoric in Simón Bolívar's: "The Jamaica Letter." Haverford.com October 28, 2009
10 Tulio Hernández, Necrofilia y personalismo, Analitica.com, Agosto 2, 2010
11 Trabajdores Petroleros:! Chávez vive, vive, vive! Agencia Bolivarian de Noticias, Marzo 6, 2013
12 Chávez sera embalsamado como Lenin y Mao, Hoy.com.ec, Marzo 8, 2013
13 Teodoro Petkoff, Miedo a los medios, Analitica.com, Mayo 2, 2010
14 Ley de cultura sancionará a medios impresos, Analitica.com, Noviembre 30, 2009
15 Preven sancionar a canalescanals de cable internacionales, Analitica.com, Octubre 13, 2009
16 Chávez llama a los medios privados enemigos de la patria y amanza a Globovisión, Elmundo.es, Mayo 30, 2007
17 Un virus llamado Globovision, Agencia Bolivariana de Noticias, Septiembre 7, 2009
18 Aram Aharonian, Medios en proceso de manipulación de la conciencia social y de domino público democratizar y masificar, Observatorio de medios.org, Agosto 25, 2009
19 Modelo de comunicación socialista debe acompañar transformación de sociedad Venezolana, Agencia Bolivariana de Noticias, Enero 17, 2010
20 El gobierno tiene a su disposición mas de 700 medios, Analitica.com, Septiembre 11, 2009
21 Media guerrilla to fire "ideological shots", Eluniversal.com, April 15, 2010
22 Andrés Simón Moreno Arreche, El riesgo de los muchachos enguerrillados, Analitica.com, Abril 15, 2010
23 Simón Alberto Cansalavi, Un capítulocapitulo de Alexis de Tocqueville, Analitica.com, Abril 5, 2010
24 L. Gordon Croviz, The Internet and Political Freedom, The Wall Street Journal, March 15, 2010
25 President Chávez: La Internet no puede ser libre, Analitica.com, Marzo 14, 2010
26 Attorney General urges Parliament to make law on the Internet, Eluniversal.com, Marzo 15, 2010
27 Designan comisión especial para investigar uso indebido y antiético de Internet, Agencia Bolivariana de Noticias, Marzo 16, 2010
28 AN aprueba investigar difusión de noticias falsas en el Web, Analitica.com, Marzo 17, 2010

29 EEUU es pionero en vigilar y castigar a usarios de Internet,Agencia Bolivariana de Noticias, Marzo 18, 2010
30 Gerver Torres, Internet socialista? Analitica.com, Abril 6, 2010
31 Rafael Díaz Casanova, Una ley para Internet, Analitica.com, Marzo 26, 2010
32 Ejecutivo tiene ley para controlar Internet, Analitica.com, Febrero 17, 2010
33 Gobierno bolivariano ha democratizado acceso a Internet, Agencia BolivarianaBolivaiana de Noticias, Marzo 18, 2010
34 Consulta popular determinará creación de ley sobre Interne, Agencia BolivarianaBolivariana de Noticias, Marzo 17, 2010
35 Eliades Acosta Resigned from his position as cultural secretary of the Cuban Communist Party, Newsgroups.cuba.com, July 21, 2008
36 Jeffrey Goldberg, Fidel: "Cuban model doesn't even work for us anymore," Progresso Weekly, September 8, 2010
37 Eliades Acosta Matos, Con Chávez y la revolución Twitter, Cubadebate, May 3, 2010, it also appeared in Agencia Bolivariana de Noticias, Mayo 8, 2010
38 Ibid
39 Michael Rowan, Twitter T, Eluniversal.com, May 4, 2010
40 Venezuela's government seeks media law to regulate the Internet, Eluniversal.com, December 10, 2010
41 Freddy Lepage, Las luchas internas del PSUV (I), Analitica.com, Diciembre 4, 2010
42 Carlos Julio Penaloza, Delenda est Internet, Analitica.com, Diciembre 19, 2010
43 Fernando Luis Egana, El lio de la LOE, Analitica.com, Agosto 16, 2009
44 Juan Carlos Aptiz, Educación roja, rojita, Analitica.com, Septiembre 3, 2009
45 Ricardo Troti, El miedo al debate, Analitica.com, Octubre 7, 2012
46 Humberto García Larrada, Comentarios al proyecto de Ley Orgánica de Educación (PLOE), Analitica.com, Agosto 18, 2009
47 Julio Andrés Borges, La educación: Problemas y soluciones, Analitica.com, Agosto 25, 2009
48 Ibid.
49 Humberto García Larrado, Comentarios al proyecto de ley de educación (PLOE), op-cit
50 Américo Gollo, Chávez, Tragedia de la universidad, Analitica.com, Octubre 5, 2009
51 Alberto Rodríguez Barrera, Agua, educación y salud, revisiones de futuro, Analitica.com, Noviembre 26, 2009
52 Sadio Garavini di Turno, Deriva totalitaria, Analitica.com, Agosto 19, 2009
53 José Antonio Rivas Leone, Inviabilidad de la Ley Orgánica de Educación, Analitica.com, Octubre 9, 2009
54 Juan Francisco Alonso, TSJ afirma que asambleas de padres tienen potestades limitadas, Eluniversal.com Octubre 14, 2009
55 Editorial Alfa presenta La Herencia De La Tribu. Del Mito de la Independencia a La Revolución Bolivariana, Analitica.com Diciembre 13, 2009
56 Obispo Auxiliar de Caracas pide juzgar en libertad a presos, Analitica.com Enero 2, 2010
57 Fernando Mires, Las venas ocultas de la dictadura, Analitica.com Octubre 29, 2009
58 Ibid P. 5
59 Fernando Mires, Dictaduras, Analitica.com, Noviembre 25, 2009
60 Daniel Lozano, Venezuela a cámara lenta, Elmundo.es, Diciembre 15, 2013
61 Andrew Cawthorne and Mario Naranjo, Opposition slams Venezuela devaluations, shoppers fret, Reuters, Febrero 9, 2013
62 Jesús Antonio Petit Da Costa, Leyes cubanas vigentes en Venezuela, Analitica.com Marzo 2, 2010

63 Editorial, Ley de las comunas=comunismo, Analitica.com, Julio 11, 2010

64 Editorial, Milicias y amargura, Analitica.com, Octubre 6, 2010

65 Venezuela es ingobernable sin Hugo Chávez Frías, Agencia Bolivariana de Noticias, Febrero 1, 2010

66 Grupo Ávila, El estado totalitario y la división de poderes, Analitica.com Octubre 12, 2009

67 Leandro F. Chique Canache, La Asamblea "Nacional", Analitica.com, Enero 7, 2010

68 Venezuelan lawyers say, President Chávez has Compromised the Judicial System, VHeadline.com, July 15, 2009

69 "En el Poder Judicial hay mafias para perseguir a la disidencia politica" Noticias24.com, Julio 28, 2009

70 Juan Fernández, El muro de Chávez, Analitica.com, Noviembre 11, 2009

71 Aníbal Romero Un pedestal para Colón, Analitica.com, Marzo 6, 2010

72 PSUV busca forzar adelanto de elecciones parlamentarias, Analitica.com, Octubre 13, 2009

73 Pedro Freites Romero, Al Totalitarismo.... ¿Y tú, quién eres? Analitica.com, Febrero 13, 2010

74 José Gerardo Guarisma Álvarez Daisaku Ikeda y el alma de la paz, Analitica.com, Febrero 7, 2010

75 Jimmy Ortiz Saucedo, La reelección presidencial, Analitica.com, Octubre 2, 2009

76 Editorial- Latin American Model, Wall Street Journal, March 12, 2010

77 Lázaro Rosa, El culto a la personalidad, Analitica.com, Agosto 7, 2009

78 Gobierno dará prioridad a proyectos de seguridad, salud e industria en 2010, Agencia Bolivariana de Noticias, Enero 2, 2010

79 The PSUV Manifesto, Eluniversal.com, Julio 23, 2010

80 Heinz Dietrich, Bolívar, Lenin y Hugo Chávez, Analitica.com, Noviembre 8, 2009

81 Heinz Dietrich, Exitosa planificación económica del socialismo del siglo XXI, Analitica.com, Marzo 13, 2010

82 Eduardo Mackenzie, Respuesta a Heinz Dietrich, Analitica.com, Noviembre 22, 2009

83 Ibid.

84 Radicalization is the roadmap directed to Chávez, Eluniversal.com, November 26, 2010

85 Ibid.

86 Colombia, Colombia! Agencia Bolivariana de Noticias, op-cit

87 Aníbal Romero, Sobre Marx y de Gramsci, Analitica.com, Septiembre 16, 2009

88 Ibid.

89 Hugo Chávez Frías, Declaración de principios del PSUV debe ser la Guía fundamental de los militantes, Agencia BolivarianaBolivariaa de Noticias, Abril 26, 2010

90 José Rafael López Padrino, Intelectuales lustrabotas, Analitica.com, Junio 11, 2009

91 Roman José Sandia, Marx y Chávez, Analitica.com, Enero 12, 2010

92 Carlos Balladares Castillo, El problema del comunismo es el comunismo, Analitica.com, Octubre 22, 2009

93 Alek Boyd,Hugo Chávez's 21st Century Socialism: Dictatorship by any other name, InfoVenezuela.com Octubre 11, 2009

94 Venezuela Congress Advocates "The End of Private Property", Universal.com Julio 23, 2009

95 Ibid.

96 Gustavo Coronel, Partido Comunista de Venezuela: Chávez es un déspota, Analitica.com, Marzo 11, 2011

97 Pablo Aure, Nazibolivarianismo, Analitica.com, Octubre 28, 2009

98   José Rafael López Padrino Once años de fracaso socialfascista, Analitica.com Enero 26, 2010
99   José Rafael López Padrino, La barbarie socialfascista, Analitica.com, Enero 8, 2010
100   Ibid.
101   Mario H. Concha Vergara, Chávez vencería a Chávez, Analitica.com Febrero 4, 2010
102   Editorial: ¿Los ricos son subhumanos? Analitica.com, Octubre 29, 2009
103   José Rafael López Padrino, Corporativismo socialfascista, Analitica.com Noviembre 5, 2009
104   José Rafael López Padrino, Nueva Arremetida socialfascista, Analitica.com Agosto 30, 2009
105   José Rafael López Padrino Autoritarismo, militarismo y lumpen proletario Analitica.com Marzo 24, 2010
106   Fernando Ochoa Antich, Crisis militar en las fuerzas armadas bolivariana, Analitica.com Abril 7, 2010
107   Presidente Chávez firmó decreto de creación de la Universidad Militar Bolivariana Agencia Venezolana de Noticias, Septiebre 3, 2010
108   High-ranking officer's remarks cast doubt on the true role of the army, Eluniversal.com, November 9, 2010
109   Ibid.
110   Alberto Barrera Tyszka, La balada de Rangel Silva, Analitica.com, Noviembre 15, 2010
111   Agustín Blanco Muñoz, , Que viva mi general Rangel Silva! Analitica.com, Noviembre 15, 2010
112   Fernando Ochoa Antich, La amenaza militar,Analitica.com, Febrero 1, 2012
113   Ningún soldado debe sustraerse de la batalla de las ideas, Agencia Venezolana de Noticias, Julio 5,2010
114   Palmer reports on low morale among Venezuelan military, Eluniversal.com, August 5, 2010
115   Analysis, The end of the professional army in Venezuela, Eluniversal.com, June 13, 2010
116   Ibid
117   José Rafael López Padrino,, Neomilitarismo populista del siglo XXI, Analitica.com Mayo 12, 2010
118   Chávez aumentó 40% de sueldo a los militares, Analitica.com Abril 26, 2010
119   Diputado Díaz: "Ministro de la Defensa pisotea la dignidad de la FANB," Eluniversal Marzo 7, 2013
120   Simón Romero, Putin Visits Venezuela to Sign Series of Deals, The New York Times, April 3, 2010
121   Oscar Arias, Carta al Presidente Mujica, Analitica.com Abril 15, 2010
122   Gustavo Coronel, Un post chavismo sin PDVSA y sin ejército, Analitica.com, Noviembre 26, 2009
123   Oswaldo Álvarez Paz, Milicianos mercenarios, Analitica.com Diciembre 10, 2009
124   Luis Ugalde, Armas contra la libertad, Analitica.com Enero 29, 2010
125   History of Canossa, Historyworld.com, Agosto 5, 2010
126   Lucy Gómez, Lo que es del Cesar y lo que es de Dios, Analitica.com, Agosto 2, 2010
127   Larry Rother, New Chávez Takes on the Church in Venezuela, The New York Times, December 19, 1999
128   Ibid
129   Rodrigo Conde Tudanca, Tensas relaciones entre la Iglesia Catolica y el Gobierno de Hugo Chávez en Venezuela 1999-2006, Simposio Hist/R12, La Historia reciente en Latino América,

130 Caracas Archdiocese reject use of religious images carrying weapons, Eluniversal. com, Mayo 13, 2010

131 Rodrigo Conde Tudanca, Tensas Relaciones entre la Iglesia Católica y el Gobierno de Hugo Chaves en Venezuela 1999-2006, op-cit

132 Ibid

133 Rodrigo Conde Tudanca, Tensas Relaciones entre la Iglesia Católica y el Gobierno de Hugo Chávez en Venezuela, Op-cit

134 Catholic Church Under Fire in Venezuela, Eluniversal.com, Julio 11, 2010

135 Ibid.

136 Bishops urge Chávez's government to stop actions to "Silence Dissenters", Eluniversal.com, Marzo 30, 2010

137 Obispo Auxiliar de Caracas pide juzgado en libertad a presos políticos, Analitica. com, Febrero 1, 2010

138 Venezuelan bishops report failure to fulfill ideas of the Founding Fathers, Eluniversal.com, Abril 20, 2010

139 Preocupación en la Iglesia Venezolana por el espiritu antirreligioso, Analitica.com, Abril 1, 2010

140 Luis Ugalda, Construir la República, Analitica.com, Febrero 14, 2010

141 Bishops Urge Chávez's government to stop actions to "silence dissenters", Op-cit

142 Venezuelan Cardinal Target of 'Verbal Aggression' Says Vatican Paper, Catholicnews. com, July 8, 2010

143 Ibid.

144 Cardenal no consignó pruebas que respaldan sus señalamientos contra el gobierno, Agencia Bolivariana de Noticias, Julio 27, 2010

145 Parliament to ask for review of Urosa's appointment as Cardinal, Eluniversal.com, July 29, 2010

146 La Asamblea Nacional de Venezuela pide la revisión de los acuerdos con el Vaticano, Infocatolica.com. Julio 30, 2010

147 Chávez Threatened To Terminate Catholic Church TV Channel License, Eluniversal. com, July 23, 2010

148 Juan Francisco Alonso Acevedo, Ruptura con la Santa Sede provocaría gran desprestigio, Eluniversal.com, Julio 8, 2010

149 Cardinal Urosa Savino: Enabling law threatens the country peace, Eluniversal.com, December 30, 2010

150 Ibid.

151 Robert J. Alexander, The Venezuelan Democratic Revolution, (New Brunswick, New Jersey, Rutgers University Press 1964)

152 Ramón Rivas Aguilar, El 18 de octubre de 1945 la instauración de la democracia representativa y del partidos del estado benefactor, Analitica.com, Octubre 19, 2009

153 Simón Romero, A Clash of Hope and Fear As Venezuela Seizes Land, The New York Times, Mayo 17, 2007

154 Ibid

155 Ibid

156 Alexander, P. 300

157 Alberto Rodríguez Barrera, Planificación es pensar en el futuro, Analitica. com, Enero 4, 2010

158 Ibid

159 Rómulo Ruiz, El Partido Militar, Analitica.com, Julio 15, 2009

160 Denuncian a Chávez por "traición a la patria" ante el TSJ, Analitica.com, Abril 30, 2010

161   Thor Halvorssen Hellum, Quisling resucitó en Chávez, Analitica.com, Diciembre 23, 2009
162   Editorial, La soberanía no comienza en la Havana, Analitica.com, Abril 17, 2010
163   Venezuela pays USD 5.6 billion for Cuban staff in 2008, Eluniversal.com, Octubre 7, 2009
164   Ibid
165   Aníbal Romero, Cuba depredadora, Analitica.com, Febrero 18, 2010
166   Diego Arria, ¿Cuál independencia celebramos los venezolanos? Analitica.com, Abril 14, 2010
167   Aníbal Romero, Cuba Depredadora, Analitica.com, op-cit
168   Mauricio Vicent, Cuba despedirá a un millón de empleados, El Pais.com (España) Enero 1, 2010
169   Baldomera Vásquez, La revolución cubana murió de fracas, Analitica.com, Marzo 9, 2010
170   Ibid
171   Cuba ordena registro de armas de fuego en poder de civiles, Analitica.com, Febrero 2, 2010
172   A. Chaplin, Terror: The New Theater of War- Mao's Legacy: Selected Cases of Terrorism in the 20th and 21st Centuries (Lanham, University Press of America, 2003)p.45
173   Venezuela Rejects Legislation of Cuban Official to Cope with Energy Crisis, Eluniversal.com February 8, 2010
174   Pablo Figueredo , ¿Quién es Ramiro Valdez? Analitica.com, Febrero 4, 2010
175   Fernando Luis Egana, El Virey bicentenario, Analitica.com, Febrero 8, 2010
176   Carlos Blanco, Chávez entregado a la mafia Cubana, Analitica.com, Diciembre 23, 2009
177   Cuba Presence in Venezuela as Neo- Colonization, Elmundo.com, Febrero 13, 2010
178   Ledezma: Maduro y Cabello reciben órdenes desde Cuba, Eluniversal.com, Enero 4, 2013
179   William Neuman, Meeting in Cuba Angers Venezuelan Opposition, The New York Times, January 15, 2013
180   Presión para mejorar a Chávez, Laprensa.com.ni, Diciembre 5, 2012
181   Julio Andrés Borges, Independencia de Fidel, Analitica.com Julio 6, 2010
182   Cuban worried about the loss of their generous Venezuelan Ally, Eluniversal, March 6, 2013
183   Book Summary of the Functions of Social Conflict, beyongintractability.org, Diciembre 4, 2009
184   President Bashar Assad Calls Chávez an "Arab Leader" Eluniversal.com, Julio 3, 2010
185   Bashar al Assad el oftalmólogo, Analitica.com, Julio 4, 2010
186   Al Assad weighs asylum in Cuba, Ecuador orVenezuela, Eluniversal.com, Dicembre 5, 2012
187   Oswaldo Álvarez Paz, El verdadero enemigo, Analitica.com, Dicembre 4, 2009
188   Sadio Garavini de Turno, Venezuela amenazada, Analitica.com, Diciembre 27, 2009
189   Sadio Garavini di Turno, Insulto a la inteligencia, Analitica.com, Enero 28, 2010
190   Chávez: Lo vuelvo a repetir, si quieres la paz, prepárate la Guerra, Analitica.com, Noviembre 14, 2009
191   Juan Carlos Apitz, Por amor al odio, Analitica.com, Diciembre 14, 2009. See also Valentín Adenas Amigo, La revolución es la obra del odio, Analitica.com, Enero21, 2010
192   William Neuman, Venezuela Warns Opposition Against Vocal Dissent, The New York Times, Enero 12, 2013
193   Andrés Simón Moreno Arreche, Chávez pa' siempre: ¿Eso es democracia? Analitica. com, Septiembre 10, 2009

194 Pentagon accuses Venezuela of using US to divert attention, Eluniversal.com, January 13, 2010

195 Ezequiel Minaya and David Luhnow, Before News of Death, Allegation of U.S. Conspiracies, The Wall Street Journal, March 6, 2013

196 Evo Morales asegura que "el imperio" enveneno a Hugo Chávez. Eluniversal, Marzo 9, 2013

197 Agustín Blanco Muñoz Somos pura muerte, Analitica.com. Agosto 30, 2009

Chapter Two

The Economic Aspects
of Chávezism

The Ideological Foundations of Chávez's Economic Policies
An array of leftist scholars and many articles in the official press emphasize Marxist elements of the country's economic policies. For example, a socialist scholarly assembly meeting in Caracas in 2009 declared that capitalism is tantamount to robbing and inflation is caused by speculation.[1] Products are sold with a 25% profit, which contributes to the rise of prices. Later in this chapter, it will be shown that inflation is a direct result of Chávez's economic policies. As was shown in Chapter one, Chávez's administration always blames external forces for his shortcomings.

Chávez repeatedly emphasized the idea that he intends to create a new financial system that will eliminate the vices of the capitalist oligarchy and bourgeoisie, allied with the mafia on both the local and international level.[2] On the international, level this is done with the cooperation of brotherhood nations, the ALBA countries (Bolivia, Ecuador, Nicaragua, and others). The creation of the Bank of the South (*Banco del Sur*) aimed at increasing the economic cooperation among these countries. The cooperation with countries such as Russia, China, and Iran is a remarkable reminder of the leadership role that Venezuela assumes in the world.[3]

Chávez's regime adopted a "new financial architecture" that would become an integral part of socialist production.[4] In 2007 Chávez proposed amending the constitution and in spite of his defeat at the ballot box this same model is being imposed. Banks are required to allocate part of their profits to community councils. According to the official government press the new financial law directs banks to invest in the country's development and not in generating profit.[5]

The official government press strongly emphasized the 2008 world economic crisis and suggested that it represents a crisis of the capitalist order.[6] The collapse of the United States financial system and the economic problems faced by the countries of the European Union demonstrated the difficulties and shortcomings of the capitalist system. Both cases represent, according to Beroes, the emergence of unsolved economic problems that are an integral part of the capitalist economic system. United States attempted to solve the problem by employing the Keynesian model, pouring huge sums of money into banks and other failed companies.

The strong ideological affinity in economic matters is emphasized by José Guerra, an economist and former head of economic analysis at the Venezuelan central bank (BCV).[7] In 2007 the Venezuelan president declared that he is breaking relations with the International Monetary Fund and the World Bank. Chávez asserted that he is cancelling a debt with these institutions that commenced in 1989, during the presidency of Carlos Andrés Pérez. These institutions, Chávez claimed are an integral part of the capitalist system and therefore rejected by the Venezuelan president. In reality what Chávez accomplished was the replacing of a cheap loan with another one that is a lot more expensive.

Chávez's socialism of the twenty-first century is an attempt to correct inefficiencies and problems that characterized Communism in the Soviet Union and Eastern Europe. The introduction of the Corporation of Socialist Markets (Corporación de Mercados Socialistas, COMERSO) is an attempt to regulate and exercise certain disciplinary capacities on public enterprises.[8] González claims that this effort is bound to fail. While the market economy is based on maximizing efficiency in order to increase profit and reduce cost; state enterprises are subsidized by the government lack incentives to be efficient. The growth of bureaucratization increases inefficiencies, which lead to shortages. The regulating state agency has no ability to criticize the central government, which is in charge of its operations. Such criticism might lead to the firing of its members. The state being in charge of economic matters implies the destruction of incentives and hence efficiency.

On July 14, 2009, Commerce Minister Eduardo Samán outlined a strategic plan of his ministry for the period 2009-2010.[9] Guerra claimed the minister of commerce relied on Marxist principles in his plan, attempting to avoid profit, which is a central theme of capitalist economy. Commercial activities cannot be performed without profit. Samán stressed the importance of barter that should become the main tool of commerce. The minister of commerce therefore becomes the enemy of productivity because he associates it with competition and the market economy. Competition as a tool to increase productivity is not in Samán's vocabulary. To be competitive means to produce quality products at low costs in order to capture an important share of the market. As a result of Samán's ideological bias he views conquering a market negatively.

Guerra concludes that there cannot be any improvement in the Venezuelan economy as long as Chávez's administration is destroying the market economy and private sector. The author of this article, an economics professor, concludes his remarks by advising the commerce minister to enroll in an elementary economics course designed especially for noneconomists.

The Organic Law of Communes revolutionized the Venezuelan political system. A new organization of the territory substituted the federal democratic decentralized model of the 1999 constitution with a centralized authoritarian one. The communes may be organized in federations containing several communes. There are also communal cities that include numerous communal federations. The Organic Law of Public and Popular Planning seeks to confirm the centralized role of the state in the economic planning. The communal council is in charge of this process and its mission is the promotion of communes' economic development. It is responsible for making sure that collective necessities are taken care of.

The Organic Law of Communal Economic System (LOSE) seeks to restrict the right of private property and replace it with communal property. The law proposed "voluntary work" and the use of the barter system. It also proposed the establishment of a commune currency as an alternative to regular money. This law is attempting to consolidate an economic system where norms and procedures will be directed toward collective property, a mechanism used to control of its activities.[10] An important theme of the communal economic system is to "eliminate the division of labor that characterizes the capitalist system."[11]

The communal state represents a specific vision of socialism that the Venezuelan government intends to impose.[12] It is based on the state's supremacy in economic activities, centralized planning, and ancestral forms of economic exchange. It follows the Marxist dogma that only the state is capable of organizing well-being and the satisfaction of human necessities. Therefore, private activities must be minimized. In a later section of this chapter a comparison will be made between the Venezuelan commune system and the Israeli Kibbutz (communal settlement).

The Venezuelan National Academy concluded that the communal economic system is a new model that institutionalizes seizure and expropriations of private property.[13] The state is responsible for allocating ownership, but in reality it does not grant proprietorship to anybody. Pedro Palm, the president of the academy, asserted, "Social property and any other forms of property just institutionalize conflict and chaos. They lead the country to deterioration and they are a step backward in its economic organization."[14]

The communal system is based on ideological grounds instead of efficiency. The idea of fighting against private property is unnatural. Division of work is a necessary condition for progress. The communal laws are filled with contradictions which are an integral part of Marxist economic thinking. The academy also criticized barter, which was viewed as inapplicable in modern societies.

The ideological underpinning of the Chávez regime manifests itself in the 2010 Organic Law on Social Comptrollership.[15] The law intends to punish private companies that charge high prices for their products or food items. It allows the national police, the National Guard, or the Bolivarian militia to enforce its rules. This law constitutes another step in the weakening of the private sector and gradually leading Venezuela, step by step, as Gramsci envisioned to a Communist regime.

Chávez's invention of a new currency, called Veguero, reveals his strong ideological orientations and his lack of knowledge in economics.[16] Labeling the Venezuelan president as a new Keynes, Huddel criticizes as futile Chávez's effort to introduce a new monetary communal unit. This currency can be used only for payment of public (state) enterprises. It is issued by a communal board and is circulated among commune members. This money is a subsidy given by the government to the members of the commune. The public enterprises can pay their workers in part by Vegueros. However, this money cannot be deposited in banks. Huddel therefore concludes that this currency (Veguero) serves no purpose. His final advice to Chávez is to leave economic matters to professional economists.[17]

A Critical View of Chávez's Economic Policies

A number of scholars and journalists combined their efforts to challenge and criticize Chávez's economic policies. In Economics 101 for Socialists (*Economía 101 Para Socialistas*), Carlos Eduardo Ruiz attempts to offer the basic principles of modern economics: supply and demand.[18] The writer tries to refute Chávez's economic ideas by criticizing the validity of Marx's writings. A new economics cannot be invented, as Karl Marx and Friedrich Engels claimed. Marxism is based on wrong assumptions. If the government or other institutions attempt to determine prices or product quality, it leads to shortages, speculation, smuggling, and inflation. Price can be determined only by the interplay of supply and demand, which leads to equilibrium. This natural phenomenon cannot be regulated by anyone

Analyzing the two Germanys prior to the fall of the Berlin Wall, King and Shulz conclude that Communism or central planning has an adverse effect on a country's standard of living.[19] Institutional support for private enterprises is another important indicator for economic success. Innovations and competition must be strongly stressed and the government must leave the private sector alone. Private profit constitutes the main source and reason for new technological innovations.

Criticizing those who claim that socialism and the increased role of the state offer the best remedy for poverty, Kling and Shulz assert that only a free market can result in eliminating deprivation.[20] The solution lies in giving jobs to the poor, which can be accomplished by the creation of entrepreneurships that will create work. Innovation is a vital key for improving the country's economics and decreasing the level of poverty.

The above authors' claim that the country's economic success depends, to a large extent, on the ability of innovators to push forward the application of knowledge. The climate for entrepreneurship depends on the legal, political, and cultural norms of the country. Chávez, in his attempt to ideologize the educational system, created strong obstacles for innovations and economic development. Chávez's Venezuela, relying on the primary role of the state, does not face competition and has no urgency to fix its problems. This is in contrast to private entrepreneurs who need to be successful in order to survive. While private business always has the risk of going out of business, governments don't have this problem. Markets, on the other hand, are more conducive to efficiency.

Hoffman analyzes Friedrich Hayek's economic views in order to refute Chávez's views on this topic.[21] Hayek, a member of the Austrian economic school who received the Nobel Prize for Economics in 1974, claimed that economic liberty depends on individual political freedom. Democracy, accordingly, cannot exist if it lacks economic liberty. In his book, *The Road to Servitude*, published in 1944, he asserted that socialism and totalitarianism are similar. Democracy is based on the supremacy of the law and the rights of individuals. Economic development can occur only if there are laws protecting liberty and freedom that enable the functioning of a free market. Communism (Socialism), on the other hand, relies on collectivism and the individual is not considered important, therefore it may approach authoritarian/ totalitarian tendencies.

The Venezuelan economist Jesús Casique presents a major criticism of those countries that opt to increase their public expenditures in order to solve the financial crisis.[22] In a reference to the Chávez regime, Casique claims that economic growth cannot be stimulated by decisions taken from a central agency. It also cannot be permanently achieved by an increase in public expenses. This will require a rise in taxes, public debt, and—worse—a rise in the circulation of money, which leads to inflation.

Economic growth according to the above Venezuelan economist is achieved when total productivity increases as a result of better machinery and tools, investment in new equipment, incorporating knowledge, and technical progress. Historically, Casique claims, a reverse relationship can be observed between public expenditures and productivity. Public expenditures are usually financed by higher taxes, which reduce incentives to work, save, or invest. Economic growth can only occur as a result of individuals and enterprises that operate in a free market. The role of the state is to guarantee the efficient operation of markets. This requires the lessening of the state's role in economic affairs.[23]

Since Chávez came to power in 1999, he has manufactured dependency on the government on a scale unseen elsewhere in the post-Soviet world. The Venezuelan president economic policies were responsible for Venezuela's having lowest gross domestic product (GDP) in Latin America, despite record high oil prices. Dependency on the government is an important explanation for Chávez's victory in the October 2012 elections.[24]

González criticizes the Chávez regime for not allowing the market economy to function without interference.[25] The process of adjusting and controlling prices by the executive branch constitutes a destructive incentive for supply. It increases the gap between demand and supply. Price control, established by Chávez's government, constitutes a threat to commerce and diverts products from the regular market to informal networks (black markets). Such activities further weaken the private sector in general and the country's economics in particular.

The shortages of basic items may also be attributed to Chávez's disregarding of market economy's rules. Chávez's overspending during his 2012 reelection campaign exasperated the shortage crisis. His absence from Venezuela for medical reasons starting on December 7, 2012, created political and economic uncertainties which increased basic items' deficiencies.[26]

Coronel criticizes Chávez's attempt to expand the public sector and calls for limiting the public bureaucracy's salaries.[27] During the period 1999-2009, $900 billion was deposited in the national treasury. Out of this sum, $50 billion was spent buying political loyalties and financing presidential campaign throughout the hemisphere. It is estimated that $100 billion was stolen by the mafia associated with public enterprises (PDVAL, MERCAL, and PDVSA) and another $100 billion was linked with inefficient oil expenses. The average annual budget has been $50 billion, which makes it $500 billion during the first ten years of Chávez being in office.

A sum of $150 billion remains uncounted for; no one knows where it is, except a small group of Chávez's loyaltists. Most likely, Coronel claims, this money is not in Venezuela but deposited in foreign banks in China, Switzerland, Iran, or Cuba. Such activities can take place because the branches of government are not independent and are ruled by the executive. Fraud and corruption are rampant and the Supreme Court is filled with members loyal to Chávez.

Coronel ridicules Chávez claim that there is a need to limit salaries. Chávez purchased an airplane that cost him $65 million. When Chávez is travelling abroad he stays at the most expensive hotels accompanied by two hundred assistants including medical doctors, cooks, and others. He gave $18 million to the American actor Danny Glover to film a movie in Venezuela. Coronel concludes that Chávez's idea of putting a limit on salaries is another excuse given by the Chavist mafia in order to continue robbing, looting, and abusing the country's wealth.

The Venezuelan economy became a prisoner of a policy, which desensitized local production. Employment was exported to those countries where expenses are lower. This was accomplished through a policy that emphasized massive imports to Venezuela. According to Guerra, the economic data in November 2010 indicates that contraction of the economy gave way to stagnation.[28]

Niall Ferguson manuscript, "The Ascent of Money,"[29] is employed by the opposition to refute Chávez's economic ideas. Ferguson claims that the evolution of credit, from ancient times to the present, has been an important technological innovation. In contrast to Chávez's views, Ferguson asserts that a world without money would hinder economic development. Poverty, the Harvard scholar claims, is related to a lack of financial institutions.

In analyzing the Argentinian economic history, Ferguson correctly asserts that a culprit for the country's economic decline was its financial management. This is especially true in the period subsequent to World War II that witnessed a severe economic decline. The major problem faced by Argentina was inflation, which should be viewed as both political and monetary phenomenon.[30] This is similar to Chávez's Venezuela, where, in spite of oil revenues, the enormous public expenses contributed to high inflation (over 20%), similar to Argentina's, which hurt the economy badly.

In an open letter to President Chávez, José Guerra summarizes the major economic problems facing Venezuela.[31] In the second quarter of 2011 the GDP increased by 2.5%. However, this raise had occurred when the market price for oil incremented by 48%, during the first three month of 2010. A major economic dilemma facing Venezuela is its enormous economic dependency on oil. In the first quarter of 2011, out of $100 in exports $95 was derived from oil. In contrast to 1998 (before Chávez came to power), which it had been $70.[32]

Relying on oil as the major source of income means Chávez's economic policies are emphasizing imports and diminishing the role of exports. Nearly all of its oil revenues are consumed by external debt. Each increase of GDP by one point causes an increment of 10 points in imports. In the near future, the service payment of the debt will amount to 50% of GDP. The fiscal deficits are the reason for the high debt. Investments are diminishing and production is contracted.

Inflation is another major predicament facing the country and should not be viewed, as the Chávez's claims, as a result of high prices, profits, and speculations. A country may have high prices and low inflation, such as in the case in Japan. Venezuela, on the other hand, has both high prices and elevated inflation. The cause of this problem is excessive government spending, which ultimately results in fiscal deficit.

Chávez's Oil Policy: The Subordination of Petroleum Activity to Political and Ideological Considerations

In an open letter to Alí Araque Rodríguez, who serves both as president of the state oil company, PDVSA, and the minister of mines and energy, Gustavo Coronel blames the Chávez regime for mismanaging this industry.[33] The first accusation involves the dual nature of Rafael Ramírez, who is both a cabinet member in Chávez's government and the president of PDVSA.

This duality has destroyed the separation between the monitoring and monitored agents, which are now the same. It makes it difficult to evaluate the company's performance. The lack of transparency becomes, therefore, a major issue; this inevitably leads to corruption and waste estimated to be a trillion dollars during the first twelve years of the Chávez regime.[34] The subordination of the oil policies to political and ideological considerations may be responsible for the problems of this industry.

During the protest and strike of the oil industry in 2002-2003 thousands of competent technical staff were dismissed. They were replaced by 100,000 incompetent persons, hired solely for being ideologically loyal to Chávez. As a result, accidents in the oil industry multiplied. PDVSA became a "socialist" oil company; it abandoned its task of exploring, producing, and transporting oil and replaced it with importing and distributing food, building houses, and other related assignments. The level of oil production decreased and was lower in 2011 than when Chávez assumed power in 1999. It also showed a reduction in the export to United States, during the period 2006-2011 by 300,000 barrels per day.[35]

Ideology plays a crucial role in Chávez's policies. Approximately 500,000 barrels of oil per day are being delivered to friendly countries that share his major beliefs, on noncommercial terms, which represent subsidies of $3-$4 billion per year. The domestic market consumes 700,000 barrels per day, with close to $10 billion subsidy. Coronel concludes his letter by claiming that Chávez's "national sovereignty," with total control and ownership of operations, is primarily utilized by regimes with a deep inferiority complex.[36]

An important issue raised by the opposition media is the differences between managing and utilizing oil funds by democratic and authoritarian regimes in Venezuela.[37] Xavier Gristani asserts that democratic regimes emphasized the importance of spending oil revenues to ensure the well-being of the Venezuelan people. The income of oil was used by democratic presidents to build a highway networks, the best in Latin America, and an industrial complex of iron, aluminum, and the electrification system.

President Rafael Caldera (1969-1974) continued the policies of his predecessors, Rómulo Betancourt (1959-1964) and Raúl Leoni (1964-1974) to invest the oil revenues for the betterment of the Venezuelan people. Indirectly referring to Chávez, who appoints assistants solely because of their ideological orientations, democratic presidents selected advisers who demonstrated expertise in their respective fields. They hired engineers, lawyers, economists as consultants, but in certain situations they preferred to get advice from workers and ordinary people. President Caldera promulgated the cooperation of science and technology in the service of the oil industry.

The conclusion reached from the data is that PDVSA does not deposit sufficient funds to cover the cost of its operations. In addition, it has to pay its partners in the mixed enterprises. It ends up with a fiscal deficit. The company is viewed by the government as a "socialist unit of production"; its aim is not to elevate the quality of people's lives, but to ensure maximum social happiness.[38]

The national government disregards the major functions that PDVSA should concentrate on exploitation, production, transport, storage, refining and commercialization. Instead the company is responsible for financing infrastructure work (pave roads, erect buildings, provide healthcare, and import food). The company mobilizes militants for diverse political actions related to the PSUV (Chávez's party), finances electoral campaign, and is in charge of foreign aid. It also pays for the state's debt and therefore needs to continue borrowing money in order to sustain its decline of oil production.[39]

PDVSA was converted into a state monopoly in the service of a political, antidemocratic project. It should concentrate its efforts on improving the commercial objectives and not the ideological ones. Coronel concludes that it needs to be replaced with a private, open industry that follows financial regulations.[40] Juan Fernández, paraphrases Coronel's ideas, claiming that oil is employed in Venezuela as a political instrument in order to expand Chávez' socialism of the twenty-first century.[41] It is not used for improving of the country's economic development, reducing poverty, or increasing the people's well-being.

José Guerra demonstrates, by using statistical data, the inefficiencies of PDVSA. Its financial debt increased from approximately $3 billion in 2006 to $25 billion in 2011.[42] During the same period the price of oil increased from $56 a barrel to $96 a barrel. While the price of oil rose by 70% the debt increase eightfold. This data indicates a failed company and the fall of production and the increase in debt suggests that the resources obtained through debt have not been employed to the purpose of increased production.

The inefficiencies of Venezuelan's oil company may have contributed to the refinery accident in August 2012, in which more than 39 people were killed and numerous others wounded. The casualties are worrisome and reflect a lack of supervision and commitment for the security of workers. Over 70% of the personnel surveyed had not participated in any security training.[43]

The opposition newspaper *Analitica* summarizes Domingo Zavala's book, *The Critical Decade* (*La década crítica*), in which he asserts that brilliant opportunities were lost, to use oil revenues as an instrument of economic growth and make Venezuela a modern country.[44] The Venezuelan economist, relying on the period 1998-2007, claims that wastefulness of resources characterized this era, in spite of the fact that oil prices registered a record high of $120 barrel in 2008. The revenues from oil which represents 90% of the country's currency weren't invested in growth, improvement of industrial production, or the service industry.

The sociologist Luis Pedro España, conducting a research on poverty in Venezuela, concluded that the country's oil boom has not favored the poor.[45] The sociological research that covered the period 1998-2008, claimed that the government lacks policies to distribute revenues among the poorest sector of society. The quality of life of households in extreme poverty worsened, according to the research. The percentage of families lacking running water increased during this period from 40% to 60%.

A plan to revise Venezuela's economy using oil revenues as a source of modernizing the country's welfare is proposed by González Cruz.[46] Cruz, indirectly criticizing Chávez's ideology, asserts that in the postindustrial age economic growth largely depends on certain characteristics. These include knowledge, technology, education, health, information, entertainment, and globalization.

Joining other critics of Chávez's economic policies, Cruz maintains that relying on a one-product economy constitutes a grave error. There is the urgent need to develop other sectors of the economy. Especially important is the service sector, which is the main producer of jobs. It is of equal value to develop heavy industry that supports the oil and petrochemical products and an agro-industry that will supply the necessary food.

In order to validate Cruz's thesis of the crucial importance of the service sector and the diversification of a country's economy he analyzes five local governments in the United States. The states under review are California, Texas, Pennsylvania, Massachusetts, and Oklahoma. He treats them as if they were independent states and attempts to demonstrate that per capita income in these states is much higher than Venezuela, primarily because of the diversification of their economy and a strong emphasis on the service sector.

For example, the per capita income of the California population is $42,548 compared to Venezuela's reduced income of $13,000. California's GDP is 5.3 higher than Venezuela ($1,846.8 vs. $348.8 billion) Even Massachusetts, a state of 6 million people, has a GDP similar to Venezuela, but the per capita income is $50,735, more than five times higher than Venezuela's. Texas, like Venezuela, is an oil producing state. However its economy is diversified and in addition to oil it produces cements, salt, and stones and has military, biomedical, information technology, and petrochemical industries. Its GDP is 3.5% higher than Venezuela and per capita income is $38,546.

Cruz concludes that in order to improve Venezuela's economy, it necessitates the return to the private sector and the establishment of laws that will attract transnational enterprises. The private business would be authentic and would issue stocks, which would be owned by both national and foreign investors. The following steps must be taken: reactivate inactive oil fields, develop oil reserves and natural gas that need to be extracted, improve production, processing, transport, distribution and commercialization of oil, develop the petrochemical industries, and accelerate drilling of oil wells. José Guerra adds to Cruz's recommendation the idea of the Venezuelan economist Zavala that petroleum must be employed as a leverage of economic development and not as a source of fiscal income.[47]

Suárez Núñez demonstrated the superiority of private initiative to state control; he compared the Venezuelan oil company PDVSA with the production of petroleum in Azerbaijan, controlled mostly by international corporations.[48] The ex-Soviet Union member has oil reserves estimated at 9 billion barrels of light crude oil. In 1999 it produced the amount of 283,000 barrels per day. In 2009 its production increased to 1 million barrels per day. In ten years, its extraction of oil multiplied five times, after the British Petroleum (BP) started to drill in 1992. The rich international corporations with their financial and technological superiority replaced the Russian state enterprise with its limited economic capacity.

The Azerbaijan state enterprise is in charge of 20% of the country's production and 80% remains with BP, which made huge investments in oil pipes and introduced sophisticated technology in order to elevate petroleum extraction and benefit the nation treasury. In contrast to Azerbaijan, which acts to increase its economic interest, Venezuela is driven by ideological motives that are in conflict with its real economic interests. For example it supplies the most expensive diesel to Bolivia with great loses to itself.[49]

López Padrino mentions that during the period 1999-2010 Venezuela received oil revenues of a superior sum of $990 billion.[50] This amount is approximately equivalent to thirty times the sum Marshall Plan spent on the reconstruction of Europe after World War II. In 1998 (before Chávez came to power), the Venezuela's internal debt was 2.530 billion bolívars (Venezuela's monetary unit) and at the end of 2010 it increased to 39.657 billion bolívars. The amount of money borrowed was also very high in respect to external debt. In 1998 the external debt was $24 billion; it is estimated that at the end of 2010 the external debt increased to $113 billion. In real terms, this amount constitutes 50% of the country's GDP.

The high amount of debt is due to financing an inefficient bureaucracy and projects outside the country. This immense volume of money spent by the government has in reality mortgaged the country. The interest on the debt in 2011 amounted to 12%, a sum higher than the combined budget for health and education (11%). The production of oil decreased from 2003 to 2010 by 920.000 barrels daily. The debt of PDVSA, which was 7.5 billion in 1999, increased to over 21 billion in 2010.[51]

Expropriations: A Gradual Path to Communism

The socialism of the twenty-first century follows Gramsci's idea of gradual transformation to Communism. Chávez's weakening of the private sector is an ongoing process in Venezuela. This course was intensified in 2006 with an increased role of the government in economic affairs. In the majority of cases the Chávez regime repaid only a small portion of the expropriated property.

The main thesis of my research is that Chávez's economic policies should be analyzed from two perspectives: short- and long-term. The Venezuelan president desires to expand expropriations in the agricultural sector which will guarantee more control over feeding the people. For example, at the end of 2011, the government planned to get control of approximately 50% of food production, import, and distribution.[52] In the long run, Chávez wants to obtain control of food distribution in Venezuela which will guarantee his political reign as well. As Petit describes it, when people who are hungry and the access of food is controlled by the state, it becomes easy to intimidate and coerce them.[53]

The justification for expropriations always uses the same "holy words," that the property rights of the citizens have been violated and, therefore, the property must be expropriated. The properties' owners are completely defenseless; not the army or any other institution will come to their help. The injustice of this situation resembles Castro's Communist Cuba.

The Government created networks for food distribution, such as Mercal and PDVAL. These institutions are rampant with corruption and 150,000 tons of rotten foods were found in the principal ports of the country. It is now the turn of private supermarkets to be added to these inefficient networks. The failure of the expropriation policy is being extended to private supermarkets.

Opposition Deputy Nora Brach claimed that the government sponsors black markets of food which enriches high-level functionaries and their friends. These ruin the Venezuelan people, who are unable to obtain basic necessities, such as milk, sugar, bread flour, oil, and other essential products. The great drama of Venezuela, like Cuba, is that food rationing became a part of their lives.

The expropriation of private supermarkets is intended to further reduce the well-being of the so-called middle class, who are continuously harassed and attacked by the regime. An uninterrupted effort exists to weaken them by obliging them to depend on the state for handouts, making them depended on the Chávez regime and hence vote for him in order to assure their economic existence.

The opposition is strongly opposed to Chávez's economic policies claiming that the private sector is massacred and harassed.[54] Mr. Noel Álvarez, the president of Venezuelan Federation of Trade and Industry Chambers (Fedecameras), labeled the government economic policies as "despotism," which will lead to the "destruction of the country."[55]

Chávez is following Gramsci's ideas is gradually suffocating the private sector. The Venezuelan president declared that he has the authority "granted by the people" and the constitution to expropriate any company. He declared, "I have been granted authority to expropriate companies."[56] Government officials are employing such terms as "excessive earning," "speculative earning," "fair prices," and others in order to weaken the private business.

The slowdown of the private sector is a result of private companies' seizures, price controls and restrictions in obtaining foreign currency. The BCV announced that imports by the private sector were down 22%, while the public sector was up 47%; amounted to $5.4 billion in the first nine months of 2010. It confirmed the gradual weakening of the private sector.[57] The availability of foreign currency was lower despite the increase in crude oil prices.

There exists an inverse relationship between the sizes of the private and public sectors. As the private sector diminishes, the opposite occurs to the public domain. In the period 2005-2011 the expropriations of private companies rose, as shown by the number of public employees by 36.2% in Venezuela.[58] The public sector had absorbed 600,000 workers during this period. In February 2011 the number of government workers was 2,273,682, in contrast to 1,668,520 workers in February 2005, just as the process of nationalization started.

The government introduced laws to enforce their demands. These statutes regulated earnings and guaranteed people's access to goods and services. Excessive profits would be forbidden. Such laws, according to the opposition, will end business practices and the system of free markets.[59] A former director of the BCV, Domingo Maza Zavala, termed these measures as "economic repression." He asserted that the attempt to restrict earnings ran counter to market laws, "because the price of goods or services should match with a total production or operating cost, with a profit margin which enables businessmen to keep on running and making investments for the company to go ahead."[60]

Twenty-six leading economists, mostly professors at Venezuelan universities, published a document claiming that the so-called twenty-first century socialism cannot be distinguished from real socialism or Communism.[61] The document, entitled "Economic Crisis and Ineffective Government: A Costly Ideology," claims that Chávez's economic policies are based on errors committed by radical socialism, which is responsible for the increased economic problems in Venezuela.

The deterioration of domestic production and economic institutions is the results of outdated political and ideological considerations. This might lead, the economists asserted, to protracted stagnation characterized by "increasing loss of productive efficiency of private and state run companies, accompanied with increase in prices, low real wages, high corruption, high social inequality and massive public debt."[62]

Jesús Seguías analyzes Chávez's expropriations, claiming that the Venezuelan president desires to have full control of the population.[63] His aim is not to improve enterprise production, but to assure that all workers depend on him and their economic security and livelihood is guaranteed as long as they vote for maintaining his power. Being in charge of the economy, Chávez will have a strong influence on voting patterns for both parliamentary and presidential elections.

Blanco Muñoz analyzes Chávez's expropriations from a psychological, sociological point of view.[64] He claims that expropriations exacerbate hatred and polarization by emphasizing the antagonistic relations between socialism vs. capitalism and popular power vs. capital authority. Chávez attempts to convince the poor that only his government can help and rescue them from the dislike of the rich.

Rivera Muñoz claims that Chávez's expropriations should be considered as an act of state terrorism.[65] He commences his article by quoting Pope John Paul II (Juan Pablo II), who asserted that terrorism is born by hatred and contempt of human life and constitutes a grave crime against humanity. The directors of Fedecamaras strongly criticized the beating of four managers in a private company that was expropriated by the Chavez's regime. The writer reiterates the fact that the government has full control of all armed groups and that they act only upon receiving instructions from Chávez's administration.

The National Assembly passed certain laws in December 2010 that will consolidate socialist production schemes.[66] According to Isabel Pereira, director of the Center for the Dissemination of Economic Knowledge for Freedom (CEDICE) the law intends to be the final displacement of private entrepreneurship by the government. Pereira claimed that, as a result of this law, inflation and imports would increase and job creation decrease.

The official government press justifies expropriations by emphasizing Chávez's declaration that capitalism is in the process of bankruptcy and is in the final stage of being replaced by socialism all over the world.[67] The seizures of private companies are justified by the ability and need to increase public benefits. In certain cases the excuse is given that the private enterprises violated the rights of the workers. The expropriation of a major aluminum company was justified because its production is essential for the construction of houses and the company was firing too many workers.

In March 2010, the Venezuelan National Assembly approved the new Organic Law of the National Financial System.[68] The major functions of the law are to permit citizen participation in financial procedures, social control of the financial system, and the promotion of the collaboration of all economic sectors in the financial system. It created the Higher National *Financial System* Body (*OSFIN*); its role is to coordinate the activities of all the major economic players on issues related to the country's development and economic stability. In reality, the law assures that the government is in charge of all economic activities.

An opposition newspaper article asserts that according to the constitution, articles 115 and 116 of the supreme law of the land, expropriations can occur only when it involves common social interests and fair compensation is awarded.[69] Professor Antonio Casanova claims that seizures of private property violate six constitutional rules.[70] In order to comply with the constitution, seizures should be reasonable, adequate, appropriate, and proportionate. It cannot be abusive and justified solely by declaring it public utility.

Professor Casanova reveals how the government by seizing the food processing company Monaca violated the rules of the supreme law of the land. The first violation is that the government paid too little, less than the actual value of the company. The Chávez's administration needed to explain and determine how the expropriation is related to the public good or social interest. The seizure should not be an abusive decision and justified solely by declaring it public interest.

The Professor correctly asserts that the seizure of the company did not transform and enhance the company's public utility. Therefore, the government's claim that it involves the public interest can be refuted on the grounds that seizures are not meant to take an industrial entity, which produces goods, services, jobs, and taxes, and turn it into something of much less public utility. As a result of the government takeover, the value of the company did not increase, but in reality decreased.

Díaz Casanova claims that expropriations constitute a violation of economic rights of the citizens guaranteed by the constitution.[71] All Venezuelan citizens have the fundamental right to own property and enjoy all their possessions which were legally acquired. Article 116 of the constitution specifically claims that confiscation of goods can only take place if crime is involved, such as illicit drug trafficking.

Chávez's expropriations are a clear violation of the constitution, and he has the complicity of the armed forces, judges, National Assembly deputies, his ministers, and variety of collaborators. These expropriations should be considered as robberies. Casanova reminds everyone that in February 1999 Chávez swore to protect and comply with the constitution and the laws of the republic. These expropriations also should be considered a violation of the law.

Writing in May 2010, Andrés Borges claimed that the accumulated value of the state's expropriations amounted to $23 billion.[72] This constitutes 40% of Venezuela external debt. This money could have been spent improving the people's well-being. For example, with this money five educational centers could be built that would narrow the gap of the needed schools in the country; two thousand kilometers of road could be constructed. Enterprises placed in the government's hand contribute to loss of employment, deterioration of labor conditions, and a decrease in the quality of products and services.

Andrés Borges laments the fact that Chávez claims that enterprises that are expropriated are the workers' property. However, when businesses are taken over by the government the workers' benefits and salaries worsen.[73] As a result of expropriations, dignity in workplaces ceased to exist.

Improving workers' well-being can be accomplished only by incentives that are an integral part of private initiative.

The nationalization of banks is viewed by Padilla as a direct attack on liberty and an important step leading the country toward misery.[74] In 2009 the state controlled 30% of the banking sector. The National Assembly approved a banking law that called for deposits of over 10,000 bolivars to be frozen. Each person who possesses such a deposit has to justify in writing to the Finance Minister any withdrawal of money. Each month there is a deduction of 1.5%. Persons who have deposits higher than 20,000 bolívars will have a tax ranging between 12%-14% imposed. On an annual basis, each depositor needs to provide 10-15 bolívars in order to help poor communities in Cuba and elsewhere. Padilla concludes that all these steps forced on individual depositors constitute a step toward totalitarianism.

Chávez would like to bring about government control of the banking industry. The Venezuelan president aims at a hegemony of public banks in Venezuela.[75] The private banks, according to Chávez, turned into financial speculators, and the government should create "a banking sector focused on development and not speculation and financial fraud."[76]

An editorial in an opposition newspaper laments the negative aspects of Chávez's administration taking over the banking industry.[77] It claims that nationalizing banks amounts to the government's playing with fire. The banking business is based on trust. The government policy toward lending institutions is eroding confidence. As a result, many depositors withdraw their money and invest it in other places or put it under the mattress. The editorial concludes that Chávez and his administration must understand that employing ideological criteria on banks is due to fail.

An important idea in the Chávez's expropriation policy is that the food industry will solely remain in government's hand. Therefore, companies that are related to agricultural products were seized. A decree was signed by Chávez to take over the Spanish farming supply company, Agroislena, which provided 70% of the country's farmer needs.[78] The justification to the expropriation was that oligopolies do not ensure food security.

The opposition reacted strongly and claimed that the seizure of the Spanish company was a severe blow to agriculture and would cause a strong decline in food production. It would impoverish the country and create a slave model of production that runs contrary to democratic principles. It will lead the country into chaos and shortages of food.[79]

Chávez declared that the need exists to liberate (nationalize) the entire Venezuelan estates and farms.[80] In order to fulfill this aim, forty-seven estates were seized by the government. The war against large estates is an important ideological issue for the Chávez's administration. As a result of the heavy rains in December 2010, many people were made homeless and the large estates could provide housing for this people.

Chávez expropriation of large estates is reminiscent of Stalin extermination of the kulaks (owners of large farms) in the 1930s in the Soviet Union. Unlike the Soviet dictator, who exterminated the kulaks, Chávez only took away their land. However, both leaders' collectivization efforts were complete failures and resulted in food shortages. President Chávez, nevertheless, was able avert hunger by using oil revenue to import subsistence items.

Imports of food and agricultural items were increased by 254%, during the period 1999-2011.[81] During the period 2008-2010 imports of food increased four times in comparison to the two years before Chávez come to power, 1997-1998. Imports are the only guarantee of the country's supply of nourishment. Agricultural exports completely disappeared. In 1998 (before Chávez came to power) agricultural exports amounted to $690 million, and in 2010 it diminished by 88.86%, to the sum of $76.85 million. Basic food items, which were placed under price control by the Chávez regime, are very difficult to find in Venezuela's supermarkets. These include basic items such as milk, meat, pasta, oil, and vegetables.[82]

A farm seizure by the Chávez regime in December 2009 was welcomed by the workers, who shouted the slogan "homeland, socialism or death."[83] One year after the government took over the farm, a third of the workers were dismissed and most of the farm assets had vanished. The workers complained that their needs were ignored. There was a general deterioration on the farm; embezzlement of funds and inefficiency were rampant.

The housing problem is an important issue in Venezuela. Fourteen million people live in slums and 74% of the population needs housing.[84] In his radio address Chávez, promised to "intensify" the seizure of land that could be used to build houses. The Venezuelan president called upon the militia to occupy abandoned plots of land.[85]

José Guerra contradicts Chávez's putting the blame on external factors and asserts that inflation and *demagoguery* are the real problems in the housing industry.[86] The official propaganda attempts to blame housing shortages on private builders, instead of faulting the government. Guerra admits that probably there were some builders who cheated, but it does not justify the expropriations of housing and apartments. Guerra claims that the government policy toward housing amounts to *demagoguery*.

According to Guerra, starting with the year 2007, the steel and cement industries as well as other suppliers of materials essential to the housing industry became state monopolies. All these industries, according to data supplied by the BCV, witnessed a strong fall in production (the steel industry fell 64%). This constitutes the main problem in the housing industry and the primary reason for continued shortages of housing. The price of construction supplies increased, which contributed to inflation. The government solution to this problem was to buy fabricated houses in Belorussia, which would improve employment in that country, but not in Venezuela.

The hatred toward private builders (capitalists) prevents the government from taking sound measures to solve the housing crisis. The solution to the housing shortages, according to Guerra, is the promotion of the private sector, while the state should assume the role of facilitator, promoting construction with clear rules, which would attract private investment in this sector. The government's employing threats and hostility can only aggravate the problem.

Cilento Sarli, writing in February 2011, claims that the residential deficit amounts to 3 million and in order to obtain 5.6 new homes for 100,000 inhabitants, the need exist to construct 160,000 housing units.[87] The goal is impossible to reach mainly because of a lack of construction materials. There are also 50,000 homes unable to be used or abandoned. The blame for the shortages should include also the governments that were in power before Chávez came to power. Current and past regimes viewed the housing deficit as it was a natural phenomenon, as if they are not responsible for the housing shortages. The lack of residential structures is caused by the absence of good public policy.

During the period 1999-2011, (the Chávez regime) 283,000 housing units were constructed. This amounts to one house for 1,000 people. In order to comply with what Chávez promised, during the period

1999-2011, 1 million houses should have been constructed. A report by the Ministry of Housing indicated that the government built 21,400 housing units in 2005, which represents only 18% of the target (120,000 housing units). In 2006 40,340 housing units were built, 88% more than the previous year but only 34% of the initial goal of building 120,000 housing units.[88]

$900 billion of oil revenues were wasted by the Chávez regime, which explains the housing deficit. One has to add to that inefficiencies, incompetence, and government corruptions, which contributed to the growth of the deficit. The criminalization of the private sector, inflation, and lack of construction supplies, were also important reasons contributing to the housing shortages.

The expropriation of property is an inappropriate way to punish those citizens who worked hard and saved money to buy their property. The government does not appreciate personal sacrifices; only collective property is valued. Venezuelans, under the Chávez regime, live in a militarized society, safeguarding a gigantic bureaucracy which victimized its people.

Farías Pucci claims that renting should be considered a partial solution to the housing shortages.[89] Pucci stresses the importance of a 1999 law of real estate renting, which emphasized the legal responsibilities of the two parties in the contract. The Chávez regime reformed this law and emphasized the rights of the renter, while diminishing the right of the property owner. It was called the Law of Regulating and Controlling Renting Property. The law aims to protect the social collective interest.

The above reform law has a socialist character, benefiting those who rent. The law creates a new constituent that has as its principal objective to defend those who rent. The prohibition of ejecting a renter is explicitly expressed in the law. It also regulates and controls the price of renting. The writer concludes that the law of renting, which restricts free market regulations, could also be responsible for the housing shortages in Venezuela.

Similar to Argentina's Perón, who ruined his country's economy and told his supporters to stop paying rent[90]; the Chávez regime took over apartments in certain residential complexes without compensating the owners.[91] According to the Venezuelan president the blame lies with developers who committed a "real estate fraud."[92]

Chávez' policies toward renting resulted in 1.5 million property owners stopping the practice of leasing.[93] The writer of this article (his name is not mentioned) claims that it is incorrect to allege that those who own rental properties are rich people. 95% of property owner's possess only one property. Only 1% of the landlords fit the category of being rich. The 2003 decision handed down by the Chávez regime to freeze rents resulted in the tenants' becoming the real owners.

Andrés Borges criticized the Chávez regime's use of the term *social property*. It signifies that the government is the proprietor of everything and the people are the owners of nothing.[94] This concept of social property is incorporated in all juridical instruments and was approved in December 2009 by the National Assembly. The government claims that land and property that the government takes over will be equally distributed to all the people. In reality, this law takes away all the people's rights and transfers them to the government. The Law of Democratization of Property reduces people's rights and gives the government full control.

Borges proposes that the law should be reversed and the people ought to become the owners of all enterprises and land. Money should be put aside so that each person can save and obtain social security in the future. Justice, the writer concludes, is distributing property for each person equally.

Is Inflation an Integral Part of Socialism?

Various scholars and writers view inflation as being inseparable from socialism. The socialists in Germany's Weimar Republic, like Chávez, mistakenly believed that devaluating the local currency would decrease inequality and benefit the poor. Eduardo Ruiz claims that inflation, a loss in the value of the currency, constitutes a secondary effect of socialism.[95] The main ingredient of this ideology is its insistence on the equitable distribution of wealth. Ruiz also claims that all states that follow socialism are heading towards the wrong direction; their economic system will sink in misery and eventually collapse.[96]

In order to prevent inflation, the increase of economic resources to the poor should follow simultaneously with increase of production of goods and services and competition among the economic agents of the society. However, in socialism production decreases, as a result of radical changes introduced in the economy. The increased role of the state in the economy and the diminishing capacity of the private sector contribute to reduced production; it creates shortages of goods and services.

Socialism also reduces competition among producers of the same product or service. The state having a monopoly, can arbitrarily fix prices without any complaint because only the government owns these goods and services. Socialist economic assumptions are based on false premises. It envisions that wealth exists and needs to be distributed equally. It ignores the fact that the cost of production needs to be less than the price of the item.

Socialism is a Pandora's box characterized by corruption, wastefulness, nepotism, inefficiency, shortages, and a dreadful quality of products. Eduardo Ruiz metaphorically suggests that socialism wants to fly an airplane that disobeys the laws of physics. It attempts to negate the fact that the economic man is motivated by egoism and the desire for profit. The economy produces wealth by obeying the laws of supply and demand, which determine prices of goods and services. Government decrees cannot accomplish this task.

The financing of social expenditures through oil income gave the government hope of a magic solution to poverty. However, Chávez's spending contributed to deficits. Chávez was incapable of creating conditions of stability in the economy. The Venezuelan president followed fiscal and monetary policies that generated the highest inflation rate in Latin America in the twenty-first century. Paradoxically, the socialism of the twenty-first century accentuates the importance of creating an equalitarian society. In reality, however, it creates wealth for some, while impoverishing the majority of the population.

Casique views inflation as a Damocles' sword that acts as a silent thief who robs the Venezuelan people of their income; it is similar to a tax that people constantly need to pay.[97] The steady rise of prices is attributed to the steady increase of consumer imports without the availability of sufficient dollars. The rise of public expenses also constitutes an important reason for inflation. In addition, Casique claims that the lack of fiscal and monetary discipline decreases productivity. Expropriations of private property also contribute to the rise of prices.

Vallenila complains that printing money in Venezuela is not related to the country's productivity.[98] This distorts the economy, which in spite of having a high 17.1% interest rate does not encourage investments in the country. All other major countries have a lot lower interest rates (United States 3.25%, Canada 3%, and the euro zone 1.25%). This high rate of interest should be an indicator for low inflation. However, Venezuela's rate of inflation in 2011 was 27.40%, which translates into a continuous rises in prices. This fact negates the possibility of employing the local currency (Bolívar) as saving or investment in a bank.

The Chávez administration claims that inflation is an integral part of the capitalist system. Therefore, it incorrectly asserts that inflation will decline as socialism becomes the dominant economic system. This view is expressed by Commerce Minister Eduardo Samán, who asserts that inflation is caused by shopkeepers and commercial agents. His solution to the problem of inflation is to close down all these businesses.[99]

Guerra concludes that the high inflation in Venezuela renders the country's economy to be outside of world commerce; it becomes safe for the country to remain solely an importer. The only profitable product is oil. By raising the internal prices, all goods imported from countries where inflation is lower seem to be cheap and therefore external buying cannot decrease. Salaries are increasing all the time because of inflation; however, buying power is diminishing constantly because the rise in salaries is lower than the rate of inflation. It especially affects those with limited resources. During the Chávez regime period (1999-2010) the buying power decreased by 162%.[100]

The Chávez administration blames speculation as the main reason for the constant rise in prices. Chávez has urged the people to fight against speculators. The Venezuelan president announced the establishment of the National Superintendence for Costs and Prices (NSCP) that will fight against high prices.[101] This act constitutes further enlargement of the central bureaucracy, which will be in charge of marking up prices.

Chávez's administration believes that consolidating a socialist government would eliminate the problem of inflation. Creating thousands of diverse companies with a socialist vision will alter the dominant perception of the need for profit and hence stabilize prices. The National Assembly plans to initiate diverse projects and laws in order to consolidate a socialist economic model. These will include an antimonopoly law, a statute controlling the buying and selling cars, and laws relating to social property and rent. These laws, according to the government point of view, will regulate speculation and the prices of products. These measures, which will be applied by the government, will bring a solution to the problem of inflation.[102]

In another government press release, Chávez called upon the people to be organized in order to be able to fight against speculators and capitalist profiteers.[103] He called upon the Bolivarian armed forces, Bolivarian National Guard, to become the vanguard in the war against speculators. Those enterprises that will increase prices will be taken over by the workers.[104]

Many economists and analysts refute the government contention that speculation is the main cause of inflation. González claims that such an idea lacks any logic and has no basis in reality.[105] This strategy intends to scapegoat the government responsibility in this matter. It attempts to divert attention from the real cause of inflation, which is macroeconomic disequilibrium, the result of faulty economic, public, fiscal, monetary, and exchange policies.

Miguel Muñoz tackles Venezuela's major economic problems including inflation from a different perspective. He claims that lack of economic knowledge by the country's leadership is responsible for Venezuela's economic deterioration.[106] In the military field, for example, one has to be familiar with war strategies. In mathematics one has to know trigonometry; a lawyer needs to be familiar with ancient Roman laws. However, those who are in charge of the country's wealth know very little about macroeconomics. They should know about monetary theories, such as the Keynesian, Austrian, and supply side theories. They need to become familiar on how to stop inflation and the problem it causes.

Muñoz proceeds to ask who produces inflation. His answer is the Venezuelan president with his ideology, the president of the BCV, and the economic ministers in Chávez's government; all these people are to be blamed for the rampant inflation in the country. The inflation is produced by the government as a result of faulty applications of macroeconomic policies, which are composed of monetary policy, price, commerce, and fiscal and exchange proceedings. The measures of fiscal persecutions, exchange control, expropriations, confiscations, less production all contribute to inflation. Price control leads to shortages and higher inflation rate.

None of all the people who are engaged in Venezuela's economic policies are economists. Chávez is a military man, the president of BCV is a mathematician, and the minister of finance is a lawyer. No one can expect these people to stop inflation. In a latter part of this chapter a comparison will be made between Venezuela's and Chile's economic systems.

One important reason that Chile's economy is one of the most developed in Latin America has to be the qualifications of its president, Sebastián Piñera. He received a Ph.D. in economics from Harvard University in 1973. Piñera, upon returning to Chile, became a very successful businessman who earned millions of dollars. These qualifications and experiences helped Piñera to modernize Chile's economic system and make the country one of the richest states in Latin America.

The government, by arbitrarily determining prices, breaks the mechanism of distribution of a free exchange between supply and demand. As a result of the government's lowering prices, it increases demand. It causes an increase of consumption of numerous items. The reduced prices constitute a disincentive for supply. Such a situation does not guarantee consumer satisfaction. It creates shortages and incentives for extracting profit from scarcity by the creation of informal merchandise distribution which is difficult to control (black markets).[107]

González strongly criticizes the Law of Costs, Prices, and Salary Protection (*Ley de Costos, Precios y Protección al Salario de los Venezolanos*) approved on May 1, 2011. Regulating profits can create enormous distortions. It affects incentives for production and supply of goods and services. This law is an indicator of a lack of basic knowledge about how to employ economics in regulating public policies. Inflation cannot be controlled vis-à-vis laws and decrees. Control of prices can only be justified in the event that there is a monopoly. Regulatory plans need to be established based on incentives in order to raise efficiency and contain cost-benefit analysis.

The Law of Fair Costs and Prices became official on July 18, 2011. It constitutes a new phase in enlarging the state's control on the private economic market. The superintendent of costs and prices has the authority to "issue an opinion on the use of methods of expenses, profits, as well as on the use of installed capacities and cost clearance."[108] This law enables the Venezuelan state to enlarge its control on all economic activities.

Alexander Guerrero views the Law of Fair Costs and Prices as a death sentence for economic liberties.[109] It eliminates market competition that is the basis for the price formation used in capitalism. The central authority assumes the responsibility to determine prices; individual and economic liberties are taken away. This law would further cause the fall of investments and increase poverty. Páez Puma claims that revising costs in order to determine a "just price" was tried before by both Lenin and Stalin in

Russia (the Soviet Union) and were an important cause for the continued economic crisis in that country.[110]

Inflation may also be attributed to Chávez's attempt to subordinate the monetary and financial policies of the BCV to his own.[111] This was done contrary to the constitution, which explicitly mentions that the central bank is independent and not subordinated to directions from the executive branch. It specifically mentions that it cannot receive or finance fiscal deficit policies.

Chávez, contrary to the ideas expressed in the supreme law, covered parts of his budget deficits with BCV's international reserves, undermining the Bolívar's support. The Venezuelan president financed the national oil company, sectional, and strategic projects with monetary resources from BCV. He forced private banks to issue credit with interest rates handled by BCV, receiving direct credit from BCV for public projects.

Chávez's policy toward the central bank is similar to the course Domingo Perón embarked in 1946, a policy that utilized the Argentinian central bank funds in order to finance his fiscal deficits.[112] Similar to the case of Perón's Argentina, the BCV was converted into a government tool for printing money according to dictates of the executive branch.

The law for reforming the central bank aims at converting this institution into an ordinary appendage of the regime with the obligation of financing the state's deficit. The past experiences of both dictators of the left and right demonstrate that such activities contributed to hyperinflation.[113]

This policy contributed to the rise in fiscal deficit, raised inflationary pressure, and increased the economic disequilibrium. It led to a sustained rise of prices, which increased poverty. It also led to the printing of money without the proper backing in order to finance the public sector. It caused a sharp decline in the currency's buying power.

José Guerra, a former economic research manager at BCV, asserts that illegal financing by the central bank has been concealed.[114] That a country sold oil for $105 a barrel in April 2011 and was unable to improve its economic status after two years of recession (2009-2011) is a monumental failure. The government's economic policy of exchange and price controls contributed to the fact that Venezuela has the highest inflation rate in Latin America.

Guerra claims that the government attempted to spread lies, such as that Venezuela has the lowest unemployment rate in Latin America. Data on unemployment from February 2011 shows that the country with the lowest unemployment was Mexico 4.7%[115], while Venezuela registered a rate of 8.8%. A second lie by the government is that inflation was reduced. In March 2011 inflation was 26.2%, a little lower than 28% the 2010 rate. However, the nuclear inflation, a measure of inflation that excludes administrative prices, shows that inflation in March 2011 was 29%. The same month in 2010 it was 30.2%. There is no evidence to affirm a pronounced decrease in inflation.

Guerra challenges Finance Minister Giordani's assertion that there are improvements in monthly economic indicators, such as a reduction in unemployment. The former central bank employee rhetorically asks, "Who calculated this data? What methodology was employed?" No one knows the answer to these questions. Therefore, doubts persist. Guerra claims that political motives were employed in order to receive favorable information.

Those in charge of economic policies and especially the BCV's managers hide information in order to be viewed positively. Where are transparency and the obligation to inform the people about economic affairs? Guerra concludes that it is of utmost importance to remove the political influence from the BCV and turn it into an independent agency.

Another important reason for the high inflation in Venezuela is the country's high debt. The service of the debt consumes 12.2% of the national budget (25.002 million bolívars). This sum is higher than the combined spending on health, public infrastructures, and social security.[116] According to Guerra, in 2010 the deficit of 31,425 million Bolivars, which is equivalent to $12.087 million (rate of exchange 2.6 Bolivars to a dollar).

Pedro Palma explains the inseparable link between devaluation of the local currency and inflation.[117] The obvious reason is that imports, which are paid by dollars, become more expensive. Another explanation is that salaries are increased, which makes production more costly, even for no importing enterprises. The government as a result of devaluation receives more income in local currency and hence embarks on expensive public ventures. The increase in the supply of money contributes to inflation and a decrease in consumer's buying power.

It is, therefore, not surprising that many analysts concur that devaluation of the local currency is based on political and economic ignorance. These decisions are made without any political dialogue or the people's participation in the decision-making process. As a result of the January 2010 devaluation of the Bolívar, the people became poorer.[118] Consequently, the government continued its wastefulness policies and raised by 25% the minimum salaries. All these activities contributed to the rise of the inflation rate. The 2013 devaluation of the currency will have similar results.

Those people earning minimum salary lost 62.3% of their buying power as a result of the January 2010 devaluation.[119] For example, if a person earned a monthly amount of 967 bolivars, or $449, before January 11, 2010, he would have a salary worth 62.3% less in terms of its buying power after January 11, 2010. The previous devaluation occurred in 2005, and from that year till 2010 the accumulated inflation was 168%. This signifies an annual average inflation of 21.8%.

José Guerra claims that in Venezuela there exists a myth that by fixing the exchange rate for dollar, internal prices would not rise.[120] President Luis Herrera's devaluation of the bolivar in February 1983 did not guarantee price stability. The government fixing an exchange rate causes inflation, exports to be reduced, and import to increase.

The government claim that devaluation will promote exports is refuted by Guerra, who asserts that the real reason is political, to resolve the immense deficits; it is a discretionary matter that imposes the regime's policies in a way similar to an institutionalized mafia.[121] In addition to fixing the deficit, devaluation takes complete control of private companies, as they become completely dependent on the government for currency exchanges.

Guerra claims that tax increases and devaluation in order to cover the government's fiscal deficit would negatively affect the economy. In spite of government's price control, inflation is on the rise. Devaluation according to Guerra is a disparate action in order to extract fiscal income from the population which would finance public expenditures.[122]

Other Characteristics of Chávez's Economic Policy

This segment will deal with economic attributes of the Chávez regime that were not previously mentioned. These will include flight of capital, brain drain, poverty, public health, trade unions, economic risk, etc. Chávez's gradual move toward Communism has had a bad effect on all economic indexes and indicators. Capital flight, brain drain, public health, and other issues worsened. Indexes of such things as political and economic risks placed Venezuela at the bottom of Latin American countries.

An important reason for flight of capital is that the private sector does not trust the Chávez regime.[123] The estimated capital flight in 2009 was $24,415 billion and in 2008 it was $21,589 billion.[124]The government envisioned that by applying a policy of exchange control it would regulate the flight of capital and safeguard international reserves. However, this policy, implemented since February 2003, had the opposite effect.[125] The flight of capital during the period 1999-2010 was $122,928 billion. On April 13, 2008, Chávez declared that exchange control of the Venezuelan currency would be permanently imposed. The Venezuelan president reiterated that he would not permit the oligarchy to take away all their dollars. Nevertheless, according to a BCV publication, at the close of the third quarter of 2008, the flight of capital was the highest since Chávez came to power in (1999).[126] How could there be an exit of capital when there were controls on currency exchange? The existence of parallel markets (black markets) where currency could be obtained through exchange operations constitutes the answer.

The following information illustrates how control of currency exchange contributed to capital flight. Without exchange control during the period 1999-2002, $28.600 million left the country; with exchange control during the period 2003-2009 the amount rose to $94.688 million. The data on capital flight reveals that during the Chávez administration (1999-2010), the flight of capital was five times greater than in 48 years prior to Chávez coming to power.[127]

The government destroyed the structural characteristics of the economy and increased dependency on one product (oil). Venezuela needs to direct the oil resources toward providing a productive, well-balanced, modern, and just economic system. Casique concludes his article by quoting Benjamin Franklin, a participant in the writing of the United States constitution, who said that the road to wealth depends on work and savings,[128] thus, indirectly criticizing the Chávez regime, which does not consider saving important.

Alex Vallenilla makes an interesting comparison between Venezuela's and Japan's capital flight.[129] He admits, however, that there is a big difference between Japan's economy (the third greatest economy in the world) and Venezuela. Nevertheless, the comparison demonstrates how people react to different ideologies.

Japan's March 2011 tsunami and nuclear crisis had an important effect on the value of the yen (the Japanese currency). The logical economic argument would claim that as a result of the national disaster, Japan must devalue its currency. However, in reality, the opposite occurred and the value of the Yen increased, breaking the 1995 record level, the rate increased to 82.71 yens to a dollar. In March 2011 the dollar was valued at 76.17 yens.

In the last years prior to the disaster, Japan followed a policy of practicing *carry trade* by using the yen in order to invest abroad. However, the disaster in Japan altered the flow of investments and a big share of this infusion of money was directed toward helping the country in its reconstruction efforts. The Japanese central bank issued 5 billion yen to assist in the recovery effort. The high demand for yen increased the value of the currency. Also important for the flow of investments in Japan was that the United States and Europe have not seemed to offer important investment alternatives.

In Venezuela, on the other hand, the flight of capital during the period 2003-2011 was around $111.5 billion. This sum of money represents half of 2010 GDP.[130] The country lives in a constant currency deficit. In March 2011 the official exchange control was 4.30 bolivars to a dollar. However, in order for the bolivar to have sufficient support it needs the BCV to maintain liquid monetary reserves of $70 billion; it has only $26,916 billion and lacks $48.084 billion, which represents about 38.64% of all flight capital resources since 2003. A part of this capital belongs to Venezuelans who maintain their wealth outside the country, to the detriment of the rest of the population.

The comparison between investment patterns in Venezuela and Japan illustrates how different ideologies affect nationalism and decision about where the money should be invested. Disappointed with Chávez's economic policies, many Venezuelans preferred to move their wealth outside the country. In Japan, on the other hand, the opposite occurred; investment was redirected toward the home country.

The brain drain is another problem that has major impact on Venezuela's economy. During the period 1999-2009, over 800,000 youngsters left Venezuela.[131] This group is mainly composed of young professionals, scientists, and businesspeople. Venezuela used to be an immigration country. However, Chávez's coming to power altered the situation. According to Professor Iván de la Vega, who conducted studies on the brain drain in Venezuela, 72% of students retain the idea of leaving the country.[132] In 2010 there were 260,000 Venezuelans residing in the United States, 30,000 in Canada, 10,000 in Australia, and approximately 200,000 in Europe.

Chávez's social investments failed in their objective of eliminating misery. Instead of being reduced poverty has increased. An example is the cost of the basic food basket, which each day becomes unattainable to those people who are poor and lack sufficient funds to buy it. Housing deficits includes approximately 2 million units.[133]

During the December 2010 National Assembly session, taxes were raised on banks, which worsened the country's economic conditions.[134] Taxes were reinstated on bank loans and the sale tax increased from 12% to 14%. Raising taxes during a recession is the wrong prescription because it inhibits aggregate demand and economic activities. This will contribute to the devaluation of the Bolívar and the government will opt for an increase in debt. All these measures will create a vicious cycle forcing the government to further calls for new taxes in order to raise sufficient revenues.

The National Institute of Statistics (Instituto Nacional de Estadística) reports that in the first quarter of 2010 poverty increased by 11.6%.[135] Those who are considered precariously poor constitute 32.5% of the population or 9,036,516 Venezuelans. The number of people who are not able to satisfy basic needs increased by 23.5% in the first half of 2010, and 11.6% of Venezuelan (791,421 families) live in accommodations that lack running water. This number represents an increase of 0.6%, in comparison to the first quarter a year before, when 6.5% of families lived in inadequate housing, the same percentage as a year before.[136]

José Padrino concentrates on the deterioration of the health system. He views Chávez's September 2009 declaration of emergency in the public health system as proof of the deep crisis in this sector.[137] The Venezuelan president inherited from the previous regime a public health system with budgetary problems, an infrastructure that requires maintaining, physical plants with questionable efficiency, duplicity, and counterproductive services. All these problems needed immediate attention.

There was the belief and hope that the Chávez government, which came to power in 1999, would implement new and unique measures that would remedy the public health system. These would include increasing the amount of investment, building more hospitals, utilizing preventive medicine, and increasing the salaries of the professional staff and workers. Chávez not only did not improve the health sector but, according to health experts, made it worse. He cut needed resources, negating the need to maintain necessary equipment.

Chávez installed popular consultants, who were not considered to be of high professional quality but were part of his political hierarchy. The Venezuelan president brought in many Cubans and put them in charge of the health sector. These people had very little practical experience and were unable to satisfy people's needs. Many health programs were cancelled, including infantile vaccination, infant-mother nutrition, and adequate levels of vaccination against AH1N1, which affects 5% of the population, twice as much as other Latin American countries, to prevent an epidemic.

As in other areas controlled by the government, corruption played an important role in determining the resources given to the minister of health. Dr. Tirso Silva (a medical doctor), a former president of the health subcommittee in the National Assembly, denounced the investments in the health sector. He claimed that the money assigned to health facilities is not coordinated with professionals who work there. Dr. Silva claims that that a major part of the money ends up in private hands, those who are privileged and close to the Venezuelan leader. (Padrino spells the word *revolution*, "robolución"; *robo* means "theft" or "robbery" in Spanish).

A report by the Cato Institute ranks Venezuela as one of the most restricted economies in the world,[138] placing 138 out of 141, and has the least free economy in Latin America. The growing number of regulations imposed on the economy and the expropriations of private enterprises and properties are two of the factors that contributed Venezuela's have become a "highly state-centered economy".[139]

Another study reveals that Venezuela is the worst place to conduct business in Latin America.[140] While Venezuela was ranked 172 on a world scale, other Latin American countries were rated as follows: Ecuador 130, Honduras 131, and Bolivia 149.

Corruption is a phenomenon that is characteristic of many countries on the globe. When it occurs, the allocation of resources to the people becomes problematic. Rodríguez Barrera analyzing corruption in Venezuela claims that is an integral part of the country's history. However, during the forty years of democracy (1958-1998) it was reduced by 80%.[141] Under

Chávez' regime, on the other hand, corruption increased to levels that there are not parallels in the country's past.

An editorial in Venezuela's opposition press asserts the anticorruption law of April 7, 2003, which defined embezzlement, established norms, and rules of conduct did not improve the situation. People are not convinced that the management of public resources is based on the principles of honesty, transparency, participation, efficiency, efficacy, and legality.[142]

The emerging new super-rich cadre is exploiting abusing the law in order to enrich themselves. Public corruption, according to the article, has grown into an epidemic, a new type of delinquency, which the writer terms *"Chavopeculador"* (Chávez embezzlement) because crimes are committed without impunity.

Álvarez Paz observed that organized crime penetrated the highest echelons of Chávez's government and was determined to manage the country's money and credit.[143] Accordingly, these mafia groups compete among themselves for the control of Venezuela's resources. These illicit groups engage in money derived from unlawful activities, such as narcotic traffic and other enterprises. As an example of his ideas, Paz mentions the detention of Fernández Barrueco and the decree that twenty bank directors not leave the country. This example demonstrates the internal struggle among various mafia groups and the ability of one camp to emerge victoriously. This idea is confirmed by the emergence of Venezuela as a mafia state, which will be discussed in the third chapter.

In a real democratic country, such an event would lead to the resignation of the head of the state. Chávez must assume full responsibility for what is happening with organized crime. It demonstrates a decayed and unethical regime. Venezuela is a lawless country without God.[144] Corruption is on the rise and norms, ethics, and morality have disappeared. Philosophers and law jurists would claim that crime was converted into the norm and violation of the law became a right.

Alvarado Griman, analyzing local elections in Venezuela, claims that Chávez's government generated funds by illicit means, such as narcotic traffic and corruption, in order to elect candidates loyal to Chávez.[145] This is similar to what happened in Colombia in the 1990s, where presidential candidates such as Samper were infiltrated by powerful drug cartels. The mafia needs to control political power in order to consolidate its economic advantages.

The disappearance of $500 million from PDVSA's pension fund was strongly criticized by the opposition press and viewed as an instance of corruption in which high government officials were involved.[146] The case of Francisco Illarramendi demonstrated the active participation of high government officials in fraud and embezzlement. Illarramendi worked in the United States for an investment company (he has dual citizenship, United States and Venezuelan) that had strong ties with PDVSA. He had strong personal relations with high officials in Chávez's government including the president (He escorted Chávez during the 1999 visit to New York).

In the District Court in Connecticut, Illarramendi was declared guilty of securities fraud and conspiracy against the Securities and Exchange Commission (SEC).[147] PDVSA's pension fund is one of the entities affected by the fraud. The losses were hidden by Illarramendi; investors and creditors were misled in order to prevent misplaced money from being reported.

PDVSA is strongly influence by Fidel Castro and his political commissar, Alí Rodríguez Araque, who has been a long-time cabinet member in Chávez's government. In the 1960s Rodríguez, as a Communist guerrilla fighter, conducted irregular warfare against Venezuelan democracy.[148] Jorge Giordani, minister of planning and Alí Rodríguez, oil minister and PDVSA's president, are very close to Chávez and share a common ideology. They are also known to have close ties with Fidel Castro; Chávez delegates major responsibilities to these two ministers.

Rodríguez and Giordani were directly or indirectly involved in Illarramendi's fraud because the transfer of such a huge amount of money ($500 million) could not happen without their approval. PDVSA's pension fund made many people rich, especially those who are close to Chávez. They illegally earned more than $10 million, an amount stolen from the country in what should be considered a criminal act.

Trade unions are an integral part of a political system. In the Soviet Union and its satellites the syndicate movement had no independent existence. In Tito's Yugoslavia the workers followed self-management, which exhibited direct democracy at the lower level. Every worker participated in the process of decision making, but similar to other Communist countries, there was not much democracy at the upper level. The Communist party controlled this direct democracy down below.[149]

Venezuela is in the process of making the transition to socialism, gradually moving toward a model that is similar to the Soviet Union. In many workplaces, there are two trade unions that operate simultaneously. One union enjoys the support of the government, while the rival one is constantly being harassed and declared to be the enemy of the revolution.[150]

Obviously, there exist tensions between these two types of unions. An investigation into the death of a worker, Remmy Rojas, exposed the tension between two trade unions. The government gives its support only to those unions that follow its ideological line. There was a controversy as to who killed Rojas, but the government sided with the version given by its own union.

Historically the union movement can be traced to the nineteenth century. The first trade union, the Venezuelan Workers Congress (*Congreso de Trabajadores de Venezuela*) was established to represent workers' interests. During the period of democracy (1958-1998), the union flourished and its power and influence increased. During periods of dictatorships, including that of the Chávez regime, unions were harassed and their influence declined.

The Chávez regime treats syndicate leaders who oppose his policies as common delinquents that need to be dealt with by criminal courts.[151] On various occasions, union leaders were imprisoned for demanding collective bargaining. Nieves concludes his article by reminding everyone that the attack against unions foreshadowed the breakdown of the Soviet bloc; the shipyard in Gdansk, Poland, was the place which the revolt against Communism began. Similarly, the struggle to resort syndicate liberty has begun in Venezuela.[152]

Robin Rodríguez expands on Nieves's idea that workers need to unite and resist Chávez's attempt to weaken them. He employs the term *labor terrorism* to indicate how workers have been treated and dealt with in the oil industry.[153] In a meeting of PDVSA's workers, the labor union expressed its determination to resist and fight for workers' rights. PDVSA's management postponed elections for union's representatives. The union urged management to allow observers, both national and international, to supervise the election process; it would be conducted by secret ballot and management should not interfere in this process.

The trade union leader directed their strong criticism of Minister Ramírez, who was labeled as the most antilabor and antisalary; who failed to recognize workers' compensations, health insurance; and did not take into account the high inflation in Venezuela, which caused a sharp decrease in the workers' buying power.[154] The rise in the minimum salary decreed by Chávez on April 2011 would cover only 48.7% of the basic food basket.[155]

The Venezuelan Workers Federation (*Confederación de Trabajadores de Venezuela*, CTV) was debilitated as a result of the oil strike (2002-2003). There were futile efforts to create new types of labor unions that would challenge the regime. In 2009 Labor Solidarity was founded; it attempted to create a coalition among several unions. In 2010 the Autonomy Front for the Defense of Employees and their Salaries (*Frente Autónomo en Defensa del Empleo y el Salario*, FADES) was created. Its platform includes the demand for higher salaries for workers, dignified employment, and a social security system. However, the Chávez regime does not recognize the existence of free syndicates.

In the first three month of 2011, the occurrences of labor conflicts increased. During this period, workers' the number of demonstrations on behalf of their unions reached 700.[156] These included strikes, marches, hunger strikes, and the capturing of workers' installations. It was projected that for the entire year of 2011 there would be 3,000 labor conflicts. The government employed the Bolivarian National Guard and police to intimidate workers and prevent them from exercising their constitutional rights.

Rafael González's article, "Market Versus Controlled Prices" (*Precios de Mercado vs. Precios Controlados*), constitutes a good summary of Chávez's economic policies.[157] Referring to the dogmatic ideological Law of Costs, Prices and Wage Protection, in which a group of bureaucrats would determine the carrying charge of each product, González asserts that these public servants have insufficient information about consumer's preference or costs structures.

The writer concludes his article by asserting that only a market economy can fulfill people's aspirations and guarantee social and economic well-being. Developed countries that enjoy a high standard of living employ the market economy model. Therefore, the question is asked: Why would Venezuela copy an economic model employed by countries with limited resources and underdeveloped economy?

The Chilean Way (Sebastián Pinera) Versus the Venezuelan Way (Hugo Chávez)

Chile and Venezuela represent opposing models of economic development. Chile is characterized by market economy, private initiatives, and the attempt to reduce the state's role in the economy. Venezuela under Chávez follows the opposite policies from Chile's. It continuously and gradually has increased the role of the state in the economy and directed its efforts to decrease the role of the private sector. Many analysts view the Chilean way as being more successful in satisfying people's needs and aspirations.

The comparison between the two economic systems reveals, nevertheless, that Chile, in spite of better economic indicators, has many social and economic challenges that it needs to overcome. The distribution of income in Chile is marked by inequality. Data from the period 2006-2009 reveals that the richest 10% people capture 40.2% of Chile's income. On the other hand the poorest 10% receive 0.9% of the country's wealth.[158] One can justly assert that the major problems facing the Chilean economic and political systems originate from the extreme unequal distribution of income.

Chile is aware of this issue, therefore, Piñera's administration created a new ministerial position on social development.[159] The minister of social development will concentrate his efforts on improving the procedures for developing social resources and will coordinate his activities with other ministers. He must assure transparency and is charged with eliminating extreme poverty by 2014.

Starting in May 2011, Chile experienced mass demonstrations that led some analysts to question the legitimacy of the country's political system. Some Chileans fear that mass rallies might lead to the restoration of the dictatorship. This idea will be further elaborated at a later stage of this chapter. However, it is important to mention that the ideal state existed only in Plato's Republic. The strong economic improvements of Chile's economy, similar to those in other capitalist countries, are not equally distributed. One can view the mass demonstrations in Chile as an integral part of a democratic society.

The mass demonstrations that occurred in both Chile and Israel (which will be analyzed at a later stage in this chapter) may be comprehended as an integral part of the globalization process.[160] The world, according to Thomas Friedman, has reached a stage of being more connected. The *New York Times* commentator notes that the slogan in the Israeli uprising represents a common denominator: "We are fighting for an accessible future."[161] Chile's mass students' demonstrations are directly linked to the Israeli slogan; education is a key element for a better future.

A headline in an Israeli newspaper, "World Protest from Bolivia to Greece, New Delhi to New York," captures the reality that demonstrations are occurring not only in the United States, but in every corner of the world, where people are demanding normal salaries, the end of government's corruption and violations of human rights, and end of state monetary assistance for bankrupt enterprises. The question arises as to why these huge demonstrations have been occurring from about May 2011.

The answer to this question is given by the authors John Hagel III, John Seely Brown, and Lang Davison. Their publication, *The Power of Pull*, constitutes an excellent explanation of the world's discontent and how this crisis can be resolved.[162] The authors claim that technological innovations, the new digital infrastructures, are transforming the business and social landscape and are beginning to reshape twenty-first century institutions.

An important distinction must be made between the previous and current technological revolutions. In the past, technological innovations experience a rapid renewal for a short time and then improvements began to flatten. This pattern enabled business to stabilize fast following the initial disruption of the innovation. At present, for the first time, the new technological inventions show no sign of stabilization in terms of price/ performance ratio improvement.

The world community, especially the developed countries, feels a great amount of stress because the system operates with institutional practices that are dysfunctional. There are new ideas and opportunities that require adjustments from both individuals and collectives. It becomes more difficult to hold a job, but there are more possibilities for starting a new company employing the world's resources. This process may continue for a definite period of time.

Competition is intensifying on a global scale, resulting in instability and uncertainty. The world has both more problems than ever and, at the same time, increased opportunities to resolve these issues. The authors are optimistic and conclude their work by claiming that the big shift created a world where more people than ever have the tools and the potential to succeed.

Chilean President Sebastián Piñera declared that Chávez's Bolivarian model is not conducive to success and constitutes an error.[163] In some ways Piñera's speech, given in July 2011, may be compared to Pericles' Funeral Oration, delivered in Athens on 430 BC. In this speech, the Athenian statesman stressed the superiority of the democratic system of government over Sparta's dictatorial rule. Like Pericles, Piñera declared that Venezuela, Cuba, and Nicaragua are free to choose their political system; however, in the twenty-first century, an economic model based on socialism, where the state is the principal vehicle of production, constitutes a failure.

In the "Chilean Route" ("*La ruta chilena*"), Antonio Muller, writing in the Venezuelan opposition press, emphasizes the great advantages that Chile's economic system has over its Venezuelan counterpart.[164] Starting in 1980s Chile embarked on a path of economic growth based on private initiatives and free market. This model was complemented in the 1990s with social policies directed to reduce poverty, inflation, and unemployment.

The 2008 world financial crisis had a minor impact on Chile. It was able to avoid the economic disaster because the monetary authorities took advantage of the high price of copper (the main export product) in order to create funds that were utilized to stimulate investments. Chile reached the highest per capita income in Latin America, approximately $15.000 per year; 33% of the homes carry internet connection; and 68% of the population is covered by public health insurance. Muller concludes his article by recommending the Chilean model be applied by all countries that strive to improve their social economic status.[165]

Torres Mega conclusions reiterated that the Chilean economic model should become an example to be followed by all the Latin American countries. Referring indirectly to Chávez, he says it is not populism that improves people's economic conditions, rather, only economic liberty allows the society to overcome poverty and enable each person to live a dignified life.[166]

Paul Bello, in "Chile's Message" ("*Mensaje de Chile*") claims that the rescue of Chilean miners in October 2010 demonstrated attributes that are characteristics only in a democracy.[167] These include transparency, honesty, and love for all people, regardless of social class. The government's acting on behalf of the people and not just for certain groups is an attribute of democracy. Such a rescue could only happen in a country where the people rule, where the government acts for the benefits of all the inhabitants. It is clear that Bello's attempts to claim that in a country such as Venezuela, where class war is a dominant theme, such a rescue would not happen.

Similarly a 2010 *New York Times* article complimented Chile's economic development.[168] In a 2010 report *Global* Competitiveness, published by World Economic Forum, Chile is ranked 30, well ahead of the United States, on such issues as political favoritism and bribes. Venezuela is placed at the bottom of the scale. Chile's economic development was accomplished in spite of the fact that in February 2010 it suffered the fifth strongest earthquake ever recorded (8.8 on the Richter scale). More than 500 people died and houses, schools, hospitals, bridges, roads, and airports were destroyed. The damage amounted to 20% of the 2010 GDP. In spite of the disaster, exports and investments grew by 20%.[169]

Chile's economic experience validates Arnold Kling's and Nick Schulz's ideas about the important link between political freedom and economic progress.[170] These scholars also emphasize the importance of innovations and entrepreneurial initiatives in boosting the country's economic standards. While Venezuela has been dominated by state control of the economy, entrepreneurialism is repressed; it is considered to be a capitalist threat to the regime. Innovations are lacking as private initiatives are negatively viewed and only the state is considered a legitimate institution that can manage economic affairs.

Referring to a 2011 law in Venezuela that attempts to control prices, Rafael González claims that it would undermine efficiency and is unable to increase productivity and abolishing any incentives that favor of innovations.[171] It is therefore not surprising that Venezuela's GDP declined almost to zero.[172] Minister of Planning and Finance Jorge Giordani claimed that in the last three quarters of 2010 the GDP fell 5.2% and blamed the decline on the global financial crisis.

The Chilean economy, on the other hand, despite also being affected by the international economic crisis, grew by 7% in the third quarter of 2010.[173] The most notable increases were shown in commerce, electricity, transportation, and telecommunication. Internal demand grew by 18.2%, headed by increase in consumption (10.3%) and, to a lesser degree, investments. Exports rose by 8% and imports by 34.4%. In spite of the world economic crisis, the GDP increased by 5.6% in 2012.[174]

In Chile a strong emphasis is given to innovations and entrepreneurship as important tools that will contribute to the country's economic development. Various renowned guests, including businessmen, high-level executives, and government officials, were invited to a conference to discuss implementing new measures to stimulate an enterprising and global competitiveness culture.[175]

The members of the conference agreed that in order to improve Chile's economy there is the need that the public sector, the business and financial communities, and the educational systems be interconnected. It is important that companies invest in research and development of new products. Because these businesses need to be able to recuperate the cost of research and development, the government should give tax incentives to assist them in reaching their objectives.

An important means of improving Chile's economy, one that is relevant to both private and public domains, is to require a reduction in the size of bureaucracy and, therefore, a reduction in costs. While a Chilean spokesman asserted that his government has made strong efforts to reduce the state's bureaucracy, the Venezuelan government's bureaucracy is growing steadily.

The journal *Forbes* analyzed eleven criteria that determine a country's attractiveness for business investment.[176] They include property rights, innovations, taxes, technology, corruption, liberty (personal, commercial, and monetary), bureaucracy, investment protection, and performance of the stock market. Chile was found to be the most attractive for business in Latin America, ranked 24 overall out of 134 countries. It was placed higher than Japan 27, South Korea 31, and Spain 32. United States was in the tenth place.

The majority of foreign visitors to Venezuela come to praise the Chávez regime and applaud its achievements. Among them one can count the American scholar Noam Chomsky, who came several times to Venezuela and delivered speeches attacking United States policies and praising Chávez. (A noted exception is Chomsky's criticizing Chávez for imprisoning judge Afiuni.) The former leader of Libya, Khadafy is another visitor, who established personal relations with Chávez and received the sword of Bolívar as an appreciation of the strong friendship between the two countries. Chávez continued supporting the Libyan leader throughout the Libya's civil war.[177]

Chile invites foreign scholars who might make a positive contribution to the country's economic development. Michael Porter, a management expert from Harvard University, came to Chile in May 2011 to offer his advice on how to improve competitiveness in the country's economy.[178] The Harvard expert claimed that Chile needs to reduce centralization in order to improve its economy. Porter, who is an expert on innovations and competitiveness, claimed that Chile is the most competitive country in Latin America.

These measures initiated by the Chilean government attempt to increase by twofold the per-capita income of Chilean people, which in 2011 was $15,000. It also aims to increase equality and further opportunities. The new initiatives aims at incentivizing energy savings, stimulating investments in utilities, increasing competition in banking and transportation, building new roads, promoting scientific research, and promoting digital methods.

Research and development is an important theme in Chilean politics. Economy Minister Andres Fontaine asked the Congress to approve a new law in March 2011 that would give tax incentives to companies engaged in research and development.[179] This initiative is expected to double the amount of investments and increase innovations and productivity. Finance Minister Felipe Larrain highlighted the fact that salaries increased by 5.8% in 2011. The rise in salary is greater than inflation, which signifies an increase in the purchasing power of the Chilean currency.[180] The Chilean Institute of Statistics (INF) reported that construction grew by 248% in the period April 2010-2011.[181]

In contrast to Chile, the BCV declared that wages in Venezuela dropped by 5.4% in 2010.[182] The worst-performing sectors were those related to real estate and business. The GDP in Venezuela grew by a slim rate of 0.36% in 2011, while inflation was 31.5%.[183] In Chile, on the other hand, the GDP grew by 6.3%, while inflation amounted to 4.2% in 2011.[184] The Chilean National Institute of Statistics reported that during the period January-March 2011, as a result of strong internal demand, especially for such items as cars and electronics, the economy grew by 9.8% in relations to the same months in 2010.[185]

The general secretary to Chilean President Christian Larroulet, in contrast to the high inflation in Venezuela, declared that the government has a zero tolerance for inflation.[186] The president's secretary declared that congress should approve a law which attempts to mitigate the rise of gasoline prices and restrain inflation. Inflation, Larroulet reiterated is the worst enemy of the poor and Chile will not tolerate it.

Finance Minister Felipe Larrain announced that in the 2011 budget, $800 million was saved, representing 1.4% of national expenses.[187] This measure will counter inflationary pressures and was received favorably by the market; consequently the pressures were removed from the central bank to raise the rate of interest. This move of cutting the budget is very beneficial to the private sector. The cuts in Chilean budget should affect all ministers, professional payments, overtime pay, telephone and cellular bills, publicity, and car rentals. However, there would not be any cuts in social programs or water and electric tariff subsidies. This policy is also beneficial to the exporting sector.

An important role of Chilean central bank, similar to its United States' counterpart, is to adjust the rate of interest. In May 2011 the central bank raised the rate of interest to 5%. Its aim was to control inflation and generate pressures on the exchange of foreign currencies.[188] Unlike Venezuela, where the central bank is not an independent institution, in Chile an official of the central bank indicated the country needs to have more capital reserves. In observing countries that are more economically developed than Chile, it found that the level of capital reserves comparative to the GDP is lower in Chile.[189] It mentions 17% of the GDP in order to improve its dealings with international economic fluctuations.

President Chávez proposed that Venezuela cease using the U.S. dollar as a currency in international trade.[190] On the other hand, in Chile, the central bank maintained a daily purchase for a three months period of $50 million in order to break the fall of the American currency.[191]

Improving the lot of the poor was an important justification for Chávez coming to power. In a 2009 speech, the Venezuelan president declared that by 2019-2020 poverty would be completely eliminated. A former member of the Venezuelan assembly, the journalist Freddy Lepage rhetorically asks what Communist revolution was able to end poverty.[192] Such revolutions not only did not improve the status of the poor, but conversely created masses of unhappy and impoverished people. A noted example is the Cuban revolution, which in the last fifty years reduced people's standard of living. Chávez's message to the poor has a political overtone. In order to escape poverty they must reelect him indefinitely.

In Venezuela 2 million people live in extreme poverty, while some who are close to Chávez were able to enrich themselves and earned millions (the Bolibourgeoisie). These are the injustices produced by the Chávez's revolution. In order to eternize his rule, he made sure the people depend on the government for their livelihood. However, this process ensures that poverty remains unchanged in Venezuela.

Piñera, like Chávez, gave a speech in 2010, describing how he imagines Chile in 2018.[193] Piñera, unlike Chávez, believed that embarking on market economy with private initiatives and hence developing the country's resources is the key element and prerequisite for solving Chile's poverty problem. Increases in investments and productivity and the creation of new employment are viewed by the Chilean president as essential ingredients that would help the impoverished. The Chilean president claims that a developed country is not only one where the average per capita income is $24,000 a year, but also (and equally important) one where poverty is eliminated.

Piñera proceeds to identify the causes of poverty: Lack of quality education, scarcity of work opportunities, and dysfunctional family structure are important causes that lead to misery. Therefore, Piñera claims that an important element in the war on poverty constitutes the strengthening of the family; human capital training is another important element in combating pauperism.

A developed country, according to the Chilean president, means that all citizens must enjoy the society's benefits and become familiar with the technological innovations. Creation of new jobs is a key element in combating poverty. In the period May-November 2010, 286,000 new jobs were created, and in 2010 the number of new places of work might surpass 300,000.[194] However, according to an editorial in the Chilean press, in order to accomplish Piñera's vision it becomes imperative that the rate of economic development average 6%. During the period June-November 2010 it was 7%.[195]

Venezuela's increase in the minimum salary in April 2011 would cover only 48.7% of the price of the basic food basket.[196] Therefore, it is estimated that those on this salary would require two minimum salaries to purchase the item in the food basket. The Chilean minimum salary was increased by 5.8%, from 172,000 Chilean pesos to 182,000 on July 2011. If inflation is taken into account the real rise is 2.5% ($1= 467.3 Chilean pesos).[197] Eleven percent of the labor force in Chile is paid the minimum salary. The information presented shows without doubt that those on minimum salary are better off in Chile than Venezuela.

According to Venezuela's central bank 25% of the poorest people in the country spent 45 out of 100 bolívares to buy food, while those of higher income disbursed only 15.[198] 25% of the most impoverished people, in May and June 2011, suffered from an accumulated inflation of 7.5%, while those of higher income the impact was less than 4.2%. In May 2011, 11 out of 100 products were absent from the supermarkets. The shortages were especially noticeable in government's supply firms (Mercal, Boual), where they reached 50%.[199] As a result of the application of the Law of Controlling Costs, seventeen basic products could not be found in Venezuela's markets. In June 2011, 62.7% of the population considered the supply of food as inadequate, while in January 2011, 51.3% of the consumers held the same opinion.[200]

Piñera's administration formulated a new plan that would supplement poor families' income. The program, which started in 2011, would also benefit people from the middle class, who encountered risks of falling under the threshold of poverty. It would give an estimated income of 250,000 Chilean pesos for a family averaging five persons.[201]

The minister of work, Evelyn Matthei, employing the thesis of *The Power of Pull*, described previously, (although it is not specifically mentioned) claimed that it is far more important to create jobs, instead worrying about minimum salary and ethical income. Chile faces the challenge of creating employment in the context of global competition.[202] How could Chilean enterprises compete with China and India? Many economic institutions, such as banks and others, face strong competition because in the era of internet, they can be managed from other countries. The actual labor legislation in Chile is a product of 1960s and did not take into account global competition. It was based on workers' versus employers' demands. Currently, this legislation should be changed and based on work in Chile versus work in India or China.

In Chávez's Venezuela education is viewed as a means of indoctrinating people in socialist values. Following Antonio Gramsci's ideas, education is an important tool in the process of society's transformation. On the other hand, the Chilean president Sebastián Piñera claims that that the role of education is to help to shape a free democratic society.[203] Accordingly, Chile is in the process of building a modern society; therefore, quality education is a right that the state must guarantee for all people.

The 2012 budget expense for education would be $11,650 billion which represents 25% of public expenses.[204] It represents the highest amount of money for education in all the country's history. It is intended to reduce inequalities. In regard to higher education, the government would like to provide a quality education to every youngster who merits it regardless of his or her economic status.

Venezuela and Israel: Transformation from Capitalism to Socialism and the Reverse

The Venezuelan opposition press published several articles applauding the Israeli economic model of development as an illustration that other countries should follow. These essays constitute an indirect criticism of Chávez's economic policies, which followed a course that increased inflation and poverty. Professor Alberto Montaner (a Cuban exiled) claims that the real revolution is not what occurred in Venezuela (although he does not specifically mentions this country) but what has occurred in Israel.

The success of the Israeli economy is attributed to its abandoning socialism (collectivism) and embracing the principles of market economy.[205] This transformation from collectivism to individualism and market economy should be viewed as a real revolution, performed without military coup d'état and barricades and without imposition of a caudillo in power. Israel is a model that needs to be exported to the world, especially the underdeveloped one. The Western countries should embrace and support the Jewish state.

The Venezuela journalist Pablo Padró analyzes Dan Senor's and Saul Singer's book, *Start-Up Nation*.[206] He asks his readers if they knew that on the NASDAQ exchange there are more Israeli companies than Chinese, European, and Indian ones combined. Israel, Padró asserts, is an economic model that needs to be imitated by others. He praises Israel's effort to create a national network of car battery switching stations that will decrease the demand for oil.

The Venezuelan opposition press published an article by the Spanish journalist, Jorge Marirrodriga, stressing the importance of new discoveries of gas deposits in the Jewish state[207] that will make Israel an important exporter of energy. The country will save 11% on electric and energy costs, which amounts to $55,000 million. This is half of what it would cost to rescue Portugal. As a result of treaties that Israel signed with Cyprus and Greece, Israeli gas can become a substitute of those derived from Maghreb union countries, which suffer from political instability. Israel, with a stable political system, might guarantee Europe's supply of energy.

While the Chávez regime attempts to increase political control by the establishment of communal systems, the Israeli kibbutz has moved in the opposite direction. As previously mentioned, this transformation from collective to individualist values should be considered a true revolution.

The kibbutz was an attempt to blend Marxist and Zionist ideas in Israel. It called for the establishment of self-governing communities, the absence of private property, the replacement of the wage system with equal allowances for everybody, the integration of physical and white collar work, and the creation a society devoid of inequalities and class hierarchies. The kibbutz for many years symbolized egalitarian and anticapitalist ideas.[208] The kibbutz's ideology emphasized shared agrarian labor, income, and meals and collective housing for children.

The defeat of the Labor party in the 1977 elections and the emergence of a right-wing party (the Herut Party headed by Menahem Begin) have drastically altered the fate of the kibbutz's movement. It hastened the decline and decreased the importance of the communal settlements in the Israeli society. The 1985 economic crisis in Israel, seventy-five years after the creation of the first kibbutz, created a feeling of despair among the communal settlements.[209] The need arose for making drastic changes in Kibbutz's structure and adopting it to the needs of market economy.

The kibbutz embraced market principles, selling part of its land to city dwellers to build private homes, on land that was previously used for agriculture. Many people left the kibbutz, looking for better-paid jobs in the cities. The communal dining hall was shut down and the principle of equal allowances was terminated and members started to be paid according to the type of work they performed.[210]

A new neighborhood was built in the kibbutz for nonmembers. The residents would own these homes. This process brought back many members who had previously left. In 2010 the kibbutz population was 127,000, up from 115,300 in 2005. The factories located in the kibbutzim produce 9% of Israel's industrial output, worth $8 billion and 40% of the agricultural output worth about $1.7 billion.

A good illustration of changes that occurred in the Israeli communal settlements is kibbutz Afikim, one of the oldest, established in 1932. It transformed itself from a collective settlement to a place dominated by private enterprises. Stores belonging to Individual members opened, such as a barber shop, a bicycle repair store, restaurants, etc.[211] Kibbutz Afikim was successful in transforming itself from a socialist venture to a capitalist profit-making institution.

In 1996 kibbutz Afikim established a committee that encouraged their members to open their own businesses. During the period 1996-2004, every three months a new business opened in the kibbutz. For example, with an investment of 20,000 shekels (around $5,500) a new fish store opened. In 2004 kibbutz Afikim started the official process of dislocation. In 2011 there were approximately a hundred enterprises. In the majority of cases, bookkeeping was done by kibbutz's administrators.

The private businesses in the kibbutz are paying rent, electric water fees and taxes and, as kibbutz members, a special communal tax. Those who open businesses need to return the loan given to them by the kibbutz. Those whose businesses are successful keep the profits. On the other hand, those enterprises that lose money face bankruptcy. According to information from the kibbutz movement, there were 270 kibbutzim in Israel with 2,500 private enterprises.[212]

An important success story in kibbutz Afikim has been transforming the dairy by introducing into a computerized system that revolutionized milk production.[213] The dairy is one of the oldest ventures; it started when the kibbutz was first established. The members of the kibbutz decided that improving the income derived from the dairy should be an important priority that could benefit all 1,500 members.

The kibbutz established a new company, Afimilk, that computerized the cow's milking process and was able to measure not only the amount of milk, but also how much fat or lactose it includes. It could measure the health status of the cow, enabling to maximize the amount of milk to be produced. This innovation made Israel the number one country in the world in milk production per cow. In developed countries, the average milk per cow per year is between 3,000 to 4,000 liters, while in Israel it is 12,000 liter yearly.[214]

When it comes to innovations, Venezuela is considered one of the less inventive economies.[215] In Latin America Venezuela is ranked higher only than Haiti. Chile is in the twenty-ninth place in the world and is considered to be the most competitive country in Latin America, followed by Uruguay, forty-ninth in the world; Mexico, sixty-first; Argentina, sixty-sixth; and Brazil, eighty-seventh.[216]

Israel is ranked twenty-first in the world, on a par with Germany and Austria.[217] While major economic decisions in Venezuela are made by the government and the private sector is in a constant declining, in Israel, on the other hand, collaboration between the government and private business is an important factor that is responsible to the economy's success.

The government in Israel encourages and supports the private sector's capacity to compete in international markets by employing intelligent use of investment incentives.

The Israeli government invests heavily in research and development and education and has implemented a program to convert research into cutting-edge businesses. The government sponsors grants for research and development, which are administered by the ministry of trade and labor. Companies can apply for such a grant, which usually includes 20 to 50% of the R&D budget. Companies must pay back the government in amounts to a defined by a percentage of the total annual sale. During the period 2008-2011, the government allocated approximately $300 million annually for this purpose. Areas of particular interest are software, biotechnology, computing, electronics, chemicals, and mechanical engineering.[218]

In the 1990s, with the arrival of close to 1 million immigrants from the former Soviet Union, a new initiative was introduced by the Government. The immigrants had high technical skills but lacked entrepreneurial experience. The new initiative helped inventors of new products to develop the skills needed to become exporters. This program was very successful; by 2009, the number of start-up companies had risen to 4,000.

The Israeli government encouraged international investors Microsoft and Cisco to build their first R&D faculties outside the United States in Israel. Motorola's R&D center in Israel is its largest worldwide. Citibank conducted international research to find a country where it could create a center of research and development in the financial field.[219] It selected Israel; the center opened in December 2011. In March 2011 Barclays announced the opening of a similar center in Israel. The finance minister claimed that building of these centers in Israel is a confirmation for the powerful Israeli human potential. Israeli scientists, engineers, and entrepreneurs are helping the United States to promote nation building and security.[220]

The Israeli Defense Forces (IDF) plays a crucial role in the country's social and economic life. Being surrounded by unfriendly countries, threatening the Jewish State's existence makes national security an important priority for the country. On October 23, 2011, the government authorized the payment of soldiers' first year of higher education.[221] Various ministers labeled this move as a revolution in education that will significantly reduce inequalities by making higher learning more accessible.

The threats to Israel's existence contribute to the rise of an entrepreneurship in the area of security. The above illustration demonstrates how military service in Israel contributed to innovation. Many credit cards companies (Visa, MasterCard, and others) are obsessed with combatting fraud. They employ thousands of employees, including at least fifty with PhDs in engineering, whose role it is to solve this problem.

An Israeli who used the computer to hunt down terrorists during his army service used his experience to start up a small company that combats credit card fraud after he completed his army service. This small company was sold to PayPal for $169 million.[222] His military experience enabled him to learn many things that escaped others with more education and experience.

The secret spying technological Unit 8200 of the Israel Defense Forces opened its door for entrepreneurs. Those who served the unit would like to open that door to the public at large.[223] Ultraorthodox Jews and Arabs are also encouraged to apply. The idea is to employ the experience of the soldiers in this unit to benefit the public at large. It is a program for any person who intends to initiate an entrepreneurial idea. It is intended especially for those people who have an idea, but lack the resources to advance their cause.

Kibbutz Sasa, a mile from the Lebanese border, was founded in 1949. It is the home of the main Plasan factory, which manufactures ballistic vests for soldiers and police and armor for Israeli Defense Forces.[224] At the closing of 2011, 90% of $500 million in orders are from Europe and the United States. Orders increased a great deal as a result of the wars in both Iraq and Afghanistan. In 2009 Plasan opened a factory in Bennington, Vermont. While the 350 workers are Americans the technology is decidedly Israeli.

A substantial amount of Iran's oil revenues are allocated to sponsor terrorism. This may also be true of Saudi Arabia, the biggest exporter of oil in the world. A large proportion of oil revenues from these countries and others are directed toward terrorism against the Jewish state. Therefore, it will not come as a surprise that Israel makes a great effort to develop innovations in alternative energy resources.

Infrastructure Minister Uzi Landau gave his blessing to the first battery-swapping station in Israel and called it the first step toward weaning the country from oil imports.[225] The minister added that revenues from

Arab countries and Iran are financing terrorism and strengthening the radical wing of Islam, which is against western culture and freedom.

Forty similar stations will be operating in the near future around the country. They will include more than a thousand swapping stations. If the experiment is successful in Israel, it may be replicated in other parts of the world. In spite of some setbacks (closing its operations in Australia and the United States). Better place continues to make progress in two core markets Denmark and Israel.[226]

Previously, the publication *The Power of Pull*, was mentioned in regard to the major changes that have occurred in the international system and how successful innovators can take advantage of the international circumstances and achieve economic success. Hagel and his partners illustrate with the example of the Israeli entrepreneur Yossi Vardi, who advanced the profitability of Google.[227]

Vardi founded his first company in 1969 and assisted in establishing seventy Israeli tech enterprises. His ability to make international connections between people and companies from around the world became an important asset and a major reason for the growth of technological innovations in Israel. Vardi is living proof of what is needed in the new international economic system—the way to proceed in order to have a successful enterprise. He is able to amplify and expand the efforts of many people. Technology-driven innovations necessitate the cooperation of many people from within or outside many countries.

The Israeli export increased by 13,400 during the period 1948-2011.[228] It increased from $6 million in 1948 to $80.5 billion in 2011. In the first years of Israel's existence exports were mainly oranges, diamonds, and small industrial products. During the period 2001-2011, Israel's main export was technology: electronics, computer programming, communication, and health. In 2010 hi-tech industries, including research and development, equaled $28.5 billion, which constituted 35% of Israeli exports. Agricultural products amounted $1.3 billion, only to 2% of its exports. This is in contrast to Venezuela, a one-product economy, where exports of oil constituting over 90% of its revenues. Israel, unlike Venezuela diversified its economy.

In 2010 Israel recorded defense exports, amounting to $7.2 billion, making the country one of the world's top exporters of arms.[229] Specializing in the production of unmanned aerial vehicles, mini satellites, and command-and-control systems, Israeli defense companies sold $9.6 billion in 2010, out of which $2.4 billion went to the Israeli Defense Forces. The Iron Dome, the country's rocket defense system attracted much attention because of its success in intercepting kassam and katyusha rockets fired from Gaza Strip in Israel in April 2011.

The continued economic crises in both European countries and the United States in 2011 had strong ramifications for both Chile and Israel. The demand for Israeli products diminished in both Europe and the United States. In spite of this, Stanley Fischer, the governor of the Israeli Bank, expressed optimism about the Israeli economic forecast.[230] Raising taxes on the rich will have negative consequences. He described the tax increase as populism, the tendency to fault the wealthy, and claimed that such a move would have negative implications on the Israeli economy. After raising the interest rates on three consecutive occasions, in May 2011, the rate remained unchanged at 3%.

In spite of huge oil deposits, Venezuela's GDP growth rate is around 2%. The World Bank warned Chávez's government that Venezuela is unresponsive to the global crisis.[231] Chile and other Latin America countries were able to build a strong line of defense against external shocks by increasing interest rates and raising international reserves. Venezuela, on the other hand, embarked on a different course. Israel's economy grew by 7.8% in the last quarter of 2010.[232] In April 2011 unemployment in Israel was 5.8%, lower than in socialist Venezuela (estimated around 8%). In 2012 unemployment in Venezuela averaged 10.3%.[233] Like Chile, private consumption in Israel was an important factor for the economic growth.

Venezuela's central bank, as previously indicated, has no institutional independence and has been used by Chávez as a tool to increase spending. Israel's central bank, on the other hand, is very efficient and plays a crucial role in the country's economic development. Its main roles are to fix the interest rate, which depends on the growth of the economy, determining monetary policies, and setting the rate of the exchange of the local currency (shekel).

Israeli economist Tamar Almor was asked how Israel was able to prevent an economic crisis. Almor pointed to Stanley Fischer, the Israeli central bank governor, and his decision to ensure that the government did not bail out any companies experiencing economic problems.[234] During the year 2008, foreign direct investment in Israel increased by 11%, unemployment declined by 1.2%, and the GDP increased by 4.1%.

Prime Minister Benjamin Netanyahu declared in November 2011 that the Israeli economy continued to grow due to the fact that the budget framework was honored.[235] He cited as an example what happened to the European countries, which faced an economic crisis resulting from an unrestrained increase in spending. By acting with responsibility, Israel was able to prevent the economic crisis facing the majority of the world.

A special report issued by the Israeli central bank entitled, "Israel and the World Economic crisis 2007-2009," recommended strengthening supervision of banks and increasing the responsibility of the institution headed by Stanley Fischer.[236] The need exists to follow a macro productive policy in order to assure that the financial system would not go into recession.

As in Chile, the finance ministry and the Israeli central bank appointed a committee to further examine competition among the banks.[237] Big businesses have no problems receiving loans with satisfactory interest rates, but small businesses face predicament on these issues. They will benefit from the reorganization of the bank system.

During the period 2008-2011, Israel's central bank purchased $50 billion in order to strengthen the declining price of the dollar in relation to the shekel.[238] As a result of this action the dollar increased in value in comparison to the shekel. Therefore, during the period July-September 2011, the bank ceased its intervention. The weakness of the euro has also negative implications for the local Israeli currency.

Chávez's Bolivarian revolution intends to correct mistakes of the Soviet Union's Communism. The new political system, which is labeled "socialism of the twenty-first century," strives to become a new model that would eliminate capitalism and be adopted worldwide by the community of nations. This task is to be achieved with the strong cooperation of the Islamic regime in Iran. Terrorism is an important instrument for achieving this goal.

In contrast, Israel's technological innovations are becoming an important instrument for mankind. As a result of many terrorist attacks on its citizens, Israel developed many programs to help these victims. It employed its vast experience in this matter to assist Japanese tsunami victims.[239] Areas affected by the tsunami disaster in Japan, would adopt an

Israeli program, which demonstrated its capabilities for coping with stress and trauma.

An Israeli company Green 2000 is teaching African countries agricultural techniques and building greenhouses to increase food production.[240] The African countries are very fertile but have very little agricultural knowledge. The Israeli company created an agronomic center in Nigeria employing the new tools and methods taught by the Israeli company, resulting in a threefold increase of agricultural production.

The first Israeli Prime Minister, David Ben-Gurion, had a dream of developing the desert in the south (Negev) and attracting many settlers to this area. Arava Power Company, a solar power company in southern Israel, is a fulfillment of Ben-Gurion's dream. The company, which was built by Israeli entrepreneurships, entered in partnership with a German conglomerate Siemens, which invested $15 million, enabling the company to become a major supplier of alternative energy.[241] The company expects to grow into a $2 billion enterprise. It eventually will supply one-third of the energy needed for the nearby city of Eilat.

An important occurrence that would strengthen Israeli-Chinese relations, especially in the economic arena, is the plan to build a train link between Israel's Red Sea and Mediterranean ports, which could serve as an alternative to the Suez Canal. The train link would spur increased trade with China, India, and other Asian countries.[242] The victory of Islamic parties in the Egyptian parliamentary elections of 2011 may increase the country's political instability and endanger the availability of the canal to all nations, especially Israel. The Jewish state has not forgotten the closing of the canal to Israeli ships by President Abdul Nasser in 1956.

Former Israel Finance Minister Yuval Steinitz asserted that it is important that China and India have another route for transporting their exports to Europe in addition to the Suez Canal.[243] A railroad would also increase the development of Israel's southern Negev desert and possibly strengthen relations with Jordan; its Aqaba port is adjacent to Eilat and could also be connected to the railroad. The estimated cost of the project, which would be built by a Chinese government company in a joint venture between the two countries, is over $2 billion. In the future, the new railroad could also be used to export gas to India and possibly China, in the event that there new discoveries. [244]

Like Chile, Israel faced mass protest demonstrations against the high cost of living, especially the cost of housing. Protests started with a person who objected to a rise in her rent. She employed the digital network to express her discontent and was joined by thousands who shared her view. The protest reached the peak of 400,000 people who demonstrated in several cities.

The publication *The Power of Pull* is instrumental in explaining the protest movement in Israel. It claims that the new technological revolution created a dysfunctional system in which economic insecurity is rampant. While general discontent among the people is a common characteristic of every country, there are a variety of issues that cause people to march in the streets. In Israel the majority of protestors were young people who claim that life in Israel is too expensive. In Chile the cost of education was the main issue. An Israeli professor described the Israeli protest movement as Aristotelian.[245] He meant that in the majority of cases the protest was peaceful, encouraging a rational social and political debate concerning Israel's future.

As had Chile's Piñera, Prime Minister Benjamin Netanyahu declared, "Social justice does not oppose a free market, it depends on it."[246] A healthy economy, according to the prime minister, is based on a vibrant private sector. He urged financial responsibility, which would not bankrupt the country.

As in Chile, an important reason for high prices is the existence monopolies.[247] Professor David Gila, who is in charge of the committee to examine monopolies, claimed that he would like to break monopolies in order to solve the problem of lack of market competition. Any market that experiences a rise in prices may have a problem with competition. However, it is important to find out if the problem relates to monopolies or normal market activity.

Prime Minister Benjamin Netanyahu welcomed the Trajtanberg report, on how to improve Israel's economy, especially the lot of the poor, reiterated his view that the government would not return to the former welfare state.[248] The government would attempt to maintain the correct balance between social sensitivity and responsible economics. The prime minister emphasized the need to have a strong economy and prevent the problems faced by the European Union. The new Finance Minister, Yair Lapid, announced (April 2013) that painful cuts would have to be made in order to close the budget deficit.[249]

The number of workers in the Israeli labor force is on the increase. Both ultra-orthodox Jews and Arab women are entering the labor market. While Venezuela suffers from a brain drain, the number of Israelis who return to their country exceeds those who leave. In 2010 the net difference amounted to 12,000 people. There are 20,000 immigrants coming to Israel annually. An important reason for this immigration is the low unemployment in Israel compared to those of Europe and the United States. The new immigrants' integration in the Israeli economy contributes to the country's economic development.

Dr. Roiter summarized the main ingredients of the Israeli economy as high financial stability; a healthy, productive banking sector; a flexible economy can adopt to changes; a hi-tech industry that brings many positive attributes to the Israeli economy; being on the road of energy independence, leading to the possibility of becoming an exporter of energy in the future.[250]

Prime Minister Benjamin Netanyahu reminded everyone that, while Standard & Poor raised the Israeli credit rating to A+ in September 2011, it downgraded the ratings of nine euro zone countries, including France on January 2012.[251] Israel's compulsory public education starts at the age of three. Unlike Venezuela, which constantly raises its public budget, Israel has achieved its goal of having each ministry cut its expenses by 4%.

This chapter attempted to demonstrate the negative aspects of Chávez's economic system, which relies on the government as the major power in economic and political decisions. It further illuminated this issue by the comparison between the economic system of Venezuela, Chile, and Israel. Without any doubt, it revealed the advantages of the economic and political systems of both Chile and Israel over Venezuela's.

However, the fact must be emphasized that the ideal society exists only in Plato's Republic. The huge demonstrations in both Chile and Israel (and other parts of the world) may have created doubts about this chapter's thesis. However, John Hagel III and his partners were able to offer an excellent explanation of this problem. He correctly asserts that the process of globalization resulting from uninterrupted innovations produced feelings of uncertainty and economic insecurity. The mass demonstration in these countries and other parts of the world is an indication of these feelings. Hagel's ideas are extremely important for both individuals and governments that want to succeed in the new international system.

The digital revolution offers an opportunity to reform the democratic system. The people, using the new system of communication, should become the real source of both political and economic power. This fact requires adjustments of the traditional working of government. The globalization process has started a new stage which requires a new outlook on how countries and individuals may benefit from this trend.

The adoption of an Israeli-sponsored resolution on entrepreneurship for development by the United nations General Assembly (December 2012) confirms that capitalism is the main instrument, which need to be applied, for reducing poverty and improving people's economic conditions. The Israeli ambassador to United Nations cited his country's experience of empowering entrepreneurs as an important cause contributing to Israel's economic development.[252] It indirectly criticized Chávez's economic policies which rely on the state as a main vehicle of economic activities and praised Chile, Israel and other countries which rely on private initiatives to improve people's lot.

Notes

1   Feria escolar socialista ha dado una bofetada al sistema capitalista, Agencia Bolivariana de Noticias, Septiembre 12, 2009
2   Nuevo sistema financiero eliminará todos los vicios económicos de la burguesía venezolana, Agencia Bolivariana de Noticias, Junio 4, 2010
3   Venezuela está contribuyendo a creación de un nuevo sistema financiero, Agencia Bolivariana de Noticias, Septiembre 22, 2009
4   Venezuelan Congress devices a socialist financial system, Elmundo.com, November 15, 2010
5   Comisión Finanza AN: Ley de Instituciones fortalecerá al ahorrista, Agencia Bolivariana de Noticias, Noviembre 16, 2010
6   Aurelio Gil Beroes, Colapso hipotecario en EEUU y crisis económica Europea: Dos caras de una moneda, Agencia Bolivariana de Noticias, Mayo 26, 2010
7   José Guerra, Chávez, Cabezaz y el FMI, Analitica.com, Septiembre 16, 2009
8   Rafael González, Corporación de Mercados Socialistas (COMERSO): Modelo económico regulatorio? Analitica.com, Julio 21, 2009
9   José Guerra, El comercio socialista según Saman, Analitica.com, Julio 21, 2009
10   Aprobaba en segunda discusión Ley Orgánica del Sistema Económica Comunal, Agencia Venezolana de Noticias, Diciembre 14, 2010
11   Parliament makes strides in consolidation of the communal economic system, Eluniversal.com, November 12, 2010
12   Miguel González Marregot, Sobre el estado comunal, Analitica.com, Febrero 28, 2011
13   Communal system is viewed as confiscating, Eluniversal.com, May 21, 2011
14   Ibid.

15 Venezuelan bill provides for militias to punish private companies, Eluniversal.com, February 3, 2010
16 Herbert Huddel, El último invento del Nuevo Keynes (Chávez) el Veguero, Analitica. com, Junio 24, 2010
17 Ibid.
18 Carlos Eduardo Ruiz, Economía 101 Para Socialistas, Analitica.com Enero 27, 2010
19 Arnold King and Nick Shulz, From Poverty to Prosperity (New York, Encounter Books, 2009) p. 4
20 Ibid. p.174
21 Rómulo E. Lander Hoffman, Involución de las democracias, Analitica.com, Noviembre 28, 2009
22 Jesús Casique, Crecimiento gasto público y libre mercado, Analitica.com, Desembre 24, 2009
23 Ibid.
24 Bret Stephens, Hugo Chávez and the 47%, The Wall Street Journal, October 8, 2012
25 Rafael González, Controles y desabastecimiento: Normar sobre los efectos y no sobre las causas, Analitica.com, Marzo 22, 2010
26 Kejal Vyas, Covert Flour Deals Show Venezuela Woe, The Wall Street Journal, February 3, 2013
27 Gustavo Coronel, Tope salarial nueva maniobra del régimen, Analitica.com, Diciembre 20, 2009
28 Ibid.
29 Niall Ferguson, The Ascent of Money, (New York, Penguin Books,2008)
30 Ibid. p. 111
31 José Guerra, Carta económica al presidente Chávez, Analitica.com, Septiembre 1, 2011
32 Ibid.
33 Gustavo Coronel, The Petroleum Policy of the Hugo Chávez Government, Eluniversal.com, February 21, 2011
34 Ibid.
35 Ibid.
36 Ibid.
37 Luis Xavier Gristani, Caldera y el nacionalismo energético, Analitica.com, Febrero 2, 2010
38 Gustavo Coronel, PDVSA 2010: cursilería, fraude y desastre gerencial, Analitica.com, Marzo 22, 2011
39 Ibid.
40 Gustavo Coronel, Un post chavismo sin PDVSA Y sin ejército, Analitica.com, Noviembre 26, 2009
41 Juan Fernández, La gira de Chávez, Analitica.com, Octubre 21, 2010
42 José Guerra, Pobre PDVSA, Analitica.com, Mayo 26, 2011
43 Diego J. González Cruz, ¿Por qué ocurren accidentes en las instalaciones de PDVSA? Analitica.com, Agosto 26, 2012
44 Se "perdió" oportunidad en economía venezolana entre 1998 y 2007, según Domingo Zavala, Analitica.com, Diciembre 9, 2009
45 Venezuela's Oil Boom Has Not Favored the Poor, Eluniversal.com, July 23, 2009
46 Diego J. González Cruz, Propuesta para avanzar una nueva Venezuela usando como apoyo los recursos de los hidrocarburos, Analitica.com, Enero 18, 2011
47 José Guerra, Ideas para Venezuela, economía y petróleo, Analitica.com, Marzo 10, 2010
48 José Suárez Núñez, Venezuela le compra al imperio, Analitica.com, enero 13, 2011

49   Ibid.
50   José Rafael López Padrino, Venezuela: un país endeudado e hipotecado, Analitica. com, Noviembre 11, 2010
51   Ibid.
52   Maibort Petit, Expropiaciones: respuesta de Chávez ante las erráticas políticas alimentarias, Analitica.com, Mayo 18, 2011
53   Ibid.
54   Employers: Venezuela Private Sector Is Slaughtered, Eluniversal.com, September 4, 2009
55   Roberto Déniz, Venezuela Business Sector Rejects State-Centered Policies, Eluniversal.com, October 13, 2010
56   María De Lourdes Vásquez, Chávez: I Have Been Granted Authority to Expropriate Companies, Eluniversal.com, October 27, 2009
57   Public Sector Imports up 47 Percent; Private Sector' Down 22 Percent, Eluniversal. com, November 22, 2010
58   Thicker Government's Payroll After Nationalization, Eluniversal.com, March 31, 2011
59   New Laws Could Suffocate Private Sector in Venezuela, Universal.com, January 29, 2010
60   Ibid.
61   Venezuelan Scholars See Rise of Protracted Stagnation, Eluniversal.com, September 21, 2010
62   Ibid.
63   Jesús Seguías, El último vagón del sector privado, Analitica.com, Junio 23, 2010
64   Agustín Blanco Muñoz, Expropiadas y usurpadas las Navidades, Analitica.com, Diciembre 25, 2010
65   Rafael Rivera Muñoz, El terrorismo de estado y sus variantes, Analitica.com, Noviembre 4, 2010
66   Laws on People's Power Are Set to Nullify Private Entrepreneurship, Eluniversal.com, December 17, 2010
67   Chávez firmó decreto de adquisición forzosa de Sanitarios Maracay y Aluminios, Agencia Bolivariana de Noticias, Diciembre 19, 2010
68   Apropada nueva ley orgánica del sistema financiero nacional, Agencia Bolivariana de Noticias, Marzo 25, 2010
69   Venezuela Has Seized 185 Industries in 2010, Eluniversal.com, October 11, 2010
70   Antonio Casanova, Seizures Violate Six Constitutional Rules, Eluniversal.com, May 17, 2010
71   Rafael Díaz Casanova, Expropiaciones inconstitucionales, June 12, 2010
72   Julio Andrés Borges, Tus 30 millones, Analitica.com, Mayo 3, 2010
73   Julio Andrés Borges, Expropiando el empleo, Analitica.com, Febrero 24, 2010
74   Carlos R. Padilla, En la ruta del totalitarismo: Nacionalización de la banca, Analitica. com, Julio 28, 2009
75   Chávez Aims at Hegemony of Public Banks in Venezuela, Eluniversal.com, December 2, 2009
76   Ibid.
77   Editorial, Otro banco intervenido, Analitica.com, Octubre 15, 2010
78   Chávez's Government Keeps Seizing Private Properties, Eluniversal.com, October 15, 2010
79   Ibid.
80   President Chávez Orders "Escalation" of Fight Against Large Estates, Eluniversal.com, December 23, 2010

81   Importación de alimentos subió 254% en 12 años, Analitica.com, Enero 30, 2011
82   Ibid.
83   Farms Adrift, Eluniversal.com, November 19, 2010
84   Everybody Wants a House, Eluniversal.com, March 25, 2011
85   Eugene G. Martínez, Chávez Order to "Intensify" Takeover of Urban Lands, Eluniversal.com. January 10, 2011
86   José Guerra, Problema de la vivienda: inflación y demagogia, Analitica.com, Diciembre 7, 2010
87   Alfredo Cilento Sarli, El déficit de viviendas, Analitica.com, Febrero 14, 2011
88   Venezuelan Government Fails to Meet Goal of 120,000 Housing Units, Eluniversal.com, March 25, 2011
89   Pedro Farías Pucci, El arrendamiento: parte de la solución, Analitica.com, Marzo 30, 2011
90   Daniel Poneman, Argentina, Democracy on Trial, (New York, Paragon House Publishing, 1987) p.71
91   Chávez: Takeover of Apartments Will Not Be Compensated, Eluniversal.com, November 15, 2010
92   Ibid.
93   1.5 millones de propietarios dejarían de alquilar, Analitica.com, Enero 12, 2011
94   Julio Andrés Borges, Propiedad social: Dueño de nada, Analitica.com, Diciembre 22, 2009
95   Carlos Eduardo Ruiz, Inflación: Inevitable efecto secundario del socialismo, Analitica.com, Octubre 24, 2009
96   Carlos Eduardo Ruiz, No se puede controlar la inflación con medidas socialistas, Analitica.com, Agosto 17, 2009
97   Jesús Casique, Espiral inflacionario en 10 años y 10 meses 707%, Analitica.com, Noviembre 6, 2009
98   Alex Vallenilla, El crédito en Venezuela está barato, Analitica.com, Mayo 4, 2011
99   José Guerra, La inflación como problema, Analitica.com, Octubre 13, 2009
100 El poder adquisitivo cayó 162% en los últimos 11 años, Analitica.com, Diciembre 3, 2010
101 Angie Contreras and Mayela Armas H., Chávez in "Fast-Track" to Legislate Against Speculation, Eluniversal.com, January 17, 2011
102 Ibid.
103 Chávez instó al pueblo a iniciar una batalla frontal contra la especulación, Agencia Bolivariana de Noticias, Enero 10, 2010
104 Ibid.
105 Rafael González, La inflación como "fenómeno especulativo", Analitica.com, Febrero 13, 2010
106 Miguel Muñoz, Inflación galopante, Analitica.com, Mayo 18, 2010
107 Rafael González, Ley de costos precios y protección del salario, Analitica.com, Mayo 13, 2011
108 Cost Law Ends With Economic Rights, Eluniversal.com, July 21, 2011
109 Alexander Guerrero, Ley de costos y precios: muerte de las libertades económicas, Analitica.com, Agosto 1, 2011
110 Oswaldo Paez-Pumar, Ley de costos y precios justos, Analitica.com, Julio 29, 2011
111 Orlando Ochoa P, Breve análisis del proyecto de ley de reforma a la ley del BCV, Analitica.com, Octubre 30, 2009
112 José Guerra, El BCV al margen de la ley, Analitica.com, Febrero 24, 2010
113 Domingo Fontiveros, Estocada blanquecida, Analitica.com, Noviembre 14, 2009
114 José Guerra, El BCV esconde las cifras, Analitica.com, Abril 15, 2011

115   The Low Unemployment in Mexico Is Explained by Damien Cave, Better Lives for
       Mexicans Cut Allure of Going North, The New York Times, July 6, 2011
116   José Guerra, El dilema: Deuda o devaluación, Analitica.com, Noviembre 9, 2010
117   Pedro A. Palma, Devaluación e inflación, Analitica.com, Enero 21, 2010
118   Freddy Ríos, La devaluación como medio de control político, Analitica.com, Enero
       20, 2010
119   El salario mínimo pierde 62.3% por afecto de la devaluación, Analitica.com, Enero
       12, 2010
120   José Guerra, El dólar y los precios, Analitica.com, Enero 26, 2010
121   Ibid.
122   José Guerra, Inflación, producción y devaluación, Analitica.com, Enero 11, 2011
123   Capital Flight Amounts to USD 8.11 Billion in Six Month, Eluniversal.com, August
       28, 2009
124   Jesús Casique, Fracaso del control de cambio, Analitica.com, Octubre 3, 2010
125   Jesus Casique, Fuga de capitales Enero- Septiembre año 2009 ,13.333 millones de
       dólares, Analitica.com Noviembre 25, 2009
126   Fugada Capitales en Venezuela Alcanza Récord, Reporte confidencial, Noviembre 15,
       2008
127   Jesús Casique, Fracaso del control de cambio, op-cit
128   Ibid
129   Alex Vallenilla, Con 39% de divisas fugadas del país se estabiliza la economía vene-
       zolana, Analitica.com, Marzo 29, 2011
130   Ibid.
131   Over 800.000 Youngsters Have Left Venezuela in 10 Years, Eluniversal.com, August
       23, 2010
132   Ibid.
133   Ibid.
134   José Guerra, 2011: dificultades y esperanzas, Analitica.com, Diciembre 20, 2010
135   Núcleo de pobreza dura sube a 11.6% en el primer semestre, Analitica.com, Noviem-
       bre 24, 2010
136   Ibid.
137   José Rafael López Padrino, La salud no es prioridad para el régimen, Analitica.com,
       Septiembre 30, 2009
138   Cato Institute: Venezuela Among the Most Restricted Economies in the World, Eluni-
       versal.com, May 19, 2010
139   Ibid.
140   World Bank: Venezuela Has the Worst Business Climate in the Region, Eluniversal.
       com, November 4, 2010
141   Alberto Rodríguez Barrera, Algunas raíces de la corrupción chavista, Analitica.com,
       Diciembre 15, 2009
142   Editorial, Peculado o soborno? Analitica.com, December 15, 2009
143   Oswaldo Álvarez Paz, El crimen organizado, Analitica.com, Noviembre 30, 2009
144   Pedro Lastra, Campo di mafia, Analitica.com, Marzo 13, 2010
145   Carlos R. Alvarado Griman, elecciones o guerra de mafias, Analitica.com, Noviembre
       27, 2009
146   Carlos Peñaloza, Enriquecerse en PDVSA (1), Analitica.com, Abril 8, 2011
147   Pdvsa Adviser Confesses to Frauds Dating Back to 2006, Eluniversal.com, March 14,
       2011
148   Carlos Peñaloza, Op-cit
149   Tudor Kuljic, Yugoslavia's Workers Self-Management, Republicart.net 2003

150 Crecen tensiones sindicales tras investigar caso Ferrominera, Eluniversal.com, Junio 20, 2011
151 Froilan Alexandro Barrios Nieves, 2010: Enjuiciamiento al sindicalismo autónomo, Analitica.com, Enero 12, 2011
152 Ibid.
153 Robin Rodríguez, Trabajadores petroleros derrotan el terrorismo laboral, Analitica. com, Septiembre 4, 2009
154 Ibid.
155 Incremento salarial sólo cubrirá el 48.7% de la canasta alimentaria, Analitica.com, Abril 28, 2011
156 Froilan A. Barrios Nieves, Autonomía sindical y las marchas de trabajadores, Analitica.com, Marzo 31, 2011
157 Rafael González, Precios de mercado vs. precios controlados, Analitica.com, Agosto 3, 2011
158 Editorial, Cifras sobre distribución del ingreso en Chile, Nacion.cl, Julio 28, 2010
159 Ingreso ético familiar de 250 mil pesos proyectado para comenzar, Cronicalibre.cl, Mayo 27, 201
160 Thomas L. Friedman, A Theory of Everything (Sort of), The New York Times, August 13, 2011
161 Ibid.
162 John Hagel III, John Seely Brown, and Lang Davison, The Power of Pull, (New York, Perseus Books Group) 2010
163 Pinera: Modelo bolivariano de Chávez "no conduce a ninguna parte." Lanacion.cl Julio 8, 2011
164 Juan Antonio Muller, La ruta Chilena, Analitica.com, Marche 13, 2010
165 Ibid.
166 Alexander Torres Mega, Aprende de Chile y de su exitoso modelo económico, Analitica.com, Abril 5, 2010
167 Pedro Paul Bello, Mensaje de Chile, Analitica.com, Octubre 15, 2010
168 Jeffrey Sachs, Chile's Lesson in Leadership, The New York Times, October 20, 2010
169 Ibid.
170 Arnold Kling and Nick Schulz, op-cit p. 90
171 Rafael González, Precios de mercado vs. precios controlados, op-cit
172 Venezuela's GDP Decline is Almost Zero, says Planning Minister, Eluniversal.com, November 17, 2010
173 Economía chilena crecio 7% en el tercer trimestre, Nacion.cl, Noviembre 18, 2010
174 Economia Chilena crecio 5.6% en 2012, Lanacion.cl, Marzo 18, 2013
175 Nora Schirmeier, Chile mira hacia adelante: innovación y emprendimiento, Nacion. cl, Mayo 29, 2011
176 Forbes: Chile es el país más atractivo de América Latina para hacer negocios, Nacion. cl Octubre 4, 2011
177 Adolfo P. Algueiro, La espada de Bolívar en Libia, Analitica.com, Septiembre 4, 2011
178 Roberto Valencia, Michael Porter: Mayor competitividad pasa por la descentralización, Nacion.cl, Mayo 19, 2011
179 Gobierno quiere triplicar créditos en empresas para investigación y desarrollo, Nacion.cl, Febrero 25, 2011
180 Larrain: "No es necesario aumento tributario para financiar la educación.", Nacion. cl, Agosto 5, 2011
181 Roberto Valencia, Empleo: asalariados sólo superan por 28 mil a independientes, Nacion.cl, June 1, 2011

182   Central Bank of Venezuela Reports 5.4% Drop in Wages, Eluniversal.com, August 12, 2011
183   Businessmen: Venezuela Economic Growth will be Meaningless in 2011, Eluniversal. com, December 16, 2010
184   Expertos bajan a 4.2% expectativa de inflación en 2011, Nacion.cl, June 10, 2011
185   INE: Crecimiento del primer trimestre fue el mayor desde 2003, Nacion.cl, Julio 12, 2011
186   Larroulet" "Gobierno tendrá cero tolerancia con la inflación", Nacion.cl, Marzo 15, 2011
187   Nicolas Westermeyer, Reducción de gasto fiscal quita presión al central en ritmo de alza en tasa de interés, Nacion.cl, Marzo 24, 2011
188   Roberto Valencia, Alza en tasa de interés aún no precipita el o Nacion.cl, Mayo 14, 2011
189   Francisco Castañeda, Tipo de cambio y pequeñas empresas, Nacion.cl, Febrero 1, 2011
190   Central Bank Proposed Replacing the Dollar to Avoid Fed Control, Eluniversal.com, August 19, 2011
191   Banco Central mantiene sin cambios programa de compra de dólares, Nacion.cl, Febrero 9, 2011
192   Freddy Lepage, Los pobres y los niños de la calle, Analitica.com, Octubre 10, 2009
193   Nicolas Westmeyer, Piñera traza agenda para que Chile sea desarrollado en 2018, Nacion.cl, Noviembre 9, 2010
194   Ibid.
195   Editorial, Una agenda para el desarrollo, Nacion.cl, Noviembre 10, 2010
196   Incremento salarial sólo cubrirá el 48.7% de la canasta alimentaria, Eluniversal.com, Abril 28, 2011
197   Aumento salario mínimo 2011-2012, Laeconomia.cl, Julio 14, 2011
198   La inflación golpea con más fuerza a las familias pobres, Eluniversal.com, Julio 9, 2011
199   Calculan que escasez de aceite y leche en polvo avanza a 42.3%, Eluniversal.com, Agosto 14, 2011
200   Ibid.
201   Ingreso ético familiar de 250 mil pesos proyectado para comenzar, Cronicalibre.cl, Mayo 27, 2011
202   Matthei: "Fácil hablar de salario mínimo, pero el tema es ver como creamos empleo", Nacion.cl, June 24, 2011
203   Piñera define la educación como "fin en sí mismo", Nacion.cl, Julio 19, 2011
204   Presupuesto 2012 de Educación será de US$ 11.650 millones, Nacion.cl, Septiembre 29, 2011
205   Carlos Alberto Montaner, ¿Qué significa Israel para occidente, Analitica.com, Julio 26, 2011
206   Pablo Pardo, El modelo Israel, derrota al de Dubai, Analitica.com, Desembre 10, 2009
207   Jorge Marirrodriga, Israel enciende la luz, Analitica.com, Mayo 4, 2011
208   James Horro, Rebuilding Israel's Utopia, zeek.net, Octubre 7, 2006
209   Ran Hakim, Kibbutzim beisrael mabat istori calcali (Otat Iad Iari, Givat Haviva) 2009 p. 184
210   Marking Centenary, The Kibbutz Reinvents Itself, The Associate Press, November 12, 2010
211   Tali Heruti Sober and Hila Weisberg Iozma lo shitufit: Cah leebha atnua akibutzit lehamemet pratit, themarker.com, June 8, 2011
212   Ibid.

213 Kovi Ben Simhon, Eih eviu aparot et havrei kibbutz Afikim laasot asakim in Vietnam, Haaretz.co.il, June 11, 2011

214 Ibid.

215 Venezuela is considered one of the less innovative economies, Eluniversal.com, November 18, 2009

216 Ibid.

217 López-Claros Agosto and Mata Yasmina, "Policies and Institutions Underpinning Country Innovation: Result From the Innovation Capacity Index, The Innovation for Development Report, 2010-2011

218 Ibid.

219 Rishmit: Hevrat Citi takim beisrael merkaz mup, ynet.co.il, September 18, 2011

220 Eisennstad and Pollock, Israel's High-Tech pipeline to America, The Wall Street Journal, March 22, 2013

221 Gov't to Pay for Soldiers' First Year of Higher Education, The Jerusalem Post, October 23, 2011

222 Dan Senor and Saul Singer, Start-Up Nation, Op-Cit p. 29

223 Gei Grimland, Irgum bogrei 8200 iasik beapril tohnit suva leiazamim setie petuha lebogrei tzaal af lemizgardim nosafim, themaker.com, February 24, 2011

224 Arthur Herman, How Israel's Defense Industry Can Help Save America, Commentary, December 2011

225 Sharon Udasin, Better Place Launches 1st Israeli Battery-Switching Station, The Jerusalem Post, March 24, 2011

226 Dubi Ben- Gedalyahu, Better Place shuts down US, Australian operations, The Jerusalem Post, February 6, 2013

227 John Hagel III, John Seely Brown and Lang Davison, The Power of Pull, Op-cit p. 89

228 Moti Besok, Mamchicim ligdol: Aietzu gadal pi 13.400 mikum amedina ad aiom, themaker.com, May 10, 2011

229 Yaakov Katz, Israel marks record defense export in 2010, The Jerusalem Post, June 16, 2011

230 Stanley Fischer: Israel able to solve its economic issues, The Jerusalem Post, September 18, 2011

231 World Bank Warns Venezuela Is Unresponsive to Global Crisis, Eluniversal.com, September 21, 2011

232 Vadim Sabidreski, Omdan slishi shel alamas: ameshek tzamah be 7.8% berivaon aaharon shel 2010, themaker.com, April 17, 2011

233 Venezuela's unemployment rate at 9.4% in January, Eluniversal, March 13, 2013

234 Tamar Snyder, Israel Economy Nimble, but Education Investment Needed, The Jewish Week, September 16, 2011

235 Yosi Greenstein, Netanyahu mudag memitun: Kiem diunim dehufim im Fiscer, nrg.co.il, November 28, 2011

236 Bank Israel: Lerachez etlenu et aahraiut al aietzivut, ynet.co.il, May 10, 2011

237 Avital Laav, Tzevet beinmisradi ivhan agbarat ataharut bein abankim, ynet.co.il, December 20, 2011

238 Yossi Greenstein, Shuk Amatah pahot tenudati- ubank Israel lo rehash matah 3 hodashim, nrg.co.il, September 10, 2011

239 Ruth Eglash, Israeli trauma program to help Japan tsunami victims, The Jerusalem Post, September 8, 2011

240 Alona Volinsky,Green 2000 teaches Nigeria, Sudan agricultural techniques, The Jerusalem Post, October 29, 2011

241 Isabel Kershner, Israel Desert Yields a Harvest of Energy, The New York Times, April 20, 2012

242 Calev Ben-David, Netanyahu Sees Red Sea-Negev Rail Spurring China Trade: Freight, Bloomberg. Com, March 6, 2012
243 Ibid.
244 Israel Okays Rail Link to Manage Suez Overflow, alarab.co.uk, February 2, 2012
245 Ushi Soham Kraus, Milekahei amehaa: Aim Paysbook iathil otanu meoni, ynet.co.il, October 28, 2011
246 Lahv Harkov, PM: Gov't Must Stop Poverty While Ensuring Free Market, The Jerusalem Post, August 1, 2011
247 Laama Sikoler, Amemune al aagbalim: Lo leases lefarek monopolism, the marker.com, October 18, 2011
248 Netanyahu vows lower prices with more competition, The Jerusalem Post, September 19, 2011
249 Lapid: I won't let Israel become Cyprus or Greece, The Jerusalem Post, April 1, 2013
250 Ibid
251 Eli Berednstein, Netanyahu: calcalat Israel boletet letova cetozthaa memediniut aahrahit, nrg.co.il, January 15, 2012
252 Amb. Prosor on UN resolution "Entrepreneurship for Development," Israeli Ministry of Foreign Affairs, December 8, 2012

Chapter Three

Chávez's Foreign Policy: Primary Objective—Expansion of His Ideology

Chávez's Views and Behavior in the International System
In an article in Analitica.com, Garavini di Turno refers to the Mexican poet, diplomat, and winner of the 1998 Nobel Prize in Literature, Octavio Paz, who remarked, "Blindness impedes seeing; but ideological blindness hampers thinking."[1] In Chávez's case the ideological blindness impedes his ability to think objectively about Venezuela's real interests in the international system. The Venezuelan president's neo-Communist ideology combined with his Bonapartist vision of his country's potential, have produced a foreign policy that is unnatural and runs contrary to Venezuela's economic and political interests.

In the 1960s President Rómulo Betancourt said that Venezuela's relations with the United States should be without submission and rudeness. Chávez, on the other hand, pursues a strong anti-United States rhetoric, amounting to vulgarity. He does not miss any opportunity to denounce U.S. imperialism. In reality, however, he is dependent on United States' imports of oil, since it is the only client that pays in cash and on time.

Guilermo Zurge claims that the Chávez regime exploits anti-American sentiments that are prevalent in Latin America.[2] With the triumph of Ollant Humala in Peru, a Chávez deputy, Calixto Ortega declared that Humala's victory confirms the fact that 80% of Latin America's population is anti-imperialist and anti-American. This fact, according to Zurge, constitutes a shameful manipulation that the Chávez regime utilizes daily in order to discredit the United States. Chávez's repeated attacks against the United States are similar to other pronouncements by the United Staes' political enemies, such as Cuba, North Korea, Iran, and others, including terrorist groups, such as Al-Qaeda and FARC (terrorist group in Colombia). Zurge concludes his article by asking a rhetorical question: Should Latin American countries ally themselves with the United States or instead choose to align with countries such as Iran, North Korea, Libya (under Kaddafi), Belorussia, and Syria? The answer is obvious.

Some analysts thought that the Obama administration would improve U.S.-Venezuela, relations. However, in spite of attempts to project a friendlier image toward Latin America, compared with the previous Bush's administration, the net results did not bring any tangible change. Since 2010 there have been no ambassadors in both Washington and Caracas. The United States' intention to send Harry Palmer to be the new ambassador to Venezuela failed because the Chávez administration did not confirm the appointment. The Obama administration responded by expelling the Venezuelan ambassador Bernard Álvarez.

A spokesman of U.S. Department of State, Phillip Crowley, strongly criticized the passage of emergency law in Venezuela, National Assembly in 2010. With this law, Chávez has undermined the people's will and became an autocrat.[3] President Obama, in an interview in December 2011, declared his concern about the Chávez government's violations of human rights and democratic values. The Venezuelan government responded by claiming that Obama is a disgrace, a great frustration for the Afro-American community, and the poor in the United States. He is also a great disappointment to the African countries that believed in him when he assumed power.

Congresswomen Ilena Ros-Lehtinen criticized the United States' State Department for secretly negotiating with Vice President Nicolás Maduro, appointed by Chaves to succeed him. The United States insisted that reestablishment of relations between the two countries must include the return of United States' anti drug agency to Venezuela. Restoring this agency may threaten Diosdado Cabello, one of the main candidates who seek to replace Chávez. Cabello, the president of the national assembly managed a macro-traffic network, implicating various high officials both in the military and civilian life. The Congresswoman emphasized the fact that United States needs to support democratic reforms in Venezuela before realizing rapprochement with the Venezuelan leaders.[4]

Enrique Krauze, a Mexican scholar, claims that Chávez considers himself the hero of the twenty-first century; a person with absolute power and a lot of money. The Venezuelan president said in 2009 that he would retire in 2021. His life, according to Chávez, does not belong to him, but to the people. His mission in life is to alter the world as it exists. Creating a multipolar world, where the Empire (United States) will become equal to other countries. Chávez considers the United States to be responsible for Haiti's earthquake, which killed thousands of people. Garavini di Turno correctly calls this accusation an insult to one's intelligence.[5]

The world, according to the Venezuelan president, is moving toward a humanistic economy, based on socialism, which promotes social and moral values in order to fulfill the necessities of the majority of people without any discrimination. This is in contrast to capitalism, which harmed humanity. Socialism will be able to solve the world's economic problems. The European Union, as a result of the economic crisis that it faces, is obliged to change in the direction outlined by Chávez. There are millions of people throughout the world who suffer from starvation. Thus socialism, according to the Venezuelan president, constitutes the only solution to their problems.

Chávez's strong support of the former Libyan dictator, Muhammad Kaddafi, and Syria's Bashar al-Assad is another illustration of the Venezuelan president's views of world affairs. Chávez is a strong believer in the thesis presented by the German journalist, Ingo Niebel, who claimed that the Libyan model of external aggression constitutes a new modus operandi of U.S. imperialism, which might be also applied in Syria and later be expanded to other countries.[6] Chávez believes that what happened in Libya may be tried in Venezuela and, therefore, he expresses strong support for the ex-Libyan dictator and the Syrian ruler.

The Peruvian scholar and statesman, Álvaro Vargas Llosa, asserted that Chávez has never hidden his imperial plans. What started as the Cuba-Venezuela axis expanded to include Bolivia, Ecuador, Nicaragua, the Caribbean Island of Antigua, Barbados, San Vicente, Granada, and Dominica. Employing Petrocaribe as an instrument for supplying oil, the Chávez regime subsidized thirteen out of fifteen islands of CARICON, in addition to Cuba and Guatemala.[7] Chávez's death brings into question the continuation of these policies.[8]

Alberto Montaner describes how Chávez is using his oil money to influence election results in South America.[9] The Chávez mode of influence varies from country to country. In Argentina, suitcases filled with money were delivered to Kirchner's campaign. Unfortunately for Chávez, the suitcases were discovered at the airport because an honorable worker insisted reporting the crime. In Uruguay, a different method was used to help his friend, the former Tumparo guerrilla José Mujica. The money did not arrive in suitcases; it was masked as a simple business transaction when a Uruguayan company headed by Mujica's wife received $32 million from Chávez.

Chávez's interference in Chile took another direction. Max Marambio is a Chilean millionaire who cooperated with the Cuban secret service. During his exile in Cuba, he maintained close relations with Fidel Castro, who permitted him to amass enormous fortune by handling dollars deriving from the tourist industry. Marambio claims that Cuba is a democratic country. In Chile he became the political director of the radical left candidate Marco Enriquez Ominari and his major financial contributor. Chávez learned about Max Marambio from his mentor Fidel Castro.[10]

During a visit to African and Middle East countries in 2009, Chávez declared that his view of the multipolar world has been modified. There does not exist a unipolar or bipolar world, nor is the international system marching toward four or five big blocs, but rather toward a multinuclear world.[11] This view may be Chávez's way of asserting that Iran and other small- and medium-size countries have the right to develop nuclear weapons. The Chávez's regime, like its Iranian counterpart, would like to produce nuclear weapons in order to deter any possibility of outside intervention. An American citizen of Argentinian origin, was detained in October 2009 in New Mexico, attempting to sell a nuclear plan to Chávez's government.[12]

Career diplomats ceased to represent Venezuela and were replaced by members of the military or party militants, converting the new state's representatives into agents for exporting the Chavist project. The Chávez regime constantly violated the principle of peaceful coexistence, contemplated in the international law, including not interfering in internal affairs of other countries. Chávez supported terrorist groups such as FARC in Colombia and Hezbollah in Lebanon.

Another important characteristic of Venezuela's diplomacy is its linkage to authoritarian and dictatorial regimes. Chávez's alliance with Castro's Cuba served as a basis for Venezuela's internal policies that reduced the country's sovereignty. The country's relations with Iran, is a major obstacle for its relations with western countries.

Chávez's First Step in Spreading his Ideology: The Creation of the Bolivarian Alliance of the People of Our America (ALBA)

ALBA represents Chávez's attempt to spread his ideology by offering the countries in it economic incentives or bribes. All these countries, which include Bolivia, Ecuador, Nicaragua, and others, are labeled Chávez's puppet states. These countries are following in Venezuela's path by gradually abandoning democratic rules and replacing it with authoritarian political systems.

In an article, entitled "Dishonest Business Called ALBA" (*"Un negocio chueco llamado ALBA"*), Emilio Nouel claims that Chávez's international behavior is solely directed by the objective of world revolution against capitalism.[13] This policy runs counter to the interests of the Venezuelan people and, according to Nouel, is contradicting the country's national interest.

In this age of globalism, economic integration among countries becomes an important priority. Its aims are to connect economies through the establishment of increased commercial relations, create wider economic integration and eliminate obstacles and discrimination among the integrated economies. The hope is to progressively obtain a common area that goods can be exchanged, policies can be harmonized, investments can freely flow and workers can circulate without restriction.

The grandiose rhetoric of Chávez about ALBA does not fulfill the above proposition. Claiming that ALBA allows the integration of the people is purely demagoguery; it is a useless declaration that does not advance the practical aims of integration. The document has no norm that regulates integration or any concrete mechanism to achieve this aim. There is no mention of tariffs, lists of products to be exchanged, unfair competition, and reciprocal investments. ALBA, Nouel claims is a political clientele group invented by Chávez to spread similar ideologies to other countries in exchange for funds that derive from oil or international support.

In order to illustrate his point of view, Nouel analyzes Venezuela's economic relations with the ALBA countries in general and with Bolivia and Nicaragua in particular. The bilateral economic relations between Bolivia and Venezuela increased especially after Evo Morales came to power in 2006. During the period 2005-2010, the Bolivian government received from the Chávez regime the sum of $8,859 million. Venezuela during the period 2007-2010 gave Nicaragua $7,920 million.[14]

The total expenses of Venezuela in all ALBA countries up to 2011 were $62,633 million, while in 2005 it was only $2,122 million. Nouel correctly describes these huge expenses as the blood of the Venezuelan people unjustly given away and contrary to the country's interests. These political ideological links are an unacceptable burden for Venezuela. ALBA, Nouel concludes, is a dreadful business for Venezuela; it is an immoral project that constitutes an insult, showing contempt for the urgent necessities of Venezuela in housing, health, education and security.[15]

Gerson Revanales expresses views similar to Nouel's, claiming that real integration among countries can only occur if it occurs among democratic states with consolidated institutions and prior political development. The process of unification will benefit the participating units if the countries are homogenous and relate to each other through diverse economic projects, infrastructure, and energy.[16] Relying on the ideas of Adam Smith, Revanales claims that division of labor and a large market reduces costs and permits the existence of a demand volume capable of encouraging the production and commercialization of goods and services. Adam Smith emphasized the importance of the market size as a fundamental variable for the functioning of the national economy.

ALBA's unification does not meet the above conditions. It does not have any relationship with other models of integration that include customs, political organization, and monetary union. The ALBA treaty should be considered a strategic alliance; a friendship accord, similar to the one signed by the organization of European socialist countries, COMECON (extinct after the fall of the Soviet Union). This union was a reaction to Western countries' Marshall Plan. Similar to COMECON, ALBA funds have come from Chávez's oil profits, which are distributed to the member countries.

Venezuela, like the Soviet Union with the Warsaw Pact, assumes primary responsibilities in the execution, materialization, and obligations in this treaty. ALBA, unlike other regional organizations, lacks a general secretary and an executive organ able to exercise its legal responsibilities and fulfill its managerial duties. It also does not have an organ in charge of solving disputes and controversial issues among its members. The death of Chávez raises questions if the huge amount of economic assistance given to these countries will continue.

Chávez gave combat mirage airplanes to Ecuador, an act that confirms the political-military character of this alliance. It constitutes an attempt to spread Venezuela's socialism of the twenty-first century to all its members.

In order to modify the international economic system, Hugo Chávez and his Ecuadorian counterpart Rafael Correa suggested in 2008 the initiation of a Unitary System of Regional Compensation and Payments (*Sistema Unitario de Compensación Regional de Pago*, SUCRE) which represents a new currency used for transactions among ALBA countries.[17] This new currency, established as a result of the continued weakening of the dollar, will attempt to end the dictatorship of the United States' currency.

Giménez Tellería claims that the new currency proposed (SUCRE) by Chávez is a dream shattered into pieces.[18] The SUCRE does not have any economic, institutional, or material support. This new currency has no chance to compete with the U.S. dollar. The only purpose of this new currency is to obtain cheaper dollars for Cuba, but not for the Venezuelan people. It constitutes a mockery of human intelligence and contempt for the people of Cuba and Venezuela.[19]

President Chávez approved, in February 2012, the incorporation of 1% of Venezuela's reserves, amounting to $300 million, into the ALBA bank. Chávez claimed that he is counting on the consent of Venezuela's Central Bank that ALBA's new economic institution will become a center of financial activities.[20]

As a result of threats from the United States (Empire) and the reaction of the fear of communism, the international system, according to Chávez, is returning to the 1960s Cold War era. NATO is still in existence; therefore, Chávez called upon the ALBA countries to create a defense alliance, a military treaty that will unite the armed forces of all these countries.[21] ALBA will create a military school that includes not only soldiers but also civilians who are interested in security and defense issues.[22]

As indicated in the first chapter, Gramsci viewed education as a necessary step in spreading communism. During an ALBA meeting that took place in Bolivia in 2009, the participating presidents issued a declaration emphasizing education as a fundamental process that would strengthen unity among the countries.[23] ALBA countries consider education as a top priority and are planning a common curriculum for basic education. Modifying people's views and altering their value system has become a top priority for ALBA presidents who want .to remain in power.

ALBA countries found it of utmost importance to discuss the creation of a common communication project in order to withstand the media's attacks on certain power centers.[24] It calls for the creation of a common press agency, radio station, television network, print publication, and information network. A special effort would be made to produce reliable reporters by training journalists to view the world from their political perspective.

ALBA leaders claimed in December 2011 that the World Chamber of Commerce follows antidemocratic policies and excludes certain countries.[25] This capitalist organization is an instrument of the big industrialized countries to dominate the rest of the world. It does not represent the interests of small- and medium-size countries.

Venezuela's opposition newspaper highlighted the economic success of Andina's Acquisition Corporation, an agreement on how to integrate Chile's, Peru's, and Colombia's stock markets.[26] It is an implied criticism of ALBA, which is based on Venezuela's redistributing its resources to other countries. The Andina's Acquisition Corporations more attuned to the ideas of Revanales and Nouel described previously.

The Andina's stock market agreement was joined by private companies, which may signal a political-economic axis restraining and slowing down Chávez's ambitions to spread his ideology and enhance his influence. The agreement deals mainly with financial investments among private companies. These countries share a common political-economic affinity, a belief in market economy, that is sharply different from the one advocated by Chávez; the use of discipline in the management of economic affairs is also different from the way it is employed in Venezuela.

The stock market constitutes the essence of capitalism. Its aim of channeling savings into investments and is based on transparency. The International Monetary Fund (IMF) in its annual report of October 2010 indicated that the best macroeconomic policies and financing condition in Latin America were found in the following countries: Brazil, Chile, Colombia, and Peru, during the period 2010-2011.[27] A Peruvian newspaper reported in December 2011 that Mexico's stock exchange would be added to the Andina's stock exchange, which already included Peru, Chile, and Colombia.[28]

Beyond ALBA: Chávez's Attempts to Spread His Ideology Throughout Latin America

On December 2 and 3, 2011, Latin American and Caribbean heads of state met in Caracas, Venezuela, to create a new organization, the Community of Latin American and Caribbean States (*Comunidad de Estados Latinoamericanos y Caribeños*, CELAC). The aim of CELAC was to develop the political-economic integration of Latin American and Caribbean countries.[29] In spite of past failures because of diverse ideological views, the hope remained that creating a permanent bloc for consultation would help to narrow the differences among the states.

The conference received a lot of commentary from both supporters (Chávez's regime and ALBA's countries) and critics. Those who supported the conference claimed that it constituted a pass to an authentic independence. The exclusion of United States and Canada was viewed as enhancing the anti-imperialist image of the new regional bloc. However, each country is free to follow its own policies.

Paéz Ávila claims that Chávez and his partners' attempt to use the conference for anti-American propaganda will fail.[30] Colombian President Juan Manuel Santos was emphatically clear when he declared that CELAC is not against anyone. Ávila concludes his article by mentioning that world progress depends on supporting negotiation and conquering new markets, not on ideological confrontations.

Latin American and Caribbean integration needs to be accomplished without hatred and exclusions.[31] The American continent, Grooscors Caballero claims, is unique and different from Europe, Asia, or Africa. From south to north, America is one unit; however, because of historical and political circumstances it became fragmented into many nations. However, the new continent was able to better understand the first great revolution of the world, the American Revolution (1776) than its European counterparts could. In order to foster America's integration, the need arises to understand the history of all the countries on this continent. This should be done without ideological confusion.

The Latin American people (especially those of the ALBA countries) need to revise their thinking in order to involve the United States. From the educational point of view it becomes necessary to combine the thinking of George Washington, Simón Bolívar, and San Martín as exemplary illustrations of how to create a common identity and coexistence of all the people in the region.[32]

Chávez's aims in CELAC, similar to what he had done in ALBA, are to use his oil revenues to foster integration and to minimize the United States influence in Latin America and the Caribbean; and to end or weaken the power of the Organization of the American States (OAS), which often criticizes his human rights violations. The OAS has less than $50,000 in order to pay its personal. Brazil owes the OAS $6.3 million and insists on eliminating the Inter-American Human Rights System. The Chávez regime owes $2.5 million to the OAS.

The Inter-American Commission on Human Rights cannot exist without the OAS. Its termination would mean the end of the Inter-American Commission on Human Rights and the Inter-American Court of Human Rights.[33] Chávez and his ALBA partners are hoping to create a new organization, which unlike OAS will lack the supervisory mechanism and the ability to criticize their human rights violations. Therefore, replacing OAS with CELAC would guarantee the uninterrupted continuation of abusing people's privileges.

Gustavo Coronel, after carefully reading the final document signed by all the participants in the conference, claimed that it created a new language, entire pages were written without saying anything important.[34] He cites as an example the plan designed to solve the poverty problem in the hemisphere. It would be formed by a ministerial committee that would address social themes. It would serve to foment cooperation, harmonization, and articulation of national public policies regarding social issues and implementation of common regional plans for social development. This declaration is mere words that have no practical meaning.

Eradicating hunger calls for combining successful government programs to be followed by other countries. Coronel rightly asks how important the accomplishments of the hemisphere in this area are. He rhetorically asks if Haiti or Cuba can be helpful. Can Venezuela ask that the state's organization for food distribution (PDVAL), which gives the people rotten food be used as a model by other countries?

Coronel expresses his opinion about how how the section of the document about improving food production and eliminating hunger should have been written. It must start with the basic assumption that food which is necessary to feed the population would be produced. This could be brought about by promoting the agricultural sector, instead of expropriating (nationalizating) ranches. Leave the variables of demand and supply in place as the major criteria for decision making instead of establishing price control. Leave the producers of agricultural items alone instead of threatening them with expropriation. Coronel views the 2012 CELAC plan of action as merely a waste.

While most of the Venezuelans, as a result of high inflation rate, are not able to cover their expenses, Chávez invited thirty-three head of states from

Latin America and the Caribbean to come to Venezuela. The maintenance of this conference involves very high expenses, which does not bring any return of capital, investment or technology. The problems facing Venezuela in the fields of health, education, security, productivity, employment and others could not be resolved by this meeting. It requires studies, equipment, decision making, financial resources, will power, and self-criticism.[35]

Venezuela, an oil producing state, lamentably does not produce the necessary food needed by the consumer. The majority of the country's demands are supplied by imports; this is a direct result of Chávez's policies of expropriating and confiscating local enterprises. Leone concludes his article by claiming that Chávez is very generous in spending the country's money and paying everyone, while the Venezuelan people are unable to balance their budget.

Barrios Nieves asks if Chávez's initiative inviting over thirty heads of states will positively impact Venezuela's economy. He then proceeds to paraphrase Chávez's United Nation speech in which he declared that governments go from one summit to another and the people remain in ruin; these events do not coincide with our people's interests, but solely justify the global power of the rich governments.[36]

In the age of globalization, one has to realize that the regrouping of countries is a legitimate need. However, with the CELAC accord, the political integration is running contrary to Venezuela's national interest. Nieves correctly claims that CELAC is propaganda, Chávez is using in order to consolidate a personal authoritarian project throughout Latin America. Chávez's double-talk manifests itself when claiming that NAFTA, the 1994 agreement among United States, Mexico, and Canada, is repulsive but the accord between Venezuela and its neighbor Colombia is considered revolutionary and socialist.[37]

A very different view on CELAC was presented by Venezuela and its partner's mass media. The Latin American and Caribbean reunion, according to Bolivian President Evo Morales, is an important step toward the liberation of Latin American countries.[38] The Bolivian president claimed that the crisis in the capitalist system is structural and terminal. The meeting of thirty-three heads of state offers a good opportunity to analyze and debate a new course of economic policies that countries should undertake. The states of Latin America and the Caribbean need to establish a new model of socialism, referred to as the socialism of the twenty-first century.

The official Venezuelan press reported an interview with the economist Luis Matos who claimed that CELAC, in addition to being a forum of political dialogue, is also a panel for commercial interchange among thirty-three countries. Venezuela's oil, (89% of Latin America's oil reserves) will be used as an instrument of social development.[39] Chávez would like to achieve in CELAC what he had attained in ALBA. However, Chávez's death and the uncertain political situation in Venezuela reduce the chance that this may occur.

Chávez's Puppet States: Bolivia, Ecuador, and Nicaragua

Bolivia, Ecuador, and Nicaragua are following Chávez's footsteps, gradually transforming their countries into authoritarian political systems. These countries are instruments in the Venezuelan president's project to buy the support of subservient followers with money.[40]

A former minister of the Bolivian government, Carlos Sánchez Berzain, describes how the Evo Morales regime transformed Bolivia into an authoritarian and tyrannical state.[41] His analysis is also applicable to Ecuador and Nicaragua, which are analyzed in a latter part of this chapter. Bolivia, according to Berzain, violated Montesquieu's theory regarding *separation of powers*. Both the judicial and legislative branches of government are controlled by the executive.

Freedom of the press was sharply reduced. If this trend continues, Bolivia will become similar to the Cuban dictatorship. Nationalization of private companies weakens the country's economy and contributes to the rise of corruption. These symptoms are also characteristic of other ALBA countries.

President Evo Morales, speaking in front of five thousand members gathered for the eighth Socialist Movement Congress (el Movimiento Socialista, MAS), declared that he would like to stay in power forever.[42] Anti-imperialist, anti-capitalist and anti-neoliberal leaders, when coming to power, do not relinquish their positions. The Bolivian president added that the congress can debate this issue. Morales position is shared by Chávez and other leaders of other ALBA countries.

Ortiz Saucedo, analyzing Bolivia's policies, claims that Evo Morales, the country's president, following in Chávez's lines, is destroying the country.[43] Bolivia, a heterogeneous country, is composed of many Indian tribes in addition to people of Mestizos and European decent. Morales, a leader of a multitribal and multiethnic society, followed primarily the economic interest of his Yoruba tribe. As a former president of the coca growers union, he turned Bolivia into a narcotic-state, (mafia state), which coincided with his tribe's interest.

Bolivia's geography contains many disconnected regions that in more than the 186 years of its independence were unable to form a real national state. This necessitates the decentralization of power, which gives local government the ability to take into consideration the country's regional difference. Saucedo's criticism of Bolivia's political centralization is similar to the French scholar Alexis de Tocqueville's emphasis on decentralization as an important characteristic of democracy. Morales, on the other hand, following Chávez's political system, is moving the country toward centralization and a homogenous vision of how to govern.

The indigenous people, from the arrival of Columbus in America, over 500 years ago, were subjugated and exploited. The victory of Morales's leftist party MAS in the December 2005 elections was an unprecedented event for Bolivia and the entire American continent. For the first time in the country's history a representative of the original people of America came to power. Some analysts compare Morales's election as president with that of Barack Obama in the United States.

After being in power more than six years, Handel Guayasamín claims, the government lacks technical experience and the political cadres required to manage the complicated needs of the Bolivian people.[44] It lacks the institutions, laws, norms, and procedures needed to manage people's demands. The government has followed authoritarian policies, attempting to hide mistakes and silencing criticism. The Morales regime conducted many persecutions against dissenters by jailing and harassing people and committing violence against those who dare to criticize his policies. In his concluding remarks Guayassamín, claims that real revolutionaries cannot commit the same errors that were committed by those who Morales fought against.[45]

Morales's government functions as an oppressive apparatus, subsidized by millions of dollars from Chávez's oil income and from narcotic traffic trade.[46] The above writer (his name is not mentioned) claims that Morales is employing propaganda similar to that used by Hitler's regime, where every means was employed to destroy the opposition and take over all the means needed to rule without opposition. Violence is employed so people become insecure. Slogans emerge everywhere so that people can repeat them.

One has to bear in mind that previous Bolivian governments did not satisfy people's needs. Evo Morales's regime is not different in this respect. The constitution Morales introduced, similar to the one in Chávez's Venezuela, destroyed separation of powers, revised the guarantees of universal liberties, and prevented it from becoming an enterprising state. Morales adopted policies that were imported from the Cuban-Venezuelan models.[47]

Antonio Gramsci was mentioned in the first chapter as emphasizing the role of education in transforming a country into a Communist one. According to the Italian scholar, if communism is to succeed, there is the need for complete reform of the educational system in order to teach and inculcate Communist values. Morales, attempted to reform the educational system. An education director, Humberto Parari, asserted in February 2012 that he was propelling an educational and cultural revolution in Bolivia.[48] A new curriculum would be written emphasizing collectivism and Bolivia's own history.

Bolivia's priorities are distorted by the Morales regime. Health is not considered to be an important priority. An important preference of the government is politics; similar to Chávez's Venezuela, the aim is to maintain power at any cost. 50.3% of the ministerial budget in 2011 was spent on matters related to the state's repressive apparatus (defense and security) and only 11.2% on health and education.[49] This statistic demonstrates the true character of multinational police state of the Bolivian government. The report that Bolivia is among the five Latin American countries with the highest cancer mortality, reaffirms Saucedo's thesis.[50]

Saucedo proceeds to ask important questions related to Bolivia's budget. Are the allocated funds for times of peace or war? How important are education and health in this budget? Is this a budget of a "socialist" government? Morales's government, similar to Chávez's in Venezuela, follows policies that violate human rights and reduce freedom of the press. It also supports coca growers. The national army is viewed as a unique source of support. Saucedo concludes his article by claiming that Bolivia continues to be a failed state.[51]

Morales's administration, like what Chávez's did in Venezuela, altered civil-military relations in Bolivia. The armed forces, according to the Bolivian president, have changed their image and are servicing all the people.[52] The head of the Air Force, General Tito Gandarillas, responded that Morales is the only leader in the country's history who identified with the military. The Bolivian president expressed his gratitude to the armed forces for enabling the state to recover capitalist enterprises and demonstrate that the government is more capable of conducting business than the private sector. Opposition members charged Morales with seeking to rule without dissent and using the armed forces for support.

Bolivia, like Venezuela, is losing its security and food sovereignty.[53] The Morales's government is destroying the agricultural sector; each day food production is decreasing. This is similar to Venezuela's importing of food, which is on the rise, increased by 52.16% during the period January 2010-January 2011. Like Chávez, who purchased expensive airplanes for his personal use, Morales bought luxurious airplanes and constructed a new palace for himself. Saucedo claims that he would not be surprised if in the near future he might build a new Taj Mahal and bigger pyramids than those in Egypt.[54]

Morales's economic policies, like Chávez, failed to improve people's well-being. The Bolivian State Oil Company lacks resources to make necessary investments to increase natural gas production. There are shortages of sugar and basic food. As in Venezuela, the government attempted to halt cost increases by instituting price controls. This policy resulted in less agricultural planting, contributing to food shortages. All these factors contributed to a decline in Morales's popularity, especially in Bolivia's principal cities.[55]

The first chapter mentioned a great increase in crime rates in Venezuela. The Chávez regime views this problem as an issue inherited from the past capitalism system. Accordingly, in their view, the transformation to socialism will make the problem disappear. However, after Chávez has been in power for more than thirteen years, the high crime rate has not disappeared.

Ortiz Saucedo demonstrates that Bolivia has similar problems; a sharp increase in crime rates and citizens' insecurity.[56] The authorities in charge of the problems do not have the political will, the sufficient resources, or the know-how to deal with the social calamity in the country. The police claim that a citizen's security is the responsibility of everyone. Saucedo strongly disagrees and cites the Bolivian constitution to defend his views. Article 16 of the constitution attributes to the country's president responsibility for preserving the security and defense of the state. The president is responsible for both internal and external security. Thus, Saucedo concludes, Morales does not comply with his constitutional obligations.[57] As these lines are written it is not clear if Morales's employment of the armed forces to combat crimes will render positive results.[58]

The employment of violence in obtaining a political goal is an important characteristic of Morales's administration. During an indigenous people's protest against the construction of a road that would destroy their way of living, the police used violent methods against the demonstrators.[59]

An important official in Morales's MAS party declared that the trials of opposition members should not be considered political persecution.[60] This announcement came as a response to a United Nations declaration condemning the trials of opposition members in Bolivia. A deputy of MAS, Lucio Marca, asserted that the ordeal of opposition members is justified. The trials of these members is based on a new law of communication, in which article 16 declared that any mass media which publishes racial and discriminatory articles is liable to face economic sanctions and license's suspension. An opposition member of the National Unity (UN) party, Jaime Navarro, praised the United Nations' declaration and claimed that political persecution constitutes a daily reality for those who oppose the government's policies.[61]

In a latter part of this chapter, an analysis will be made of narcotic trafficking in Chávez's Venezuela. Bolivia has been following the same policy, especially after the expulsion of the United States' Drug Enforcement Agency (DEA) in 2008. Evo Morales criticized the United States, antidrug policies in Latin America and claimed that the real purpose is to advance the American interests in this region. Morales repeated the 2005 Chávez declaration that the United States' Drug Enforcement Agency is using its agents for espionage on Venezuela.[62]

It is important to note that chewing coca leaves constitutes part of the indigenous culture. The attempt to differentiate between coca leaves and cocaine is problematic. The leaves constitute the basic ingredient of cocaine. Bolivia did not sign the 1961 convention related to narcotic traffic.[63] It is difficult to comprehend how protecting those who grow coca leaves will help solve the country's drug problem.

Morales called upon the United Nations to repair a historical error and legalize coca in Bolivia.[64] The Morales regime claims that it is working relentlessly to eradicate the narcotic trade. The evidence nevertheless is clear that in Bolivia the drug lords coexist with the government's structures.[65] As corruption is rampant the narcotic money reaches the highest officials in Morales's government.

The approval of building a road in Tipnis sharply increased conflicts among the indigenous tribes. Saucedo claims that this decision was motivated by Morales's desire to expand the agricultural land of his tribe's coca growers.[66] It calls for the destruction of 2 million trees, which may cause the genocide of Tipnis's indigenous tribes. As a result of mass protest, Morales decided to cancel the deal.[67]

In this respect, it is important to note that the Morales's government approved a law (in 2011) to increase the cultivation of coca leaves from 12 to 20 thousand hectares.[68] This decision may be very helpful for the drug cartels and weaken the war against narcotic traffic; it will also lead to the growth of narcotic and a failed state.

A former Bolivian Defense minister, Ernesto Justinian, claimed that narcotic traffic is caused by inequalities of conditions, lack of control, and the absence of a real government policy to combat this trend.[69] During the period of the Morales administration, cocaine production increased by 50%. This becomes evident when one views the construction of luxurious apartments and expensive cars belonging to the cocaine mafia, who enjoy free movement in the country. When the United States' DEA was present in Bolivia, it paid $50 thousand to informers. It ceased to work in the country, after Morales ordered the American agency to leave. United States identified twenty countries as producers or places of transit for narcotic trafficking in 2010. Both Venezuela and Bolivia are included on this list.[70]

The president of the Social Democratic Party in Brazil accused the Bolivian president of sponsoring narcotic trade in Bolivia. He criticized former Brazilian president Lula da Silva, of the Workers' Party, for ignoring what is happening in Bolivia.[71] Lula da Silva was prepared to finance the construction of a road on the Brazilian-Bolivian border that would facilitate the cocaine traffic in Brazil.

Further proof that Bolivia is a narcotic (mafia) state is presented by the Brazilian journal *Veja*, translated to Spanish through an opposition Venezuelan newspaper.[72] Only a third of the coca planted in Bolivia is used for local consumption. The rest is purchased by organized crime. The lives of 1 million Brazilians are ruined as a result of this illegal drug. A private company of public opinion research, in a poll conducted in 2012, found that 64% of the respondents claimed that the executive branch is losing the drug war.[73]

The Bolivian government, according to the article, is directly involved in narcotic traffic. A strong link exists between organized crime and officials of the Morales's government. The Brazilian journal indicates that an important assistant to President Morales, Ramón Quintana, serves as a coordinator with the organized crime units in Bolivia.[74]

In the first chapter, it was observed that Chávez is using United States (Empire) as a scapegoat, responsible for all the failures of his policies. Bolivia adopted a similar line, blaming the Empire for discontent among its people. The building of a road in Tipnis brought a sharp conflict between the local indigenous population and the government. Bolivian Vice President Álvaro García Linera, in an interview with a Mexican newspaper, claimed that the United States is behind the mass indigenous protest.[75] The vice president claimed that United States would like to safeguard the Amazon as a water reserve territory. This could be accomplished by promoting divisions and conflicts among the indigenous people through governmental organizations, such as United States Agency for International Development. This accusation was strongly denied by the United States.

Deputies of the Movement for Socialism (*Movimiento Pro Socialismo*, MAS) suspected that police officers were implicated in a U.S. revolt against the government of Evo Morales.[76] A government minister claimed that some police commanders had not committed themselves to the process of transformation in their department. The government would not permit these officers to harm state security, conducting acts of terror, through the transfer of arms and ammunition. This infringes the penal code and constitutes an armed insurrection, terrorism, and conspiracy that need to be investigated thoroughly.[77]

In Ecuador, as in Venezuela and Bolivia, gradual transformations have taken place that turned the country into an authoritarian political system. Rafael Correa's administration is following Chávez's style of state-dominated socialism and dictatorship.[78] Following his mentor Chávez, Correa launched a referendum in which the people were asked to express their opinion on various proposed issues. Many human rights activists viewed the referendum on May 7, 2011, as an attempt by the Ecuadorian president to grab power and weaken democratic institutions. Correa dismissed his critics by emphasizing that he proceeded democratically.

Correa took advantage of his popularity in order to advance a Chávez's-style governing system. Among the proposals voted on, there were two articles that were intended to further strengthen his power and weaken the opposition. In all democratic states, the judicial branch plays a major role because of its ability to control and check the other branches of government, especially the executive.

Correa's referendum included a question that allowed him to weaken the Supreme Court and put it under his control. Another measure that weakened democracy allowed the president to control the mass media. A government commission would be created monitoring and regulating the media's content. It would oversee television, radio, and the press.

Gustavo Coronel claims that with the referendum's approval, Correa had converted Ecuador into an authoritarian system; freedom of expression would be persecuted and those who protest would be considered enemies of the state.[79] The state became the dominant institution, resembling North Korea, and following the path of both Evo Morales's Bolivia and Hugo Chávez's Venezuela.

Control of the mass media has weakened the opposition press and exposed the people to a one-sided opinion. This is a strong characteristic of authoritarian and totalitarian political systems. The sanctions against the television station Teleamazonas in 2009 were a warning that the authoritarian process has started.[80] The reason for shutting down the station was that it supposedly reported that PDVSA's drilling for natural gas in Ecuador's Puma is harmful to the environment and causes the death of fish. The television station was accused of presenting false information, which is considered to be a violation of citizens' rights to be freely informed.[81] The decision was strongly criticized by the president's brother, Fabricio Correa, who claimed that it constitutes a barbaric act.

Correa' abuse of the press manifested itself when Emilio Palacio, the editorial page director of the newspaper *El Universo*, was charged with "aggravated defamation of public officials."[82] He accused Correa of ordering the army to fire on a hospital during a police protest.

The Bolivian opposition press (*Hoybolivia*) reported that the judge assigned to the case, Mónica Encalada, fled to Colombia because Correa's lawyers pressed her to rule in his favor.[83] She was offered a bribe of $3,000 monthly if she ruled in the president's favor. Encalada claims that she was threatened for refusing to accept the bribe and, therefore, left the country and may ask for asylum in Colombia. She was replaced by another judge who ruled in Correa's favor. The court awarded $40 million to the president for compensation and sentences the editor to three years in prison.

In spite of the fact that President Correa pardoned those at *El Universo,* he asserted that the "abuse press has been defeated."[84] His change of mind is attributed to the strong pressure by human rights and press freedom groups in Ecuador and around the world. Correa also mentioned that he would drop the case against those who wrote a book exposing the government's contracts with his big brother. In spite of these pardons, freedom of expression remains a problem in Correa's Ecuador.

In a visit to Peru in February 2012, Correa emphasized that his pardon of *El Universo's* editor should not be viewed as an ideological conversion. The Ecuadorian president called upon the Latin America's citizens to rebel against their countries' communication media, which reflect only interests of the rich.[85] In Latin America there exists the dictatorship of the communication media and the time is ripe to rebel against this abuse.

In reference to the pardon of *El Universo's* editor, Correa reiterated his view that the government leaves open the possibility of suing any newspaper that distorts the news. The government calls upon journalists not to defend the indefensible—those who insult and vilify the news. Referring to the Inter-American Commission of Human Rights (*Comisión Interamericana de Derechos Humanos,* CIDH), Correa asserted that he would not allow an international bureaucracy, which passes impudent decisions coming from Washington, to enforce its decisions on a sovereign state.[86]

In February 2012 a new law was passed that aims at silencing the press during elections. The law is intended to silence the private press during election periods. Article 21 of the law orders the mass media to refrain, directly or indirectly, from influencing public opinion. It is forbidden to express favorable or unfavorable opinions about any political candidate.[87] Press association in both Ecuador and abroad denounced the law, claiming that it violated the constitutional rights of free expression and opinion.

The Correa's administration created a new body to prosecute journalists, the National Electoral Council (*Consejo Nacional Electoral*), which by virtue of the new law would determine if a journalist's article could directly or indirectly benefit a political candidate or the electoral process.

An opposition legislator called upon Ecuador's Constitutional Court to declare this law unconstitutional, contradicting the democratic codes that would regulate the presidential voting of 2013. Correa repeated his claim that journalists are corrupt and liars.[88]

An opposition newspaper in Nicaragua, evaluating the fifth anniversary of Correa's coming to power, claimed the Ecuadorian president weakened the opposition, criminalized protest, and increased the authoritarian and totalitarian tendencies of the government.[89] In conjunction with this anniversary (January 14, 2007), was announced that 5,000 citizens' revolutionary committees were to be created and that they that should be in place before the 2013 elections. These committees were needed to reinforce citizens' participation in neighborhood communities and for implementing the official policy. In reality, like in Venezuela, the aim is to create citizens loyalty and readiness to fight in defending the regime.[90] The reelection of Correa in Ecuador in February 2013, similar to Chávez's reelection in October 2012, demonstrated that dependency on the state for people's livelihood was an important reason why these authoritarian leaders were reelected.[91]

As previously mentioned in the cases of both Venezuela and Bolivia, an important step in the weakening of democracy is the strengthening of the central state and decreasing the power of local governments. Bejamín Dang claims that Correa intensified the conflict between the central government and the Ecuadorian indigenous population.[92] The original Ecuadorian people believed that the state must be multinational, recognizing all tribes and ethnic groups in the country.

Correa embarked on modernizing projects, ignored the rights of the indigenous communities. The Ecuadorian president shut down the environmentalist group Ecological Action (*Acción Ecológica*) in his attempt to weaken dissent. Indigenous protests to the president's policies were followed by police repression and brutality. As a result of the confrontations with the indigenous people, the leader of the original population declared, "We reject President Rafael Correa's racist, authoritarian and anti-democratic statements, which violate the rights of [indigenous] nationalities and people enshrined in international convention and treaties."[93]

The indigenous leaders complained that the government accuses many of their people of being terrorists.[94] This is a grave accusation coming from a government that calls itself socialist. They cited an example of members who were accused of terrorism because they protested during a reunion of ALBA countries in Otavalo, Ecuador.[95] While Ecuador, unlike other countries, has not experienced episodes of terrorism, those who attempt to change the country's policies are labeled as committing acts of terror.

Antonio Gramsci was mentioned in the first chapter, emphasizing the crucial role of education in the process of transforming a country into communism. Like Chávez, Correa embarked on the process of changing education, especially university learning. The institutions of higher learning, as they did in Venezuela, resisted changes and called for mass protests. In October 2009 students, professors, and rectors from various universities mobilized in Quito (the country's capital) to express their opposition to the government's higher education law.[96]

A university rector declared that the proposed law is dangerous because it contains many elements that are unconstitutional and risky to the fundamental principles required if institutions of higher learning are to fulfill their duties. The government, on the other hand, claimed that the law is necessary for revolutionizing universities and so the state can restore its role in regulating superior education. The protests, according to the government, are directed by those who are afraid of losing their privileges.

The higher education law was amended several times. Important changes were introduced that attempted to further increase the government's role in the educational process. Article 70 of the 2010 amendment claimed that those who work in institutions of higher educational are considered to be public servants subjected to the government's laws.[97]

The president of the National Council of Higher Education (*Consejo Nacional de Educación Superior*, CONESUP) declared in 2010 that he would continue to fight for universities' autonomy and universal principles that govern institutions of higher learning. He claimed that the government decision to create an institution to supervise universities is unconstitutional.[98]

The first chapter contained a detailed analysis of civil-military relations in Venezuela. Chávez understood the importance of having a military that shares his basic beliefs and ideology in protecting his regime. The failed coup d'état against the Ecuadorian president on September 30, 2010, convinced Correa that he needs to follow steps similar to his Venezuelan counterpart's to ensure his regime's continued existence. The Ecuadorian president announced changes in the military hierarchy, denouncing those who were responsible for the attempt to oust him.[99]

Officers in the armed forces were implicated in the coup. The resignation of General Patricio Cárdenas on January 31, 2012, is directly linked to the failed attempt to oust the president. Correa will make structural changes in the armed forces. There are too many soldiers who do not understand their duties; some of the servicemen are in contact with the opposition, who want to generate discontent among the armed forces. According to the government's information, 1,199 police and military personnel participated in an attempt to oust the president,.[100] They received from two to eight years in prison depending on their direct involvement in the rebellion. Some claimed that the sentencing was not a judicial decision, but rather a political one.[101]

The failed coup of September 2010 was supposedly due to a salary dispute in the police department. Correa, like his Venezuelan counterpart, claimed that it was financed by the United States.[102] Chávez also made a similar claim in 2002. A year after the unsuccessful coup, Correa claimed that out of a police force of 40,000, only 1,000 officers participated in the revolt. Those who participated shouted slogans, chanting down with Venezuela and Cuba. The discord also involved certain military groups and the Ecuadorian press. On orders from certain military officers, the Quito's airport was closed.

Ecuador is a volatile state with fragile institutions. Since Correa assumed power, the bond market and direct foreign investment have been continuously falling. According to the economic analyst, the coup against Correa is a direct result of social and economic policies that reduced the president's popularity. Ecuador has not had access to external finance since the 2008 stoppage of payments on global bonds worth $3.2 billion. The problem in countries such as Ecuador is the lack of business pressure groups, capable of functioning as a political counterbalance.[103]

An illustration on how the Ecuadorian government is conducting its economic policies, how easy it is for an enterprise to operate in a country, is given the publication *Doing Business 2012*. Ecuador was placed in the 130th place out of 183 countries.[104] Other Latin America's countries, such as Chile, Peru, and Colombia gained higher places, 39, 41, and 42 respectfully. These countries are attempting to institute regulation reforms, in contrast to the majority of Caribbean countries and Ecuador. The criteria analyzed by *Doing Business* includes right to property, protection of investors, regulatory efficiency, the enterprise's openness, property registry, and the management of contractual permits.[105]

As previously mentioned, when analyzing Evo Morales's government, it revealed beyond any doubt that Bolivia is a narcotic-state. A similar tendency can be observed in Ecuador, there is a strong partnership between the Colombian terrorist group FARC and the Correa regime. Some analysis views this cooperation as Ecuador's moving in the direction of becoming a narcotic democracy.[106]

Several of Correa's assistants had direct links with FARC. The International Institute for Strategic Studies (London) reported that during the 2006 campaign President Correa received the sum of $100,000 as a financial contribution from FARC.[107] The information was gained from 8,382 electronic documents found in the computer of Raúl Reyes, a top FARC commander who was killed in March 2008 by the Colombian army across the border in Ecuador. Chávez was also involved, but both Correa and the Venezuela president claimed that the files were faked. Interpol nevertheless vouched for their authenticity.[108]

Fernando Carrión, a security expert, claimed that Ecuador has been converted into an important platform of narcotic traffic.[109] The country exports 270 tons of cocaine yearly. Narcotic traffic is a problem shared by all Latin America's countries. Mexico and Central America have suffered from violence generated by drug cartels and mafias, which also operate in Ecuador.

There are several important reasons why narcotic traffic flourished in Ecuador. The country's geographical location among producing and consuming drug's countries is an important reason. The Amazon zone has many maritime routes that bring drugs to Brazil. Ecuador's official currency, the dollar, is another factor that contributes to the increase in narcotic traffic. All financial services can be performed by the same currency. The weakness of Ecuador's institutions is another factor contributing to narcotic traffic. The debility of the judicial branch and lack of sufficient police and armed forces to combat this phenomenon are also contributing factors. The lack of intelligence work and a broad strategy to confront this problem constitute other factors.

Previously, the term Bolibourgeoisie was mentioned, referring to Venezuela's new class that emerged as a result of Chávez's policies. These people became rich as a result of their close relations with the president. A similar trend can be observed in Ecuador.

A diplomatic suitcase with 40 kilograms of cocaine, belonging to the Ecuadorian Foreign Minister Ricardo Patiño was discovered on its way to Ecuador's general consulate in Milan, Italy.[110] A foreign ministry spokesman claimed that the suitcase was opened en route to Italy. He asserted that the suitcase's seal was changed and contained the mark of Chile's foreign minister.[111] This official view was disputed by experts on diplomacy and security, who asserted that shipments of diplomatic suitcases are rigorously protected.[112] The claim was made that the travelling suitcase was sealed and was not opened until its arrival in Milan.

Opposition members of the Ecuadorian legislative branch asked the general comptroller to investigate the matter by having a special audit should be performed at the Ecuadorian embassies located in Italy, Holland, and Belgium for the period September 2011-March 2012. The opposition members called upon the foreign minister to resign. An article on this topic emphasizes that it is of utmost importance to investigate people in high positions in the narcotic traffic trade. These include Correa's sister, Piñera Correa, and Pedro Delgado, the director of Ecuadorian central bank and a first cousin of the president, as well as Jorge Luis Redrobán Quevedo, an Ecuadorian owner of two restaurants in Milan. His dinning places were used as distribution centers for illegal drugs. The Italian police detained these people. Pictures of the restaurant owner with all the people close to president Correa were circulated on the Internet.[113]

An editorial in the opposition newspaper *Hoy.ec* strongly criticizes the Correa government for not taking a serious step to shed a light on the capturing of a diplomatic valise containing 40 kilograms of cocaine.[114] The investigation proceeds very slowly without providing any information to the public. Attorney General Galo Chiriboga has not taken any concrete action in this case. The crime of putting cocaine in a diplomatic suitcase was committed in Ecuador and it affects the country's reputation. It is an embarrassing scandal and calls for immediate clarification.[115]

In Ecuador there have not been an indictment against Foreign Minister Ricardo Patiño; the Italian police, on the other hand, arrested four Ecuadorians citizens implicated in this illegal activity. They are implicated in the crime of transporting cocaine in a diplomatic suitcase and expected to receive prison terms of between six to twenty years.[116]

The January 2012 visit of the Iranian president to ALBA countries is viewed merely as a propaganda device. The article mentions that Vitoria Muland, from the U.S. Department of State, after the Iranian President Ahmadinejad, concluded his Latin American tour, asserted that those countries which hosted the Iranian president would be exposed to new sanctions from the United States.

Nicaragua, like to other ALBA countries, has gradually proceeded toward an authoritarian regime. The world mass media publications and the Nicaraguan opposition press strongly condemned the November 2011 elections and viewed them as a fraudulent. Luis Calleja, the director of Nicaraguan Democratic Movement, said that it has been obvious that Ortega's November 2011 election violated the constitution, as well as the country's laws.[117] He defined a democratic state as a country where the executive branch is elected through free elections and that has transparency and independent institutions. These conditions, lamentably, do not exist in Nicaragua.[118]

Joel Hirst offered a detailed analysis of the 2011 electoral campaign in Nicaragua. Harassment of the opposition has been an important characteristic of Daniel Ortega's regime. A family that was known to be a supporter of the opposition Liberal party, headed by Fabio Gadea, was approached by the local police, and together with the local chapter of Ortega's party (FSLN) and people from the Municipal Electoral Authority, shouted that they intended to kill all the liberals.[119]

Two people were assassinated in the encounter. When members of the Nicaraguan Center of Human Rights (el Centro Nicaraguense de Derechos Humanos) arrived at the scene, they found more than eighteen bullets. The matter is under investigation, but reflects how Ortega's supporters are attempting to intimidate voters.

Ortega's candidacy was illegal because the constitution prohibits presidential reelection. The Nicaraguan president claimed that the constitution violates human rights. The Supreme Electoral Council (*el Consejo Supremo Electoral*) controlled by Ortega did not grant accreditation to all national electoral observers. The European Union and observers from the Organization of American States (OAS) called the elections opaque and worrisome. The U.S. State Department claimed that the elections were not transparent.

The fraud became obvious during the congressional elections. The candidates for the legislative branch received 100,000 more votes than the president. This allowed Ortega's party the Sandinista Front (FSLN), to receive fourteen additional seats in congress and obtain the majority. According to an organization observing the election, 34% of voting centers lacked a process for eligibility verification; 13% of the voters could not arrive at the designed voting areas; 20% of the voting places did not have observers from the opposition parties; in 20 municipalities, the voters were intimidated by the police and progovernment forces.[120]

Another article written before the November 2011 elections claimed that Ortega's regime adopted illegal procedures to assure their victory in the forthcoming elections.[121] The Supreme Electoral Council adopted a procedure of requiring citizens to have identity cards in order to vote. Those who are members of Ortega's party received preferential treatment in obtaining the card. More than 450,000 Nicaraguans lacked identity cards five month before the elections and there is no estimate of how many people are eligible to vote.

In the 1990 elections, Ortega lost with 40% of the vote. In 1995 he received 38% of the vote, but won as a result of the fragmentation of the opposition parties. In 2008 Ortega's party was defeated in the municipal elections, but won as a result of fraud. Carache correctly predicted that the November 2011 elections would be marked by fraudulent practices.[122] In 1989 Daniel Ortega could not manipulate the elections and gave power to Violeta Chamorro, who replaced him. He made sure not to repeat this mistake.

Sergio Ramírez, writing before the November 2011 elections in Nicaragua, did not have any doubt that Ortega would win the elections.[123] There has never been an electoral campaign in Nicaragua characterized by such inequality of resources. Chávez gave Ortega $4.6 million during the period 2007-2011. With the Venezuelan president's oil money, Ortega was able to buy, equip, and renew five television channels and ten radio stations, which were continuously praising the Nicaraguan president. It also financed street advertisements, shirts, flags, and hundreds of vehicles that carry Ortega's messages. The state's ambulances, official government cars, and the health system were mobilized during the electoral campaign to assist in Ortega's reelection.

Ramírez asserts that democracy is in danger and may disappear after Ortega's reelection. Many people in Nicaragua risked their lives to free themselves from the Somoza's dictatorship. The Nicaraguans need to fight and not to return to a government similar to the one they disposed. Commander Tomás Borge, in presenting Ortega's presidential candidacy, said the following: "The revolution is a source of rights and its positions are always legitimate and just beyond the formal and concrete."[124] In other words, in behalf of the revolution, everything is allowed.

The ideas advocated by Antonio Gramsci on the need to advance the cause of communism gradually have been implemented in Nicaragua. Gradually, attempting to control the mass media, Ortega is following in Chávez' footsteps, in aspiring to establish an authoritarian regime. While the 2011 elections were marked by irregularities and criticism of many international observers, the majority of local media has exhibited a different perspective.[125] The election result was described as a "resounding victory." Ortega's government was able to control half of Nicaraguan television stations. His greater presence in the media contributed to his electoral success.

In the first chapter, Milovan Djilas' 1950s book, *The New Class*, was analyzed and applied to the situation in Venezuela. The Chávez regime is creating a new class (Bolibourgeoisie) composed of those people who are in close relations with the Venezuelan president.

A similar trend can be seen in Nicaragua, where the vast resources which derive primarily from Chávez's oil money are not directed toward improving people's standard of living, but are channeled toward Ortega, his family, and his supporters.[126] Ortega's families are in charge of funds deriving from the Venezuelan oil accord, communication media, and oil distributions.

Yadira Leets Marín, Ortega's wife, and his first-born son are administrating the oil distribution company bought by Venezuela. Juan Carlos Ortega Murillo, the president's son is director of a television station, channel 8. Members of Ortega's family are in charge of mixed Venezuelan-Nicaraguan companies that import oil from Venezuela. Alba Caruna, a family member, is in charge of the Sandinista's state bank. A lot of the bank's money is used to enrich Ortega's family.

While Ortega, his family, and associates are enriching themselves, the rest of the population does not benefit from the vast money coming from the Chávez regime. Only 12.5% of the population claims that they were aided by the country's social programs. 87.5% assert the opposite.[127]

Salinas Maldonado, a journalist from Spain, visited Nicaragua in November 2009. He witnessed big billboards of smiling Ortega (similar to those showing Mao-Tse-Tung in China). Some of the placards announced the end of poverty, while misery could be seen from the window of a bus.[128]

Starting in 2006, when Ortega assumed power, his promise to reduce poverty and bring more justice was not fulfilled. 79% of the population lives on $2 a day. Poverty contributed to the atmosphere of political uncertainty. Many donor countries, as a result of the fraud in the municipal elections of November 8, 2008, reduced their assistance to Nicaragua. Ortega decided to reduce the country's budget, especially in the area of health and education.

The government attempted to increase revenues by imposing tax reforms. The reforms encountered general discontent. Taxes were raised on stores, saving accounts, pensions, and foreign remittances. Most of the country's economic problems could have been solved with Chávez's monetary assistance, which in 2008 amounted to $457 million. However, as previously mentioned, the Venezuelan economic assistance is used in a discretionary manner. With the Venezuelan funds, Ortega bought two MI-17 helicopters made in Russia, with an estimated price ranging $3 to $5 million. Some claim that the helicopters are solely used by Ortega and his family.[129] Maldonado concludes his article by claiming that Ortega is the prototype of a new Latin American authoritarian leader, who employs the military to harass, repress, coerce, and frighten his opponents.

While Ortega, his family, and associates enrich themselves, the country's infrastructure, especially the schools, are deteriorating rapidly. The Nicaraguan government claims that only 40% of the country's schools have shortages of qualified teachers and infrastructure problems. This claim is disputed by the director of the World Bank for Central America; Felipe Jaramillo asserts that 80% of the schools in the country lack competent teachers.[130] Eight out of ten schools are in bad shape.

According to Luis Fleischman and Nancy Menges, Ortega has followed in Chávez's footsteps in strengthening relations with drug cartels.[131] According to these authors, Nicaragua under Ortega may turn into another narcotic state; providing key transit routes to drug cartels and hence increasing anarchy and chaos in the region.

Roberto Cajina, an expert on security and defense, insists that Nicaragua faces a danger from small narcotic retailers. While the police exert great efforts on and attention to drug cartels, the small narcotic retailers are ignored.[132] Narcotic drugs are used as a replacement for money and bribery and given to those who are supposed to fight this phenomenon. The drug cartels are operating and prosper in a culture of corruption, lack of proper institutions, and a fragile justice system. More cocaine is sold locally, which steadily increases the number of drug addicts.

The importance of the armed forces as a protector of Ortega's regime was previously mentioned. Unlike Costa Rica, which decided not to have an army, Ortega decided to follow in Chávez's footsteps and establish obligatory military service.[133]

Education of the youth is of crucial importance for the regime's survival. In the first chapter, Antonio Gramsci was mentioned as one who understands the primary role of education in the establishment of communism. Ortega's regime is using the Sandinista youth in an attempt to legitimize and assure the continuation of the regime. The youngsters, who are dressed in pink and white, are compared by Amalia del Cid to similar movements in Hitler's Germany, Mussolini's Italy, Stalin's Soviet Union, and Fidel Castro's Cuba.[134] There are certain differences among these groups. The Ortega's youth, for example, do not persecute Jews. Those who join receive many benefits; among them the opportunity to land a government job. During the period 2007-2012, Venezuela gave approximately $2 million to this movement.[135] However, in spite of the assistance received it is always short of funds.

In the first chapter, a detailed analysis was done on the conflict between church and state in Chávez's Venezuela. The main idea that the church is opposed to Chávez's attempts to modify Venezuela's social and political culture was emphasized.

In Nicaragua a similar trend can be seen as the church opposes the Ortega government's efforts to shape family life and politically indoctrinate them.[136] Ortega's party, the Sandinista Front, intends to subordinate various state institution to the Council of Citizens' Power (*Consejo del Poder Ciudadano*), directed by Ortega's wife Mrs. Rosario Murillo. Archbishop Leopoldo Brenes, a Nicaraguan church leader, said that the family is in danger when groups with certain political orientations interfere in the domestic domain, which the church considered as a sacred place. The

Archbishop asserted that parents, the father and mother, need to be the only ones who decide their children's future.[137]

Venezuela's Chávez and Iran's Cooperation in International Terrorism
The views of Hugo Chávez and his Iranian counterpart, Mahmud Ahmadinejad, are not similar in their attempt to create a new international system. However, they share a common attribute, the need to weaken the United States as an important player in the international arena. The strong cooperation between Chávez and Ahmadinejad attempts to achieve this aim, a precondition for their ability to form a new international order. In order to achieve this goal, strong cooperation between the two countries and terrorist organizations such as FARC, Hezbollah, Islamic Jihad, Hamas, ETA, and others have been established.

Chávez would like to create a new international order where socialism of the twenty-first century would become the dominant force among nations. Ahmadinejad, on the other hand, would like to create a world theocracy ruled by his version of the Koran. During a meeting in Tehran in February 2012, Iranian President Mahmoud Ahmadinejad and Hezbollah's leader Hassan Nasrallah jointly declared their view of how the future international system should be. Every Muslim, according to them, has the duty to wipe Israel off the map. "If all Jews gathered in Israel, it would save us trouble of going after them worldwide."[138] Israel, according to the Iranian view, is a "cancerous tumor that should be cut and will be cut."[139]

According to Hezbollah's view the elimination of Israel and the world's Jewry constitutes a precondition for the creation of a worldwide Islamic state. The terrorist attacks by Iran (Hezbollah) against the Argentinian Jewish Committee (1992 and 1994) are an illustration of this tendency. The Iranian Supreme Leader admitted that his country assists Israel's enemies such as Hezbollah and Hamas. It is interesting to note that the Iranian President Mahmoud Ahmadinejad visiting Egypt in February 2013 claimed that his country has no intention of attacking Israel.[140] In order to understand this declaration, it is important to comprehend that lying is permitted if it advances the cause of Islam.

In 2011 Chávez wrote a letter to the UN Secretary General in support of a Palestinian state. In this letter, he shared the opinion of many Third World countries, which claimed that Zionism is a form of racism. The United Nations' resolution 181 of 1947 declared that two states should be established, one Jewish and the other Arab. According to Chávez, this is illegal.[141]

Chávez's close relation with the Jackal further proves the Venezuelan President's support of terrorism. The Jackal allied himself with pro-Palestinian radicals who plotted terrorist attacks in Europe, in the 1970s. He later joined the Red Army faction. The kidnapping and assassination of the Italian Prime Minister Aldo Moro in 1978 revealed the Red Army's far-reaching arm. The Venezuelan terrorist praised Osama bin Laden as a "symbol of modern Jihad."[142] Chávez praised the Jackal as a "revolutionary fighter" and claimed that his government would defend an honorable citizen who participated in fighting for great causes.[143]

The Jackal was considered in the 1970s the public enemy number one in Europe. He received support from both the Eastern Europe's Communist states and the Arab radical countries such as Libya and Syria. The Jackal's pronouncement "long live Chávez" is an indication of the affinity between the Venezuelan president and the terrorist.[144] The pictures of Che Guevara and Carlos the Jackal inundated Western Europe. However, Europe was able to free itself from such type of revolutionary terrorism.

There is no question that these models for a future international system, if implemented would clash with each other. Some analysts predict conflict, which would face the Venezuelan leader and his Iranian counterpart. Pilar Rahola asks important questions relating to the close ties between Chávez and the Iranian regime. How can one reconcile Karl Marx's writings with those of the fundamentalist interpretation of the Koran?[145] How can there be a compromise between the ideas advocated by Che Guevara and those by the most tyrannical version of Islam? Referring to the Iranian president's January 2012 visit to Venezuela, Rahola claims that the applauding in Caracas of a regime that stones females is absurd.

This cooperation between Chávez and the Iranian regime is labeled by Rahola as "the evil alliance." It is based on shared totalitarian traits. The two countries suppress individual liberties, the opposition is debilitated, and critics are threatened. While poverty is on the rise, those in power are increasing their wealth.

Chávez enables the radical Shias to enter South America and convert the indigenous people to Islam. The Venezuelan leader is the guarantor of the spread of extreme Islam all over Latin America, and together with his ALBA partners, supports the delirious Iranian nuclear program. How can one accept the ideological perversions that unify Islam with Bolivarism? How can the stoning of women and gays be related to Chávez's ideas? Rahola concludes his article by claiming that the ability of Iran to obtain nuclear weapons may be compared to Hitler with an atomic bomb.[146]

Vivian Akel claims that Venezuela's social blindness prevents the country from noticing the true intentions of the Persian Empire.[147] The aim of the Persian Empire (Iran) is to expand its religion in Latin America. Venezuela allied itself with the enemy of the West. The Venezuelan people need to be proud of their heritage and not emulate a reactionary model, which will force the teaching of Islam in schools on all educational levels and force women to wear burkas.

Marion González expresses the view that Chávez is ignorant and does not understand the true intentions of the Iranian regime. The Venezuelan President claims that Iran eventually will embrace socialism. The truth is that Iranian President Ahmadinejad is a conservative, a believer in a theocracy, an enemy of Socialism and Communism.[148] Islam, according to González, wants to spread and impose itself with blood and fire; this is the meaning of the sword of Islam.[149]

In the Persian Empire, Christians were worth half the value of Muslims. During the Iran-Iraq war (1980-1988), children less than twelve years old were used to remove explosive from mined fields. The kids were brainwashed to believe that if they died, a secure place in paradise would be waiting for them. The mothers, who came to collect the dead bodies, complained that the corpses were dismembered.[150]

There are about six million Muslims who reside in Latin America. The majority of Muslims are Sunni and the minority Shia. Muslim population centers with Shia concentration form a convenient recruitment center for Iran's terrorism.[151] Iran is also engaged in extensive social, cultural, and religious activities aimed at exporting the Islamic revolution and converting people (especially Indians) to Shia Islam.

Hezbollah, an Iranian proxy, is directly engaged, according to intelligence reports from several countries, in South America's cocaine trade.[152] Hezbollah, for years received $200 million annually from Iran, with additional aid from Syria. However, as a result of the economic embargo on Iran, the aid to Hezbollah has been diminished. The Syria's civil war and the damages caused to Lebanon as a result of the 2006 war with Israel extenuated the need for additional funds to the terrorist organization. This caused a stronger reliance on criminal enterprises, especially relying on South America's drug trade.[153]

The Iranian president extended a strong effort to deemphasize the differences between their outlooks of future world. In a visit to Ecuador on January 2012, Iranian President Ahmadinejad declared that capitalism is on a dead-end street and will face the same fate as Soviet Union's Communism.[154] According to the Iranian president the decline of capitalism will create a new world order dominated by justice, peace, and friendship. The religious perceptions of brotherhood and solidarity among nations will be attained.

Chávez is used by the Iranian government as a tool of promoting its interests in Latin America. According to a U.S. House Committee of Foreign Affairs Iranian President Ahmadinejad asked Chávez to interfere with the former Argentinian President Néstor Kirshner, in order to change the country's policy and allow Iran access ot Argentinian nuclear technology.[155]

Starting back in the 1980s, Iran and Argentina collaborated on nuclear programs, which were cancelled by former President Carlos Menem, after the Iranian (Hezbollah) terrorist attack in 1992 and 1994 against the Argentinian Jewish Center and the Israeli Embassy in Buenos Aires. Argentina was asked to abandon the judicial investigation and renounce bringing to Justice Iranian Defense Minister Ahmad Vahidi, who played an important role in these attacks. In exchange, Iran would invest in an Argentinian economy.

The improved relations between Chávez and Argentinian President Cristina Fernández were able to achieve the Iranian objective. In the reunion of South American countries (Mercosur) in August 2010, the Argentinian president modified her views about Iran and rapprochement occurred. Fernandez's government decided to freeze investigations regarding Iran's terrorist attacks on Argentinian soil.[156]

The visit of Iranian President Mahmud Ahmadinejad to Venezuela and the ALBA countries in January 2012 received a lot of criticism from the opposition press. Maibort Petit claims that what unites the Venezuelan president and his Iranian counterpart is their anti-American sentiment.[157] Ahmadinejad referred to Chávez as a "real brother" and assured that both countries will join hands in fighting imperialism. Both leaders are united in fomenting hatred; the two countries sharply increased the purchase of arms.

However, Petit correctly asserts that these relations do not serve Venezuela's interests or those of other Latin American countries. They only serves those corrupt leaders who mortgaged the future of their countries in order to pursue political objectives alien to the collective well-being of their people. Chávez and his ALBA partners handed the future of their countries to the radical Iranian cause, without taking into account the consequences of their actions.

Venezuela and its partners do not realize that they are hosting a dictator with blood on his hands. In 2011, 552 people were executed in Iran, the second highest number in the world after China.[158] Helping Iran to violate sanctions against it and comply with its objectives against Israel and the United States constitute acts of insanity which will be punished when sanity returns to the region.

The economic accords between Iran, Venezuela, and its partners proclaimed that their agreements differ from neoliberal globalization practices. It is based accordingly on the need for sustainable development, social justice, sovereignty of all the countries involved, and the right of self-determination.[159] The author of this article (his name is not mentioned) refers to such statements as being propaganda. It is too early to predict how the death of Chávez will impact Venezuela-Iran relations. It is also, not yet clear how the new elected Iranian President will alter the country's policies.

Milos Alcalay asserts correctly that Venezuela and its ALBA partners applauded Iran's attempt at blackmail with a threat to close the Strait of Hormuz, which constitutes a clear violation of the international right of free navigation.[160] The official visit of the Iranian president to the "Bolivarian Alliance" demonstrated the arrogant and stubborn attitudes of these governments, which have been marching against the direction taken by civilized nations.

Several opposition articles on Venezuela and its allies stressed the fact that Ahmadinejad's 2012 trip to Latin America did not include Brazil.[161] The previous Brazilian president, Luis Ignacio Lula da Silva visited Iran in 2010 and negotiated a deal for Iran to receive uranium. This visit stirred a lot of internal criticism; the agreement was used by the Iranian as a tool for derailing the United Nations sanctions against their country. Lula's replacement, Dilma Rousseff decided not to follow in the predecessor's steps. She did not sympathize with the Iranian cause and decided to freeze Brazil's and Iran's relations.

President Rousseff decided publicly to emphasize that she preferred to have close relations with the United States rather than with Iran.[162] The Brazilian president figured that her country's economy will further benefit from good relations with Western countries. Rousseff manifested its preference when, in March 2011, Brazil supported a United Nations investigation of Iran's violation of human rights. The Iranian government lamented the fact that Rousseff destroyed the good relations established during Lula's presidency.

Juan Arias further elaborates on the reasons why Ahmadinejad did not visit Brazil. He claims that President Rousseff, unlike her predecessor, is practical and less influenced by ideology.[163] In 2012 the Brazilian president had reduced her country's commercial relations with Iran by 73%. The president of the Brazilian Foreign Trade Association, José Agosto de Castro, pinpointed the major difference between President Rousseff and her predecessor. Lula, the former president, is more political and Rousseff has her feet on the ground; in commerce there is no ideology.[164]

In an interview, Rousseff was decisive and expressed her moral indignation against the stoning death penalty given to women in Iran (she cited the stoning of Sakineh Ashtiani as one example of this brutal practice). She is appalls and cannot accept such barbaric acts, which are characteristic of the Middle Ages.[165]

Chávez and Narcotic-Terrorism

A Chávez inner circle member, Minister of Interior and Justice Pedro Carreno, claimed that in spite of the capitalism crisis, imperialism has not declined. It employs the terms *terrorism* and *narcotic traffic* as an excuse of invading or interfering in the internal affairs of other countries.[166]

It is my intention to disapprove the minister's thesis and demonstrate that narcotic traffic has been employed by the Chávez regime as a tool for weakening the United States and enriching those who are close to the Venezuelan leader (Bolibourgeoisie). In some respects, the Chávez regime is following the nineteen century British policy toward China, introducing opium to the Asian giant country in order to weaken the will of the people to defend themselves. It led to the Opium War, which was characterized as a Western conspiracy against China.[167]

The Chávez regime did not invent narcotic traffic as a tool to weaken the United States. The Communist leadership of Cuba learned the lessons from the Opium War. In the mid 1960s at a meeting between Cuban Defense Minister Raúl Castro and the Czech Ministry of Defense, the issue of drug trafficking was discussed as an ideological weapon to be used against the United States.[168]

Cuba's drug involvement started in 1961, when high-ranking officials discussed the setting up of a cocaine traffic network. In 1982 a Federal Grand Jury in Miami indicted four senior Cuban government officials on charges of conspiring to use Cuba as a safe haven for transporting drugs into United States via Colombia.[169] On February 7, 1983, a former Cuban intelligence officer confirmed in his testimony Cuba's involvement in the drug trade as a deliberate campaign to destabilize the United States.[170] The trial of the strongman Manuel Antonio Noriega revealed that Fidel Castro's brother Raúl was linked to drug trafficking.[171] Fidel Castro used the drug trade as a tool to enrich himself.

It is not surprising that Chávez, who considers Fidel Castro as a father figure and model, followed similar policies in using his country as a haven for narcotic trafficking. Similar feelings were expressed, by Fidel Castro who said that he considered Chávez to be a true son.[172] As will be described in a later stage of this research, Castro also used drug trafficking as an instrument to enrich those people whom he favored. Chávez would probably partially agree with the Iranian revolutionary guard proclamation, "We are told that the drugs will destroy the sons and daughters of the West, and we must kill them. Their lives are worth less because they are not Muslims."[173]

Elizabeth Burgos reaffirms Cuba's employing of narcotic traffic as influencing Chávez's policies.[174] She claims that the decision of the Inter-American Commission of Human Rights, (CIDH), an autonomous organ of Organization of the American States (OAS), that the Organic Law against Organized Crime and Financing Terrorism (March 2012), constitutes the reason why Chávez was forced to abandon this organization. This law runs counter to Castro's and his mentor Chávez's belief that they can gain access to power by imposing a totalitarian system. Venezuela needs to ensure that the country is not under the surveillance of International organization.

A 2010 report claims that Venezuela became a secure bridge for drug traffic in South America.[175] As mentioned previously, Morales expelled the United States' Drug Enforcement Agency (DEA) from Bolivia; Chávez decreased their presence in Venezuela. Bolivia and Venezuela are the only countries that are labeled by the United States as failing to combat illegal drugs.[176] Venezuela is used as a departure point for half the cocaine going to Europe by sea. General Henry Rangel Silva was accused by the U.S. Treasury Department in 2008, working closely with the Revolutionary Armed Forces of Colombia (FARC), helped to transport drugs through Venezuela. On January 2012 General Rangel was appointed Defense Minister.[177]

In September 2008, the former Venezuelan Minister Ramón Rodríguez Chacin and the director of the intelligence services were added to the list of active narcotic traffickers by the U.S. Department of Treasury for links with the terrorist organization FARC.[178] In 2009 the Treasury Department sanctioned two Venezuelan citizens of Lebanese origin, including one with diplomatic credentials, who were accused of supporting the terrorist organization Hezbollah; while Venezuelan-Colombian relations have had their ups and downs, under the presidency of Santos there were significant improvements. In 2009, however, the former Colombian Defense Minister Gabriel Silva claimed that Venezuela is used as a drug route to Central America.[179]

Whereas there have been improvements in Venezuelan-Colombian relations, especially after the Makled affair, which will be later discussed, the Chávez regime has allowed the country to be used as a preferred route of cocaine traffic in South America.[180] Although there were some improvements in the antinarcotic cooperation between Colombia and Venezuela, the collaboration with the United States on this matter remains at a minimum level. According to a U.S. State Department report, the weakness of the Venezuelan judicial system and the increased corruption of high-level officials makes the country a preferred route for drug trade in South America.

Former Mexican president Vicente Fox accused President Chávez of facilitating drug trafficking toward the northern area of western hemisphere and indirectly contributing to the rise of crime rates in Mexico.[181] Similar accusations were made by former Venezuelan Supreme Court Judge Eladio Aponte, who defected to the United States. He claimed that Chávez's government is a bastion for narcotic traffic.[182]

Hezbollah, also known as the "Party of God," decided to fully engage in criminal activities, cooperating and making business transactions with Colombian drug cartels. How can a party claiming to be religious engage in criminal activities? The answer given is that any means that advance Iran or its proxy Hezbollah's main objective, which is to spread the Islamic revolution, is permissible. Like other authoritarian and totalitarian movements (or states), it is permitted to use any available means in order to achieve its aim. In this respect it becomes of utmost importance that the chairwoman of the House Foreign Affairs Committee, llenna Ros-Lehtineni called for changing the traditional view of drug cartels as a law enforcement issue and classify them as a foreign terrorist organization.[183]

Chávez's relations with the Colombian terrorist Revolutionary Armed Forces (FARC) are an illustration of both his populist tendencies and his not having clear guiding principles. Ideologically, there exists a great deal of affinity between the Venezuelan president and FARC. Political interests were the primary cause that determined these relations. FARC is a narcotic trafficking terrorist group operates freely in Venezuela and has an office in the presidential palace (Miraflores).[184]

FARC is a Marxist group that originated in the 1970s with the aim of taking over the government in Colombia by violence. FARC supported Chávez before his election in 1999 and contributed money for his campaign.[185] In 2001, Ramón Rodríguez Chacin, who at that time was the second in command of the Venezuela intelligence services, became the main liaison between FARC and the Venezuelan government. Chacin, who later was appointed interior minister, in a public farewell speech gave full support to FARC and declared, "Keep up your spirit and fight, we are with you."[186]

On March 1, 2008, the Colombian army, as previously mentioned, crossed the Ecuadorian border and raided a group of FARC members, including a senior commander Raúl Reyes. During 1990s Reyes was the leader of an international network representing sympathizers of FARC. Starting with the year 2000 Reyes maintained an archive of electronic mail that included thirty years of strategic documents, records of periodic conferences, and other reunions that constitutes essential milestones in FARC's evolution.[187]

The Colombian authorities gave the captured materials to INTERPOL, which conducted a forensic investigation in order to validate the documents' integrity. The captured information revealed that FARC intended to develop an ambitious plan in order to come to power. It included spreading guerrilla warfare in all Colombia's rural zones, manipulating political and social tensions in the cities, exploit the interest of other parties to reach a peaceful agreement, and using any available means in order to achieve a military victory. To obtain political and military support from countries bordering Colombia was considered of primary importance. The military impact of FARC reached its peak in 1998 when Colombia was declared a failed state.[188]

FARC's international strategy was to assure financial and military support. During the Cold War, it achieved its aim by receiving aid from countries with similar ideologies such as China, the Soviet Union, and North Korea. Subsequent to September 11, 2001 (9/11), FARC has been considered a terrorist organization. A concerted effort was made to exploit the tensions between Colombia and its neighbors.

The fall of the Soviet Union forced FARC to look for new sources of income. These included political sympathizers all over the world, narcotic trafficking, and support of foreign armed groups, such as the Spanish terrorist assemblage, ETA. Chávez allowed FARC to utilize Venezuela as an operational staging ground. The Venezuelan government supported FARC's office in Caracas by furnishing intelligence reports, providing documentations, and giving other forms of assistance.

After the 2002 failed coup d'état in Venezuela, FARC was able to exploit the atmosphere of fear and paranoia in the country, providing its experience in urban guerrilla's warfare to the Chávez regime.[189] In the event of a U.S. invasion of Venezuela, FARC was viewed as a strategic ally. Chávez gave $50 million to FARC as an advanced payment, promising to give $250 million later. The captured documents also indicate that Venezuela asked Colombian rebels to kill opposition members.[190]

Gustavo Coronel stressed the criminal nature of FARC. Four hostages captured by the terrorist organization were assassinated in 2011.[191] This barbaric act verifies once more the criminal character of this group. The cruelty of FARC should influence the Chávez regime to abandon its protection of the terrorist organization. This, Coronel claims, has not yet happened.

The new FARC's leader Timoshenko was Chávez's guest for some time. Coronel asks how it is possible for the Colombian president to plan a visit to Chávez, a criminal, who plotted with FARC to damage Colombia. One cannot understand how President Juan Manuel Santos reversed the policies of his predecessor Álvaro Uribe. The assassination of the hostages,

Coronel claims must remind Santos that crimes committed by FARC are not reconcilable.[192]

U.S. Department of Treasury warned in 2011 of the danger posed by FARC members' presence in Venezuela. It revealed the strong link between financing terrorism and Venezuela's assistance to FARC. The connection between Chávez and FARC deserves a special attention.[193]

Venezuela under Chávez became a center for international terrorism. While previously the links between the Chávez regime and Iran, Hezbollah, Hamas, and Palestinian Jihad were described, there are also connections with European terrorist groups, such as ETA[194] (a terrorist group in Spain, which wants to bring independence to the Basque people). Two of ETA's members, Iraiz Gesalga Fernández and Urtiaga Valderrama, were arrested in France.

The Spanish newspaper *El Mundo* reported that these ETA members were interviewed in Caracas and lived in Venezuela from September 11 to October 11, 2008. Their role was to establish secure channels between ETA and the Venezuelan government. Their aim was also to consult FARC members.[195]

Judge Eloy Velasco from Spain's antiterrorism court asserted that "Venezuelan governmental cooperation" with ETA and FARC, finances its activities through narcotic traffic.[196] Evidence exists that the Chávez regime is coordinating an illegal association between FARC and ETA, the magistrate claimed. In 2007 ETA members were escorted to a Venezuela jungle where they taught their FARC counterparts how to handle explosions.[197]

Moisés Naim, a famous journalist, whose articles have been published in many countries, was quoted in 2007 as saying," Whenever the narcotic traffic economy flourishes it produces political consequences. The huge sum of money involved in this trade produces high levels of corruption and complicity in the highest echelons."[198]

In May 2012 Naim further elaborated on this idea and coined the important term *mafia state*.[199] Mafia states are not states that criminal networks take over, but inversely, ones where the government takes control of drug cartels and other illegal groups in order to promote and defend the national interests, especially those of the ruling elite. The criminal networks are put at the state's service. In addition to Venezuela, the list of mafia states includes countries such as Bulgaria, Guinea-Bissau, Montenegro, North Korea, and Afghanistan.

While history furnishes ample examples of monarchies using pirates and mercenaries; democracies recruited mafias to achieve their objectives; a noted example was U.S. CIA's decision to recruit the mafia in order to assassinate Fidel Castro in 1960. These examples differ sharply from what has been happening in Venezuela, for example, where the criminal networks are an integral part of the government. Venezuelan former Supreme Court Judge Aponte, as previously mentioned, offered ample evidence which confirmed that high-level state functionaries are the principal bosses of important transnational criminal groups.[201]

Naim concludes his article by asserting that contemporary mafia states acquired importance that obliges us to rethink traditional concepts, which view the world as composed of nation-states and nongovernmental organizations that are constantly interacting with each other. The coduct of new mafia states is not yet completely understood, partially because not enough attention was paid to its existence.[202]

The Makled affair is a classic example of Naim's mafia state concept. Naim furnishes examples from the Makled affair in order to illuminate the concept of mafia states. Makled's scandal received a lot of attention, especially from the Venezuelan opposition press, and it shed an important light on the operations of the Chávez regime and his inner circles.

Walid Makled, a Syrian-Venezuelan narcotic terrorist was arrested in August 2010 in Colombia. U.S. authorities had visited Makled at least three times in a Colombian jail. Both the United States and Venezuela demanded his extradition for crimes such as cocaine trade; extortion; kidnapping; terrorism training; and cooperation with FARC, Hezbollah, and Iran's ongoing attempt to develop nuclear weapons.[203]

The official Venezuelan view was that Makled was a criminal engaged in narcotic traffic and, therefore, needed to be investigated and brought to justice by the country's judicial system. In reality, as Luis Egana correctly described, Makled has been a good illustration of how the Chávez regime operates. Makled's crimes implicated high-level officials—generals; admirals; members of the legislative branch; high-ranking officials in the police department; and judges, including those who serve on the Supreme Court.[204] In summary, a sample of the highest echelons, the elite of civil and military strata. These accusations do not solely derive from what Makled testified; there also exists ample evidence to support this evidence.[205]

Makled was very helpful to Chávez in ending the 2002-2003 oil strike. He embarked on a process of accumulating political and economic power, with the direct support of the Venezuelan state. The Chávez regime gave Makled special privileges, such as permission to operate in the international port of Cabello. He also received authorization to function in the Valenci Airport. Makled was able to buy the airline Aeroposthal, which enabled him to further increase his narcotic traffic. He was able to transport drugs from one place to another with the complicity of Venezuela's power structure.

The huge fortune that Makled assembled is directly linked to Venezuela's operation of its political system. He was able to form strong alliances with important, influential figures. Makled was able to bribe many officials and in return he was able to enrich himself. He is not only rich in money but also in state's secrets.

In an interview with the Spanish-language television network Univision, Makled claimed that he paid $5.5 billion to the general commander of the Venezuelan army and in addition he gave $1 million to a group of forty generals, colonels, and majors.[206] The list of important people who were bribed by Makled includes Fizar el Aissami, the brother of the interior and justice minister Tareck el Aissami; the director of the national Drug Office, General Luis Reverol; and many others. The list includes, as previously mentioned the former military chief, Henry Rangel Silva, who later was appointed defense minister. The commander of the navy, Admiral Carlos Aniasi, granted a warehouse to a company owned by Makled.[207]

Makled's extradition to the United States could have shed light on the Venezuelan narcotic traffic links with Hezbollah. A Venezuelan diplomat of Syrian origin, Ghazi Atef Nassereddine Salame, the second in command of the Venezuelan embassy in Syria, was in charge of directing the growing numbers of Hezbollah networks in South America. The United States accused four enterprises directed by Makled of dealing in narcotic traffic.[208]

Moisés Naim furnished testimony of former Supreme Court Judge Eladio Aponte, which was previously described, to provide proof of Venezuela's being a mafia state. Betancourt Oteyza, refers to and interview of the former judge on Globovision, in which he claimed that Venezuela lacks independent branches of government; Chávez is in charge of every governmental activity, judges, journalists, and citizens are harassed in order to spread fear among the people. Chávez appointed colonel and lawyer,

Eladio Aponte, to the Supreme Court. He was removed from his post in March 2012 supposedly for his links with Makled's narcotic traffic.

According to Aponte, the government conceals its responsibility in the drug trade, in reality converting itself as an accomplice of crime.[209] Vladimir Mujica claims that the former judge's testimony validates Makled's testimony that Venezuela is a mafia stste.[210] Chávez's regime, similar to Castro's Cuba, has employed narcotic traffic to weaken the United States, enrich itself, and trusted subordinates.

An important question under consideration is why Colombian President Juan Manuel Santos decided to extradite Makled to Venezuela and not to the United States. The Colombian president made this important decision a week after Chávez invited him to come to Caracas.[211] At this meeting, the two presidents signed a bilateral trade agreement that increased their economic cooperation by $6 billion. Since the Venezuelan judicial system lacks independence, the fate of Makled will be solely decided by Chávez.

Colombian President Santos claimed that U.S. President Barack Obama did not express reservations on his decision to extradite Makled to Venezuela.[212] Venezuela, according to Alcalay, has an international obligation to terminate narcotic traffic networks operating in its territory. The aim should be not only to imprison Makled for thirty years, but more importantly to destroy the narcotic traffic empire and the complicity of the Chávez regime. This will reduce the severity of crimes against humanity.[213]

In spite of the fact that Chávez was a strong supporter of the terrorist group FARC, subsequent to the extradition of Makled, the Venezuelan president responded by delivering a FARC member Joaquín Pérez Becerra to Colombia.[214] Members of Venezuela's Communist Party who usually support Chávez, such as Deputy Oscar Figueroa, questioned the decision. Becerra living in Europe, decided to move to Venezuela, realizing that it offers him a safe haven, where he can engage in narcotic trafficking without being arrested. Reyes concludes his article by claiming that a true revolutionary government would not betray Becerra.[215]

The Spanish newspaper *El Mundo* cited Wikileaks' revelations that Chávez was forced to cut his relations with FARC in order to secure Makled's extradition to his country.[216] According to this report, high-level officials in the Venezuelan armed forces pressed Chávez to negotiate with the government of Juan Manuel Santos for the extradition of Makled to

Venezuela. Makled accused the Venezuelan armed forces of being directly involved in transporting drugs. This information was obtained from millions of emails obtained by Wikileaks.

Makled, according to the information given by Wikileaks, had valuable records of transactions that could incriminate high-level officials in the Venezuelan government. He possessed detailed information on the increased cooperation between Venezuela and Iran, especially about the Iranian presence in Venezuela.[217]

U.S. Senator MarcoRubio of Florida asked an important question concerning the expulsion of the Venezuela's Miami consul: Was the breach of security by the Venezuelan diplomat an isolated case or an ongoing, repeated activity?[218] My findings indicate that Venezuela in cooperation with Iran, its proxy Hezbollah, and other terrorist groups is constantly attempting to weaken the United States, by using any available means including terrorism. Chávez' behaviors in the international arena, similar to his domestic policies, are based in some cases on nonideological factors and populism. As A. C. Clark correctly asserts, describing Chávez as a hypocrite is an understatement.[219] Naim's mafia state gives the best explanation for Chávez's behavior, which is to enrich himself and his followers and expand his version of socialism of the twenty-first century.

Chávez's death raises questions about the future course of Venezuela's foreign policy. Maduro's expulsion of two United States' attaches indicates that changes will not occur in the short run. The political future of Venezuela, Chávezism without Chávez, is a new page in Venezuelan history. However, similar to Peronism, which was not eliminated after the death of Peron, Chávezism will remain, in some form, an integral part of the Venezuelan political culture.

Notes

1 Sadio Garavini di Turno, Chávez y su política exterior, Analitica.com, Septiembre 15, 2009
2 Guillermo A. Zurge, El antinorteamericanismo latino, Analitica.com, Julio 16, 2011
3 Maibort Petit, Chávez anhela escándalo mediático tras sus amenazas de posible rotura diplomática con USA, Analitica.com, Diciembre 31, 2010
4 Ros-Lehtinen critica negociaciones secretas, Laprensa.ni, Enero 5, 2013
5 Sadio Garavini di Turno, Insulto a la inteligencia, Analitica.com, Enero 28, 2010
6 María Teresa Romero, Contra el mundo desde la trinchera del ALBA, Analitica.com. Septiembre 29, 2011

7   Álvaro Vargas Llosa, El ajedrez imperial de Hugo Chávez, diariolasamericas.com, Agosto 12, 2009

8   Petroamigos estan en serios aprietos, Laprensa.com.ni, Marzo 8, 2013

9   Carlos Alberto Montaner, Hugo Chávez, al gran elector en el cono sur, Analitica.com, Septiembre 7, 2009

10   Ibid.

11   Carlos Dallmeier G. Multipolaridad, descansa en paz, Analitica.com, Septiembre 13, 2009

12   Detienen en EEUU a físico que pretendía vender proyecto nuclear a Chávez, Analitica.com, Octubre 21, 2009

13   Emilio Nouel, Un negocio chueco llamado ALBA, Analitica.com, Febrero 25, 2011

14   Ibid.

15   Ibid.

16   Gerson Revanales, La nueva estructura de la integración latinoamérica, Analitica.com, Diciembre 21, 2009

17   Presidente venezolano destaca valor supremo del sucre para acabar con dictatura del dólar, Agencia Bolivariana de Noticias, Agosto 3, 2011

18   Carmen Jacqueline Giménez Tellería, SUCRE: "Un sueño que se deshace en pedazos, Analitica.com, Junio 2, 2010

19   Ibid.

20   Reservas internacionales venezolanos estarán en Banco de ALBA, Agencia Bolivariana de Noticias, Febrero 4, 2012

21   Chávez insta a crear Consejo de Defensa Militar de los paises del ALBA, Analitica.com, Octubre 18, 2009

22   ALBA to Create Military School to Train Soldiers in the Region, Eluniversal.com, November 29, 2010

23   El ALBA considera a la educación como fundamental para dinamizar la unión de los pueblos, Agencia Bolivariana de Noticias, Octubre 20, 2009

24   ALBA se propone crear red de medios de comunicación para fortalecer integración, Agencia Bolivariana de Noticias, Febrero 3, 2012

25   El ALBA acusa la OMC de ejecutar prácticas antidemocráticas, Agencia Bolivariana de Noticias, Diciembre 15, 2011

26   La Bolsa Andina, un nuevo eje sudamericano, Analitica.com, Octubre 17, 2010

27   Ibid.

28   Mexican Stock Exchange Aims to Join Peru, Chile, Colombian Exchange, Andina.com.pe, December 5, 2011

29   Ramón E. Azócar A, Una América Latina para América Latina, Analitica.com, Diciembre 4, 2011

30   Juan Páez Ávila, La ALBA y la CELAC, Analitica.com, Diciembre 10, 2011

31   Rafael Grooscors Caballero, La integración de América debe ser alcanzada sin odio y sin exclusiones, Analitica.com, Diciembre 23, 2011

32   Ibid.

33   Carlos Ponce Silent, Quiebra la OEA, Analitica.com, Diciembre 11, 2011

34   Gustavo Coronel, Plan de acción de la CELAC para 2012: un larguísimo mojón, Analitica.com, Diciembre 6, 2011

35   José Antonio Rivas Leone, La cumbre del CELAC, Analitica.com, Diciembre 4, 2011

36   Froilán Barrios Nieves, La integración y la CELAC, Analitica.com, Diciembre 8, 2011

37   Ibid.

38   Evo Morales: Nos reunimos para buscar la liberación de nuestros pueblos, Agencia Bolivariana de Noticias, Diciembre 3, 2011

39 Economista Matos: Celac consolida al petróleo como instrumento de desarrollo social, Agencia Bolivariana de Noticias, Diciembre 10, 2011

40 Maibort Petit, Los cómplices de Irán en América Latina sacan sus cuentas, Analitica. com, Febrero 2, 2012

41 Carlos Sánchez Berzain, Gobierno de Evo Morales tiene un exceso de tiranía, Hoybolivia.com, Febrero 23, 2012

42 Morales dice que se quedaráen el poder para siempre, Hoybolivia.com, Marzo 25, 2012

43 Jimmy Ortiz Saucedo, 2011, un pésimo año de la Bolivia plurinacional, Analitica. com, Diciembre 25, 2011

44 Handel Guayasamín, El Gobierno del MAS, Analitica.com, Enero 15, 2011

45 Ibid.

46 "Evo Morales gradúa la violencia para imponer su constitución, Analitica.com, Junio 11, 2009

47 Ibid.

48 Para el gobierno es crucial la revolución educativa, Hoybolivia.com, Febrero 6, 2012

49 Jimmy Ortiz Saucedo, La salud, otro embuste plurinacional, Op-cit

50 Bolivia entre 5 países latinomericanos con mayor mortalidad por cáncer, Hoybolivia. com, Febrero 3, 2012

51 Ibid.

52 Gandarillas: Evo "es el único que se identificó con las FFAA," lostiempos.com, Mayo 29, 2012

53 Jimmy Ortiz Saucedo, Cada día producimos menos alimento, Analitica.com, Febrero 19, 2012

54 Ibid.

55 La inflación, la escasez y los escándalos le pisan los talones a Evo Morales, Analitica. com, April 6, 2011

56 Jimmy Ortiz Saucedo, La seguridad ciudadana no es tarea de todos, Analitica.com, Marzo 7, 2012

57 Ibid.

58 Ramy Wurgaft, Evo Morales saca el ejército a las calles para combatir la delincuencia. Elmundo.es, Marzo 17, 2012

59 Centa Rek L, Van por Cumbre, Analitica.com, Diciembre 12, 2011

60 MAS: procesos a opositores no es persecución política, Hoybolivia.com, Febrero 6, 2012

61 Ibid.

62 Presidente boliviano critica real interés de EEUU en lucha antidroga, avn.ve, Enero 16, 2013

63 El presidente de Bolivia anima a masticar la coca, Elmundo.es, Febrero 21, 2012

64 Morales pide en la ONU reparar error histórico y despenalizar coca en Bolivia, Hoy. com.ec, Marzo 12, 2012

65 Maibot Petit, Gobierno de Evo Morales penetrado por el narcotráfico, Analitica.com, April 1, 2011

66 Jimmy Ortiz Saucedo, Potencial genocidio en el TIPNIS, Analitica.com, Marzo 3, 2012

67 Bolivia: Amazon Road Deal Canceled, The New York Times, April 11, 2011

68 Jimmy Ortiz Saucedo, Quieren más coca para la cocaína, Analitica.com, Diciembre 17, 2011

69 Maibot Petit, Gobierno de Evo Morales penetrado por el narcotráfico, Op-cit

70 Ibid.

71 Jimmy Ortiz Saucedo, La marcha de la coca ilegal, Analitica.com, Diciembre 31, 2011

72   Duda Texeira, Bolivia: La república de la cocaína, Analitica.com, Julio 11, 2012

73   Gobierno boliviano pierde Guerra contra las drogas, Hoybolivia, Noviembre 29, 2012

74   Ibid.

75   EEUU desmiente injerencia sobre el conflicto del Tipins, Hoybolivia.com, Febrero 8, 2012

76   MAS: policías estarían implicados en complot de EEUU contra Morales, Hoybolivia. com, Marzo 29, 2012

77   Ibid.

78   Daniel Sayani, Ecuadorian Socialist President Rafael Correa's Power Grab, thenewamerica.com, June 13, 2011

79   Gustavo Coronel, Ecuador: en camino a ser una Corea del Norte, Analitica.com, Enero 2, 2012

80   Directivo de Teleamazonas teme que la democracia esté llegada a su fin en Ecuador, Analitica.com, Diciembre 23, 2009

81   Ibid.

82   An Assault on Democracy, The New York Times, January 23, 2012

83   Ecuador: Jueza reitera que Corea la presionó contra El Universo, Hoybolivia.com, Febrero 24, 2012

84   William Newman, President of Ecuador to Pardon Four in Libel Case, The New York Times, February 27, 2012

85   Corea pide en el Perú "rebelión" contra medios, Hoy.com.ec, Marzo 1, 2012

86   Corea vuelva su ataque contra la Comisión de Derecho Humanos, Hoybolivia.com, Marzo 31, 2012

87   Ecuador: una ley calla a la prensa en elecciones, Hoybolivia, Febrero 7, 2012

88   Ibid.

89   Dolores Ochoa, Corea festeja aniversario de su llegada al poder y "revolución." La prensa.com.ni, Enero 14, 2012

90   Ecuador celebrara 5 aniversario de la revolución ciudadana el 14 de Enero, Agencia Bolivariana de Noticias, Enero 5, 2012

91   Ivan Sandoval Carrión, Por que gano? Eluniverso.com.ec Febrero 19, 2013

92   Benjamin Dang, Ecuador's Challenge: Rafael Correa and the Indigenous Movements, upsidedownworld.org.ec, October 21, 2010

93   Ibid.

94   Con pedido al fiscal general concluyó la movilización indígena, Eluniversal.com, Marzo 24, 2012

95   Ibid.

96   Ecuador: Movilización contra Gobierno, Analitica.com, Octubre 19, 2009

97   Modifica Ley de Educación Superior en Ecuador, iesalc,unesco.org, Octubre 18, 2010

98   Ibid.

99   Rafael Correa anuncia cambios en cúpula militar, Agencia Bolivariana de Noticias, Febrero 10, 2012

100   Un tribunal emite las primeras condenas por la sublevación de 2010 en Ecuador, Elmundo.es, Junio 28, 2011

101   Ibid.

102   Corea acusa a EEUU haber financiado revuelta policial, Eluniversal.com, Septiembre 29, 2011

103   Ibid.

104   Ecuador ocupa el puesto 130 entre los 183 países donde es mas fácil hacer negocios, Eluniversal.com, Marzo 1, 2012

105   Ibid.

106 Daniel Sayani, Ecuadorian Socialist President Rafael Correa's Power Grab, ThenewAmerican.com, June 13, 2011

107 Ecuador President May Have Sought Money From FARC for Elections, Says Report, Latino.Foxnews.com, May 11, 2011

108 Ibid.

109 Fernando Carrión Mena, Ecuador exporta unas 270 toneladas de cocaína al año, Hoy.com.ec, Abril 6, 2012

110 La oposición inicia acciones para indagar origen de valija con droga, Eluniversal.com, Marzo 1, 2012

111 Valija diplomática ecuatoriana llegó a Italia con droga y sellos cambiados, Hoybolivia.com, Marzo 12, 2012

112 Alijo de droga en valija diplomática de Ecuador, Hoy.com.ec, Febrero 10, 2012

113 Ibid.

114 Opinión de Hoy, Esclarecer sin dilación caso de valija diplomática, Hoy.com.ec, Marzo 29, 2012

115 Ibid.

116 Hasta 20 años de prisión para acusados en caso de valija, Hoy.com.ec, Mayo 25, 2012

117 Ortega provoca la exclusión del país, Laprensa.com.ni, Enero 24, 2012

118 Ibid.

119 Joel D. Hirst, Fraude en Nicaragua, Analitica.com, Noviembre 21, 2011

120 Ibid.

121 Douglas Carcache, Síntomas de fraude, Analitica.com, Junio 1, 2011

122 Ibid.

123 Sergio Ramírez, Las elecciones más inverosímiles del mundo, Analitica.com, Octubre 18, 2011

124 Ibid.

125 Blake Schmidt, Nicaragua's President Rules Airways to Control Image, The New York Times, November 28, 2011

126 Impacto Alba solo en la fortuna de Ortega, Laprensa.com.ni, Enero 17, 2012

127 Ibid

128 Carlos Salinas Maldonado, Nicaragua se hunde en la miseria, Elpais.com.es, Noviembre 10, 2009

129 Ibid.

130 Ocho de 10 escuelas estan en mal estado, Laprense.com.ni, Enero 20, 2012

131 Luis Fleischman and Nancy Menges, Silence On Fraudulent Rule In Nicaragua Detrimental to Latin America and U.S. Interests, The American Report, December 1, 2011

132 Elizabeth Romero, Naecomenudeo en el "paraíso", Laprensa.com.ni, Enero 2, 2012

133 Oposición de Nicaragua denunció que el Gobierno pretende aplicar estrategias militares de Chávez, Analitica.com, Octubre 25, 2009

134 Amalia del Cid, Las tropas de Daniel Ortega, Laprensa.com.ni, Mayo 6, 2012

135 Ibid.

136 Gloria Picón/ José Denis Cruz, Iglesia rechaza control a familias, Laprensa.com.ni, Abril 23, 2012

137 Ibid.

138 Robert Bernstein, Irwin Cotler and Stuart Robinowitz, Inciting Genocide Is a Crime, The Wall Street Journal, May 1, 2012

139 Alex Spillius, Iran's Supreme Leader Vows to Confront 'Cancerous Tumor' of Israel, The Telegraph, February 3, 2012

140 Iran is a nuclear state but has no intention to launch attack on Israel—Ahmadinejad, RT news, February 6, 2013

141 Sadio Garavini di Turno, Las cartas de Chávez, Analitica.com, Octubre 11, 2011

142 Nicola Clark, Carlos el Chacal Goes on Trial for Bombing in France, The New York Times, November 7, 2011

143 Carlos el Chacal", ante tribunal francés: "Soy un duro", Lanacion.cl, Noviembre 8, 2011

144 Milos Alcalay, Ilich Ramírez Versus Carlos el Chacal, Analitica.com, Diciembre 21, 2011

145 Pilar Rahola, La alianza del mal, Analitica.com, Enero 15, 2012

146 Ibid.

147 Vivian Akel, Irán.... Resurrección del imperio persa en América Latina, Analitica.com, Enero 14, 2012

148 Rafael Marrón González, La secta siniestra, Analitica.com, Enero 16, 2012

149 Ibid.

150 Ibid.

151 Lt. Col. (ret.) Michael Segall, Latin America: Iran's Springboard to America Backyard, jcpa.org, June 2011

152 Jo Becker, Beirut Bank Seen as a Hub of Hezbollah's Financing, The New York Times, December 13, 2011

153 Ibid

154 Ahmadinejad cree que el capitalismo está "en un callejón sin salida", Laprensa.com.ni, Enero 13, 2012

155 Maibort Petit, Irán penetra Latinoamérica, Analitica.com, Julio 24, 2011

156 Ibid.

157 Maibort Petit, Irán y Venezuela unidos contra el imperio, Analitica.com, Enero 13, 2012

158 Que busca Ahmadinejad en América Latina? Hoy.com,ec, Enero 14, 2012

159 Relación ALBA Irán se apuntala en la propaganda, Hoy.com.ec, Enero 16, 2012

160 Milos Alcalay, Ahmadinejad y el ocaso del ALBA, Analitica.com, Enero 5, 2012

161 William Newman and Simón Romero, Increasing Isolated Iranian Leader Set to Visit Allies in Latin America, Op-cit

162 Maibort Petit, Los cómplices de Irán en América Latina sacan sus cuentas, Analitica.com, Febrero 2, 2012

163 Juan Arias, Por qué Ahmadinejad no irá a Brasil, Analitica.com, Enero 12, 2012

164 Ibid.

165 Ibid.

166 La criminalización es el arma política del imperio para preservar su patio trasero, Noticias24.com, Julio 29, 2009

167 Joyce Hor-Chung Lau, Highlighting Differences in Interpretations of the Opium War, The New York Times, August 18, 2011

168 Emilio T. González, The Cuban Connection: Drug Trafficking and the Castro Regime, scholarlyrepository.miami.edu, January 1, 1997

169 Ibid.

170 Ibid.

171 Knight Ridder, Castro Brother Linked to Drugs in Noriega Trial, Chicagotribune.com, November 21, 1991

172 Cuba: Chávez "acompaño a Fidel como un hijo verdadero, Lanacion.cl, Marzo 5, 2013

173 Iranian Drug Ring Funding Terror, ynetnews.com, November 18, 2011

174 Elizabeth Burgos, De Petro-Estado a Narco-Estado, Analitica.com, Mayo 20, 2012

175 Mexican and Colombian Drug Traffickers Operate in Venezuela, Eluniversal.com, November 25, 2010

176 John Lyons, Cocaine: The New Front Lines, The Wall Street Journal, January 14, 2012

177 Ibid.
178 Venezuela acumula diez sanciones de EEUU y la UE, Eluniversal.com, Mayo 29, 2011
179 Narcotráfico: Colombia apunta a Venezuela, Analitica.com, Octubre 24, 2009
180 Venezuela: Ruta predilecta de los narcotraficantes, Hoybolivia.com, Marzo 8, 2012
181 Former Mexican President Accuses Chávez of "Facilitating Drug Travel," Eluniversal. com, February 9, 2011
182 Venezuela pide a Interpol capturar a ex magistrado, Hoybolivia.com, Abril 21, 2012
183 Jennifer Scholtes, Iran and the Drug Cartel, actforamerica@donationnet.net, October 17, 2011
184 Humberto Marcano Rodríguez, Penetración Narco-Terrorista, Analitica.com, Mayo 29, 2012
185 IISS: The FARC Financed Chávez Before 1999, Eluniversal.com, May 13, 2011
186 Aleksander Boyd, Hugo Chávez and the FARC Boost Uribe's Popularity, vcrisis.com, January 24, 2008
187 Mickel Inkster, Los documentos de las FARC, Analitica.com, Mayo 11, 2011
188 Ibid.
189 Ibid.
190 Simón Romero, Venezuela Asked Colombian Rebels to Kill Opposition Figures, Analysis Shows, The New York Times, May 10, 2011
191 Gustavo Coronel, La barbarie de las FARC y su influencia sobre la relación de Colombia con Venezuela, Analitica.com, Noviembre 30, 2011
192 Ibid.
193 Maibort Petit, Departmento del Tesoro de EEUU advierte sobre el peligro de los vínculos Irán-Venezuela FARC, Analitica.com, Noviembre 23, 2011
194 ETA en Venezuela, Analitica.com, Enero 18, 2011
195 Ibid.
196 Anna Mahjar-Barducci, Basque ETA Terrorists Move to Venezuela, Team Up with Colombia's FARC, stoneageinstitute.org, January 19, 2011
197 Ibid.
198 Rafael Rivera Muñoz, Walid Makled García confirmado y silenciado, Analitica.com, Mayo 26, 2011
199 Moisés Naim, Estados mafiosos, Analitica.com, Mayo 7, 2012
201 Ibid.
202 Ibid.
203 Michael Rowan, The US $6 Billion Man. Eluniversal.com, November 30, 2010
204 Fernando Luis Egana, Los carceleros de Makled, Analitica.com, Mayo 14, 2011
205 Ibid.
206 Public Prosecutor Office Investigate Walid Makled's Claims, Eluniversal.com, April 5, 2011
207 Opposition Deputy Points to Links Between Makled and Senior Officials, Eluniversla.com, January 14, 2011
208 Roger Noriega, ¿Existe una red terrorista de Chávez a las puertas de Estados Unidos? Analitica.com, Marzo 23, 2011
209 Luis Betancourt Oteyza, La lección de Aponte Aponte, Analitica.com, Abril 25, 2012
210 Vladimir Mujica, El magistrado, Analitica.com, Abril 27, 2012
211 Michael Rowan, The US $6 Billion Man, Op-cit
212 Milos Alcalay, Makled y el crimen de Lesa Humanidad, Analitica.com, Abril 24, 2012
213 Ibid.
214 Lus Mely Reyes, La deportación express de Pérez Becerra, Analitica.com, Mayo 2, 2011
215 Ibid.

216   Chávez cortó con las FARC en 2011 para que Bogotá le entregara a Walid Makled, Elmundo.es, Marzo 9, 2012
217   Ibid
218   Países asociados a Irán juegan con fuego, Laprensa.com.ni, Febrero 16,   2012
219   A. C. Clark, The Revolutionary Has No Clothes, Hugo Chávez's Bolivarian Farce, (New-York, Encounter Books, 2009) p.139

Conclusion:
The Transformation from
Democracy to Mafia States

This study analyzes the Chávez regime from three main perspectives: political, economic, and international. The death of Chávez in March 2013 enables us to evaluate his regime and the lessons that can be deduced from his fourteen years in power. The first chapter attempts to explain *Bolivarism*, a term that characterizes the regime. In essence, *Bolivarism* is the philosophical and political underpinning that justifies his policies. Chávez was elected democratically as president in 1999, and he gradually transformed the country into an authoritarian/totalitarian system. Changes have been introduced to the country's political, economic, and external behavior. These alterations to the Venezuelan political system weakened those democratic institutions that functioned to balance power. This enabled narcotic traffickers and organized crime to freely integrate them into the country. As Moisés Naim correctly asserts, the mafia states are countries in which the government takes control of organized crime in order to promote and defend their national interest. This is especially true in promoting the interests of the ruling elite.

Chávez claims that he follows Simón Bolívar's ideas, which are compared by many analysts to the ideas of U.S. President George Washington. The need for legitimacy, especially for authoritarian regimes, constitutes an important element of their political behavior. Claiming that his policies have been a continuation of Bolivar's ideas has increased his acceptance among the people.

After extensive research of the literature related to Latin America's hero, it becomes apparent that Bolívar changed his views at different times. In the last part of his life, he abandoned his liberal beliefs and endorsed authoritarian ideas that Chávez appropriated.

An important idea found in this research is the strong influence of the writing of Italian Communist scholar Antonio Gramsci on the Chávez regime. Commenting on the Communist revolution in Russia (1917), Gramsci stated his belief that the Bolshevik uprising should not be imitated in Europe. New values and reform of the educational system are needed in order for the people to reorient their thinking and value systems. This process may take a long time but it is a precondition for a successful Communist revolution.

It is important to note that the Chávez regime received support from international organizations. An important objective of these organizations, especially after the 2008 economic crisis, is to promote a new ideology that will take into account the errors committed by Soviet communism. Heinz Dietrich, a Communist scholar, is considered to be an important leader of the organization attempting to promote communism. While claiming that Chávez should be considered a "new Lenin of Latin America," after the legislative elections of 2010, he changed his mind.

Opposition scholars have outlined the importance of nineteenth century French expert Alexis de Tocqueville's emphasis on decentralization as an important attribute of democracy. Chávez, on the other hand, stresses centralization and the weakening of local governments as a mean of strengthening his rule. The communal system was Chávez's way of increasing control over people's lives. If reelected in October 2012 Chávez promised that by 2019, 68% of the Venezuelan people will live under such systems.[1] Because the central government is in charge of funds allocated to these organizations, it assumes control of people's livelihood.

It is my conviction that the Chávez regime embarked on the process of changing people's way of thinking; the control of the mass media and the educational process were necessary tasks to reach this goal. Gradually Chávez has eliminated newspapers and radio and television stations that opposed his rule. Educational reform has attempted to ensure that all levels of learning are exposed to the principles of Marxism. This interaction will assist in the creation of a "new man," guaranteeing the indefinite rule of the Chávez regime. These changes contributed to the emergence of the mafia state.

Similar to the totalitarian governments of the twentieth century, the Venezuelan government has demonstrated the dangers involved in attempting to control both the mass media and the educational process. In order to combat criticism by the private media, the Chávez regime organized "media guerrillas," high school students who became "activists for the truth" for the government.

The armed forces have played an important role in Latin America's history. Chávez, a military commander, understands the importance of this institution in helping him to hold power. The military was restructured; assuring that the armed forces would adhere to the same ideology as the Venezuelan president. The former chief of the armed forces and current defense minister, Juan Manuel Santos, has declared that the military is "married" to Chávez.

The Catholic Church also constitutes an important institution that played an important role in Latin America's history. Chávez's attempt to change Venezuelan society by increasing the role of the state and decreasing the family's function, encountered strong opposition from the church hierarchy, in both Venezuela and the Vatican.

A comparison between the Chávez regime and Rómulo Betancourt's administration (1959-1963) demonstrates the superiority of the democratic model of modernization over the authoritarian one. The rule of law characterizes democratic governments. Political and economic development depends on strict rules that everyone needs to obey. The Chávez regime, however, has violated laws and expropriated private property, which contributed to budget deficits, inflation, and economic stagnation.

As a result of inconsistencies in Chávez's policies, different scholars characterize his rule differently. Whereas some claim that he is a Communist, others label him as a fascist. Although Chávez claimed adherence to Marxist-Leninist principles, his policies have not always matched his stated ideology. Unlike Fidel Castro, who was versed in Marx's writings, Chávez has never read important books by the Communist founder, such as *Capital*. Lack of serious academic background (he was accepted to the military academy based on his skills as a baseball player) was another factor contributing to the inconsistencies.

Chapter two analyzes Chávez's economic policies, comparing them with the literature on this topic. A good illustration of Chávez's economic philosophy is expressed by Bolivian president Evo Morales, a follower of the Venezuelan president, who called upon the world's government to nationalize the natural resources of their countries, claiming that state should assume the main role in economic development.[2] According to one of Morales's followers, the idea that the state is a bad administrator of public funds is the invention of imperialism, which aims to take away the country's natural resources.[3] Chávez's view, shared by his followers, is that central planning constitutes the main vehicle of economic development.

Several Western and Venezuelan economic scholars were employed by the opposition press to refute Chávez's economic philosophy. The main point was to present the superiority of market economy over central planning. Niall Ferguson's book, *The Ascent of Money: A Financial History of the World*, was used to demonstrate the strong link between the development of capitalist institutions and economic development. His book, which surveys the development of capitalist institutions, such as banks, demonstrates their contributions to the countries' economic development.

Ferguson emphasizes the important link between property rights and political rights, which are a precondition to a successful economy. This is in contrast to Chávez's policies of expropriations and the abuse of people's rights. In contrast to Chávez, Ferguson claims that private ownership is a precondition of economic progress. The increase of people's dependence on the state will result in increasing poverty.

Arnold Kling and Nick Schulz's book, *The Hidden Story of How Markets Work*, is also a manuscript used by the opposition press to refute Chávez's economic ideas. Contrary to Chávez, these authors emphasize that reducing the state's role is a precondition for economic development. They claim that communism had an adverse effect on people's standard of living. Innovative improvements in the country's economy depend on incentives given to the private sector. Profit and gain are natural human motives that provide the impetus for improving the economy.

Kling and Schulz compare the functioning of two types of societies, one governed by the rule of law and the other by organized crime, which employs extortions that weaken business and the country's economy. In the case of the Chávez regime, the government is the criminal organization, a mafia state threatening those who dare to oppose its rule, considering them "enemies of the state." The arrest of Judge María Lourdes Afiuni in December 2009 because she ruled contrary to Chávez's order is a case in point.[4] The judge was held in deplorable conditions in prison for over a year.

In Venezuela and its affiliate countries, where the public sector has been constantly on the rise and businesses and private initiatives have been drastically reduced. On the other hand, there are many similarities between Germany, Chile, and Israel, where the culture of entrepreneurship and competition is strong. As is emphasized in *The Power of the Pull,* innovations and entrepreneurship are essential elements for a country's economic success.

Venezuelan economist Jesús Casique criticizes Chávez's economic policies by presenting a comprehensive economic theory. Analyzing the 2008 world economic crisis, Casique claims that many countries decided to increase their budget in order to solve their economic crisis.[5] The economic crisis caused some analysts to resurrect the ideas of John Maynard Keynes, the failure of whose recommendations has been demonstrated by history. The demand for a quick solution manifested itself in the policy of increasing public expenditures. As a result of these activities, regulations on economic and financial institutions increased, causing the creation of additional bureaucrats and waste of needed resources.

Economic growth cannot be permanently achieved by the increase of public expenditures, which require raising taxes, public debt, and worst the amount of money in circulation, leading to inflation. The source of the creation of wealth, Casique insists, is determined by work and knowledge. The state needs to create the conditions for the efficient operation of markets. The government needs to assure that each economic unit is fulfilling its function. Those who promote government intervention, injecting money into the economy, believe that it will increase demand and, therefore, production. However, one must ask where the resources derive from to sustain the expenses. This resort does not create a new source of wealth, but only redistribution of income from one group to another.

The government cannot create buying power; it redistributes income, which increases inefficiency. Only the work of a free market can remedy the situation. Public expenses can replace private investments and discourage economic growth as a result. An increase in economic activities will occur only when total productivity increase as a result of better machinery, investments in new equipment, and technical progress. Contradicting Chávez's economic philosophy, Casique asserts that historically one can observe that when public expenses are reduced there is a rise in long-term economic productivity.

Government expenditures, which are mostly financed by taxes, reduce incentives to work, save, and invest. All activities are taken over by the state, in contrast with what Bolivian President Morales asserted, it reduces efficiency. The inefficiencies in health care and education in Latin America, which is nationalized, validates Casique's theories.

Indirectly referring to Chávez's idea, economic growth cannot be achieved by decisions taken by a central agency. It can only result from individual entrepreneurship operating under free market conditions. Casique uses Chile as an example of a country that achieved economic success by following such policies. On the other hand, the European Union economic crisis illustrates economic policies that the Venezuelan economist had warned against following.

Andres Volpe reinforces Casique's ideas and gives a good summary of the ideas presented in the second chapter. He claims that free markets, have evolved in the most advanced evolution of humanity.[6] Without a free market, countries could not survive in a globalized world.

Volpe contends that rescuing banks or other businesses is a violation of free market principles. It runs counter to the elements of efficiency. When an economic actor is inefficient, market forces act to remove it from the system. Chávez's policies of nationalization and expropriation of enterprises have increased inefficiencies and unemployment. Without private property there is no free market. Those who blame capitalism for the economic crisis have forgotten that modern life evolved as a result of this system.

Capitalism, Volpe claims, is an economic system that rewards the capacity of reason and the pursuit of benefits. However, it punishes the tendency to make bad decisions and illegality and immorality. Those who intend to eliminate capitalism and the free market aim to exclude people's rights at the same time. Capitalism necessitates the institutionalization of people's rights; only through peace and order is it possible to operate and create wealth. The 2008 international financial crisis caused the abuse of capitalism. In the United States, for example, the judicial system should have brought to justice those who manipulated the financial system, falsifying information to enrich them, and thereby brought on the crisis.

Analyzing Chávez' economic policies, Trino Márquez claims that the country's economic problems have little to do with the international economic crisis.[7] Surveying the period 1980-2003, Márquez asserts that during this interval there were thirty-eight financial crises affecting nearly all the countries in the region. However, some countries, such as Brazil, Chile, Colombia, and others, introduced changes in their economic policies that enabled them to be less affected by the 2008 world economic crisis. These changes included the following: reducing the size of the government sector, expanding the participation of the private sector, putting public finances in order, producing a balanced budget, minimizing fiscal deficits, increasing control of public expenses, increasing efficiency, punishing corruption, and controlling inflation through fiscal discipline.

Venezuela's economic problems are not related to the international economic crisis. They are a consequence of an irrational model that emphasizes state intervention in the economy. Chávez's political model has destroyed democracy and ended the market economy. It established repressive institutions, which harassed the private sector. These policies have devastated the economy. Private investments, both foreign and domestic, are the lowest in South America.[8] In spite of huge amounts of oil deposits, the Chávez regime rejected the structural reforms that permitted other Latin American countries to confront the 2008 international economic crisis. Chávez's economic policies, Marquez concludes, have generated poverty and the destruction of the productive apparatus.

While Chávez claims that his policies have helped the poor, the reality is different. According to information given by the Venezuelan Central Bank (BCV), 25% of the poorest people in the country spent 45% of their income on food, while those in a higher income bracket spent 15%.[9] Inflation, which is common in Chávez's Venezuela, is hurting the poor more. Shortages of food are noted, especially in stores run by the government. In January 2011, 51.3% of consumers considered the supply of food as insufficient. In June 2011 the percentage rose to 62.7%.[10]

An important suggestion to break the state's monopoly and help the poor in Venezuela is given by the scholar Francisco Mondali. The Harvard professor claims that oil revenues should be directly distributed to the citizens. This should be accomplished with "universal transparent and regular payments."[11]

The Venezuelan opposition press contrasted Chávez's economic achievements with those of its neighbor Colombia. As a result of Colombia's free trade agreement with the United States an important increase in direct foreign investment has occurred. In 2011, Colombia's Gross Domestic Product (GDP) was 4%, while inflation in 2010 was 2.8%. According to the World Bank, Colombia is ranked thirty-seventh in the world and the highest in Latin America in reference to friendly atmosphere for business investments and protection of them.[12] During the period 2002-2009, Colombia experienced a 40% growth in foreign investments, while at the same time the Venezuelan stock exchange (a capitalist institution) has constantly declined.

Chile's President, Sebastián Piñera, warned about the negative economic consequences of nonindependent central banks. When such a bank finances the budget deficit, it is like giving morphine, which initially alleviates pain, but later has the grave consequences of creating dependency on the drug.[13] The governor of the Israeli central bank, Stanley Fisher, correctly asserted that fiscal deficits negatively affect economic development in the long run.[14]

Chávez completely ignored the warning of these two economic experts. He converted the BCV into an institution that finances the government's deficits. He followed similar policies toward Central Bank of Argentina initiated by Juan Domingo Perón, which had a negative impact on the country's economy. In spite of the international rise in oil prices during 2010, the Venezuelan state oil Company's (PDVSA) debt reached $10 billion in 2011.[15] In 2011 the Venezuelan budget increased by 67%.[16]

An important conclusion reached in analyzing political systems that follow a different ideological path, such as Chile and Israel, is that although capitalism aggravates social inequalities, it is the best system.[17] Cycles of expansion and slowdown are an integral part of capitalism. The debate among economists revolves around the extent of government interference in economic decisions. As previously mentioned, the government must assure that all economic units are working in harmony and that ethical norms are observed. The European Union's economic crisis demonstrated the shortcomings of social democracy, and its idea that markets must bear a high level of taxation, regulation, unionization, welfare spending, and subsidize health care and education.[18]

Chávez further accentuated people's dependence on the state for their livelihood. In a public opinion poll conducted in Venezuela (2011), it was revealed that 45% of the country's households depend on the government for their sustenance.[19] Unlike European leaders, Chávez gradually embarked on initiatives that abolished democratic institutions and replaced them with his authoritarian personal rule.

The comparison between Venezuela's economic system and those of Chile and Israel demonstrates that following responsible economic policies, such as avoiding budget deficits and reducing taxes in order to encourage investments, would bring economic benefits. President Sebastián

Piñera declared that Chile, unlike countries in Europe and the United States, has not followed the irresponsible policies that brought many countries to economic crisis.[20] Chileans, the president declared, should be proud that in spite of the world economic crisis economic growth is continuing. This has created employment and integration in the globalization process and advancement toward making Chile an industrialized country without poverty before the end of this decade.

In spite of high levels of economic development, Chile has faced mass protest demonstrations. Ernesto Ottone claimed that Chile's problem is political; the government needs to increase political legitimacy, confidence, and credibility.[21] Chile's predicament is not lack of economic growth. Its urgent need is to increase citizens' participation in politics. This can be accomplished by establishing primary elections. People need to be more politically informed, enabling them to participate in debates on issues concerning their future. The educational system also needs reform.

Contrasting Venezuela's and Israel's economic systems shows two types of governments heading in opposite directions. While Venezuela has continuously increased the state's role and reduced private enterprise, Israel has moved in the opposite direction. Many of Israel's founding fathers left Russia and came to what was then called Palestine, attempting to build a proletarian society and hence implement socialism in the new land. The creation of the kibbutz movement was strongly influenced by Karl Marx's writings and the 1917 Russian revolution.

The 1977 elections in Israel, which led to the victory of the right wing party Herut headed by Menachem Begin, produced a peaceful political revolution. The emphasis has shifted to privatization and weakening of the public sector. The kibbutzim were transformed to ventures that emphasized profit and entrepreneurship. Equality among kibbutz members ceased to be an important priority. The changes introduced into Israeli society enabled the country to achieve high levels of economic development.

Israel's economic achievements were manifested both in 2010 and 2011; it showing the fastest economic growth of all developed countries (4.8% GDP growth).[22] It is the only Western country that lowered unemployment and upgraded its economic ranking by Standard & Poor during this period. While Venezuela suffers from a brain drain as a result of the 2008 economic crisis, immigration to the Jewish state and the number of Israelis returning have increased.

Referring to the topic of research and development (R&D), Dr. William Colglazier, science and technology adviser to U.S. Secretary of State, Hillary Clinton, said the following, "Israel is a world leader and a model not only for small countries but for all countries."[23] Similar pronouncements came from scientists from Brazil and the European Union. Human resources are the most important factor explaining Israel's economic development.

The Islamist uprising in the Arab world strengthened Ayatollah Khomeini's 1991 statement that Iran and its affiliates have replaced the Soviet Union as the main opponent of Western democracies. In Egypt, one of the principal Arab countries affected by the rise of the Islamists, the election of Muslim Brotherhood's Mohamed Morsi as president brings into question the free passage of navigation in the Suez Canal, especially for Israeli ships. Therefore, creating an alternative to the Suez Canal by building a railroad from the city of Eilat to Tel-Aviv's port is an important contribution to international trade in a globalized world.

Coser's ideas about the functions of social conflict were discussed on several occasions in this manuscript. Venezuela named the United States as the country's enemy intending to invade in order to depose the Chávez regime. Therefore Venezuelans need to stay united in order to repel the "enemy."

Israel does not need to invent the enemy. Iran and its proxy Hezbollah, Hamas, and other groups, will not compromise when it comes to the Jewish state's destruction. The declaration by the deputy chief of staff of the Iranian armed forces, Brigadier General Mostafa Izadi, that no pressure can deter the Islamic regime from its commitment to the full annihilation of Israel represents the uncompromising attitude of this regime.[24] Similar statements have been made by high Iranian officials, including the spiritual leader, Ayatollah Khomeini. The hatred exhibited by these countries and groups promoted Israel's internal unity, which contributed to the country's economic development.

However, in spite of repeated threats to its existence, thousands marched in 2011 to protest economic inequalities in Israel. If the current Iranian regime is replaced and animosity toward Israel replaced with political and economic cooperation by the Arabs states, the internal division in the Jewish state will intensify. It is a known fact in Jewish history that internal fighting contributed to the national disaster of the destruction of the second Temple in 70 A.D.

The book, *The Power of Pull: How Small Moves, Smartly Made, Can Set Big Things in Motion,* gives an excellent explanation as to why there have been mass protests in the United States, Chile, Israel, and other countries. Insecurities in these countries are enhanced by the rapid changes and innovations of the globalization process, bringing unprecedented modifications to the workplace.

In a conference on renewing energy, Professor Eugene Kandel, the head of the National Economic Council in the office of Israel's Prime Minister emphasized the role of the oil industry as an "engine of growth" both in Israel and elsewhere.[25] Countries should maximize their internal oil exploration, reducing foreign petroleum export, specifically from Iran and other Arab countries. This is of the utmost importance in winning the war on terror.

Israel's renewable energy industry, including solar power and electric cars (produced by Reuven Agassi's Better Place company), makes an important contribution to a peaceful international system. Agassi has contracts with many foreign countries to export his innovations. A delegation of U.S. experts on energy toured Israel in June 2012. One of the delegates, Brian Wynne, commenting on Israel's achievement in renewable energy, said "Israel is obviously a great microcosm of many energy challenges and there is some terrific innovation going on here that will have a big impact on the world."[26] It is therefore not surprising that the outspoken Bolivian President Evo Morales declared in an international conference (June 2012) in Brazil that the "green economy's" environmentalists are attempting to subjugate the anticapitalist governments.[27]

Chapter three attempted to analyze Chávez's behavior in the international arena. Anti-United States rhetoric is the most prominent characteristic of the Venezuelan president's pronouncements. A great effort is directed toward creating a new international order, where American influence would diminish. Another important component of Chávez's external behavior is to expand and export his ideology in Latin America and beyond. Oil revenues have been used to influence the outcome of elections in Latin America and other places. Chávez's Bolivarian revolution is considered an alternative to capitalism that should be adopted everywhere.

Another important attribute of Venezuela's diplomacy is the strong relations with authoritarian and dictatorial regimes. Chávez's close interactions with Cuba, Iran, North Korea, Syria, and Libya (under Kaddafi) demonstrate the Venezuelan authoritarian regime's alliance with governments similar to his own.

The creation of the Bolivarian Alliance of the People of our America (ALBA) in 2004 is considered to be the first step in spreading Chávez's ideology. Chávez's aim at a December 2011 CELAC conference in Caracas, where all the Latin American and Caribbean countries participated, was an attempt to further increase the spread of his ideology. The United States and Canada were excluded from the conference. As was the case with ALBA, his aim was to use his oil revenue to spread his ideology and foster integration.

Another important aim has been to reduce United States influence in the region, and to end or weaken the power of the Organization of the American States (OAS), which often criticizes Chávez's human rights violations. In this respect, the Venezuelan National Assembly rubber stamped the Venezuelan president's decision to withdraw from the Inter-American Commission on Human Rights (CIDH), which is a part of OAS.[28]

In the final document of the CELAC's conference, which was prepared by Venezuelan bureaucrats, Venezuela was mentioned as a model that other countries should emulate. The criticism from opposition circles correctly claimed that the country's state companies are wasting food and giving rotten food to its citizens. Another criticism was that the United States and Canada were excluded. In order to foster real integration, the need arises to understand the history of all the continent's countries. Therefore it is important to combine the political philosophy of George Washington, Simón Bolívar, and San Martín. This would create a common identity and help foster coexistence among the entire region's people.

Chávez's puppet states, Bolivia, Ecuador, and Nicaragua, were analyzed in order to demonstrate that these countries have evolved in a process similar to Venezuela's. Gradually these regimes have been transformed into authoritarian states. All these countries are using Chávez's oil revenues to weaken and harass the opposition.

Narcotic traffic is important in Venezuela and its puppet states. Drug trafficking from Mexico, Colombia, and Brazil has been operating in Bolivia.[29] Colombia's Chancellor María Angela Holguín confirmed the existence of her country's drug cartels in Bolivia.[30]

General René Sambría, who headed the Bolivian antidrug unit which was abolished in 2008, testified that high-level officials in the Morales government have been engaged in corruption and narcotic traffic.[31] The General was captured in Panama and brought to the United States, where faced accusations of conspiring to bring illegal drugs to the United States. In a federal court in Miami he was sentenced to fourteen years in jail. All these accusations make Bolivia, a mafia state, like Venezuela.

The close link between the regime of Ecuador's Rafael Correa and FARC, a narcotic trafficking terrorist group, shows traits shared with Bolivia and Venezuela; illegal drugs play an important role in the country's political process. A diplomatic suitcase with forty kilograms of cocaine belonging to Ecuadorian Foreign Minister Ricardo Patiño was discovered on its way to the country's consulate in Milan, Italy. In spite of calls from opposition members to investigate the crime, no serious attempt was made to resolve this issue. High-level officials in Correa's administration, including his wife, were involved in this incident. According to United States information, Ecuador is not only a transit place for illegal drugs, but has also become a drug producer.[32] The 2009 closing of an American military base in Ecuador contributed to an increase of narcotic traffic.

An editorial in an Ecuadorian opposition newspaper warned of the negative consequences of the increased penetration of narcotic traffic in the country.[33] An egregious increase in organized crime and narcotic traffic is evident in Ecuador. The first hint of this malady was observed in 2009 when the president of the commission that investigated Colombia's military attack on Angostura, Ecuador, observed that FARC and narcotic traffic have penetrated various political, judicial, cultural, and social organizations.

In 2011 Jay Bergman, director of the U.S. Drug Enforcement Agency (DEA) in the Andean region, asserted that drug trafficking from Albania to China uses the Ecuadorian soil as a platform of narcotic negotiation. Ecuador, geographically located between Colombia and Peru, the major world producers of illegal drugs, makes the country a convenient place for negotiation. This information confirms Ecuador's classification as verging on becoming a mafia state.

Further proof that Ecuador is on verge of becoming a mafia state is furnished by the Mexican journalist Anabel Hernández, author of *The Man of Narcotics* (*Los señores de los narcos*). After arriving in Ecuador in late July, she claims that Ecuador is a warehouse of narcotics.[34] Drug cartels are flourishing and important illegal drug transactions are executed with no fear from the authorities.

Ortega's Nicaragua has followed in Chávez's footsteps in strengthening relations with drug cartels.[35] There are many indications that Nicaragua is on its way to becoming a mafia state. Crime cartels have been established in Nicaragua. These groups deal with money laundering, prepare cars with hidden compartments to carry drugs, and expand their social bases by further contributing to the weakening of state's institutions.[36]

Freedom of the press is of great concern in Venezuela and its ALBA partners. Journalists in these countries live in constant fear of being sued for criticizing their governments. When reporting bribery among government officials, a Nicaraguan journalist was accused of slander.[37] Election fraud is another issue of concern in these countries. Chávez was reelected as president by falsifying elections results. Ortega is labeled by opposition members as the unconstitutional president because his reelection was in violation of the supreme law of the land.

Like Venezuela, the ALBA countries have increased government interference in economic affairs and expropriated private enterprises, which has contributed to a sharp economic decline. A new small class emerged in these countries composed of those who benefited from the government's activities. In Nicaragua Ortega's extended family is in control of key economic positions. The weakening of government institutions enables a great deal of public funds to be directed toward those people who have close relations with their leaders.

All these countries violate human rights. As Ecuadorian President Correa expressed, in the forty-second assembly of the OAS, human rights are viewed differently by the ALBA states. These countries wish to withdraw from this organization and create a new Latin American system of human rights. This network would favor the interest of Latin America people and not the hegemonic power (indirectly referring to the United States).[38] The Venezuelan National Assembly rubber-stamped Chávez's proposal to withdraw from the CIDH.

Previously, it was mentioned that Fidel Castro advised Chávez that having nuclear weapons is of utmost importance in assuring his regime's survival. The Soviet Union did not allow its satellite states to develop nuclear weapons; Fidel Castro was not able to convince the Soviet Union to attack the United States with nuclear arms. Therefore, Israel's accusation that the Chávez regime is financially contributing to the Iranian nuclear military program is not surprising.[39] Iran promised Venezuela that it would share the technological advances it acquired in this field.

In spite of the fact that Chávez and Romanian President Nicolae Ceausescu lived in different historical periods, they displayed many similarities in their ideas and policies. Chávez's constant fear is that the United States will invade his country in order to depose his regime. During the Cold War, Ceausescu feared that the Soviet Union would interfere in his country, as it did in Czechoslovakia in 1969. He worried that his independent foreign policy would not be tolerated.

The former Romanian president was a strong advocate of the creation of a new international system where small- and medium-size countries would be free to follow their own policies without the interference of the superpowers. Romania adopted a defense law that called upon the entire population to participate actively in fighting an aggressor. The "popular war" doctrine, which was adopted in 1972, was aimed at deterring a possible Soviet invasion. Chávez adopted similar ideas, training the population in the event of a possible invasion. People at worksites were given military training so that they woud be able to defend their country.

The United States should be very concerned about the close cooperation between Chávez and the current Iranian regime. Both countries have exerted a strong effort to weaken the United States. Narcotic traffic is an important tool used by these countries to debilitate the American people. U.S. residents who purchase illegal drugs are indirectly contributing to the rise of terrorism directed against their own country. Hezbollah, an Iranian proxy, and the Colombian terrorist group FARC have been using narcotic funds to sponsor terrorism.

In this respect, it is important to note that on a visit to Bolivia in June 2012, Iranian President Mahmoud Ahmadinejad declared that his country intends to replace the DEA, which the Morales administration expelled in 2008.[40] This will assure that Hezbollah will be able to increase its narcotic trade, which is being protected by Iranian troops stationed in Bolivia.

An important factor that contributed to the rise of narcotic traffic in these countries was the successful effort by Colombia, with United States' help, to combat this malady. The drug cartels, recognizing the obstacles imposed on their activities moved to Venezuela and its ALBA partners. In these countries corruption is rampant and state institutions are weak, enabling the cartels to operate freely. This process precipitated the establishment of mafia states, where the drug cartels have become an integral part of the ruling elite.

The assassination of Venezuela's ambassador to Kenya, Julio Olga Fonseca, further confirms the thesis that the Chávez regime is a mafia state. The Kenyan police established links between Venezuela's diplomatic delegation and local and international narcotic traffic.[41] According to the International Committee of Narcotic Financing (*Junta Internacional de Fiscalización de Estupefacientes*) of the OAS, 50% of the illegal drugs reaching Europe pass through the Venezuelan-African route.[42]

Venezuelan Defense Minister Henry Rangel Silva was accused of being involved in narcotic traffic by the United States. The former Colombia President Álvaro Uribe declared that Venezuela has been converted into a paradise for narcotic traffic under the dictatorship of Hugo Chávez.[43] A report submitted by the international Financial Action Task Force, claimed that Bolivia remains on the "black list" and Ecuador is about to join it there; Venezuela also risks being added.[44] These countries are accused of money laundering and financing terrorism. Both the Colombian president's announcement and the international organization's report, further support Moisés Naim's concept of a mafia state. Venezuela and Bolivia, as previously mentioned, have already reached this stage. Ecuador and Nicaragua are on the verge of joining the list.

One byproduct of Venezuela's becoming a mafia state is the sharp increase in crime. Caracas has become one of the most violent cities in the world. In 2011 there were 17,000 assassinations in Venezuela.[45] From the time Chávez came to power in 1999 through the end of 2011, 136,000 people have been murdered in Venezuela; 90% of these cases have not been brought to trial.

The Makled affair is a classic example that proves that Venezuela is a mafia state. Makled, who bribed high officials from both the civilian and military sectors, was able to transfer illegal drugs from Venezuela to his final destinations. He established strong cooperation with terrorist groups such as FARC, Hezbollah, and others. Colombia eventually captured Makled, which led to the demand for his extradition by both the United States and Venezuela.

If Makled had been extradited to the United States, he could have delivered important information about Hezbollah, FARC, and Chávez's inner circle. His information could have been of great assistance in the war against terrorism. If Colombian President Juan Manuel Santos is right in his assertion that President Barack Obama did not object to Makled's extradition to Venezuela; a great error has been committed. As the judicial system in Venezuela is dependent on Chávez, Makled's fate will remain in the hands of the Venezuelan president. In a related manner, President Obama declared on July 10, 2012, that the Chávez regime represents no danger to the United States.[46] This is a misleading statement, which does not take into account the true nature of Chávez's regime.

Another factor that favors Chávez's reelection has been the strong dependency of Venezuelans on their state. These people, whose livelihoods depend on the regime, could vote for Chávez in order to perpetuate their benefits. In this respect, it is important to note that a Venezuelan analyst asked if there exists the possibility of democratic Chávezism .[47] The idea is to retain the dominant role of the state, but at the same time increase people's real participation in the government's decision-making process. The European Union can be used a model, where people enjoy many economic benefits, while democracy is maintained. However, the economic crisis in the European Union demonstrates the inefficiencies of this model. The only solution lies in the return of a real democracy and the establishment of a market economy. The oil revenues should be used to develop the country's infrastructure and not as a donation to foreign countries.

The death of Chávez in March 2013 raised the question of Venezuela's political future. Can Chávezism survive without Chávez? It is interesting to note that two scholars from opposing ideological spectrum, Moises Naim and Heinz Dietrich (a former Chávez's consultant) reply to the above question similarly. They claim that "Chavismo without Chávez can only exist for a short time."[48] Dietrich asserted that Chávezism without Chávez can remain only for one presidential term and then follow the path of traditional political parties, such as Democratic Action (Accion Democratica) in Venezuela.[49]

Dietrich claims that there exist a similarity between the situation in Venezuela, after the Chávez's last surgery (December 2012) and the situation in Russia after the death of Lenin. This comparison is also relevant after the death of the Venezuelan leader. In Russia two candidates were competing to replace Lenin, Stalin and Trotsky. In Venezuela Nicolas Maduro and Diosdado Cabello are contending to replace Chávez. Maduro, the candidate of the international left, believes in continuing Chávez's policies, especially the close relations with Cuba. Cabello, on the other hand, an ex-military officer, will prefer nationalistic policies benefiting Venezuela. Dietrich compares Cabello to Stalin.[50]

Reforms in Argentina's government introduced during Christina Fernandez's presidency may turn the country into a Chávez-style government. A notable example is the seizure of the oil company YPF from Spain Repsol. This further increases the importance of my research.[51] Her attempt to imitate Correa's Ecuador by introducing legislation to control the mass media is an additional step in this direction. Fernández called for establishing a new ethical law regulating the mass media.[52]

Comparison between Chávezism without Chávez and Argentina, after the death of Peron in 1974, enables us to shed an important light on Venezuela's political future. Argentina, in post-Peron era, was never able to abandon Peronism. The rule of law was replaced by strong influence of pressure groups, such as big labor, domestic producers and the corrupt political class. Christina Fernández's administration is a noted example.[53]

Chávezism in similar fashion will continue to influence the Venezuelan political system. However Peronism similar to Chavism has no clear demarcation lines. More than one interpretation can exist regarding the practical application of these ideologies. Therefore a split may be an important possibility. Chávez's brother Adan may follow in this path and form his own party.[54].

Mafia states, as Naim correctly asserts, have become a new entity in the international system. The inefficiencies of many governments, both in economics and institutional organizations, have produced a void that the drug cartels have been able to exploit. The huge sums of money earned enable those who are engaged in illegal drug activities to become an integral part of the ruling elite. In this respect, it is important to note that the forty-second Assembly of the Organization of American States proposed in June 2012 that the hemisphere countries declare that narcotic traffic and corruption constitute crimes against humanity.[55]

Chávez hoped that his political model would not only influence Latin America, but also impact the entire world. Reality, however, indicates that those leaders in Latin America, who followed market policies and even a pragmatic brand of leftist politics, have been more successful in developing their economies. Chávez's style is being replaced by a more moderate and market friendly version. Socialism of the twenty-first century lost its appeal because it failed at home.[56] Chávez's legacy is that his project, similar to the twentieth century Soviet Communism, failed. The selection of a new Pope Francis, with his emphasis on helping the poor, may further weaken Chávezism. The demise of Chávez's model allows the United States to rebuild its influence in South America.

Moisés Naim gave an accurate explanation regarding Chávez's electoral victory of October 7, 2012. He emphasized the "curse" of the Venezuelan oil wealth. The Venezuelan president is the head of a petro state and controls the legislative and judicial branches, the electoral tribunal, and the oil industry, which generated 98% of the country's wealth without any checks and balances. Defeating such an authoritarian leader becomes an impossible task.[57] Many Venezuelans are hoping that what occurred in Spain, after the death of the dictator Francisco Franco, might take place in their country.[58] The death of Chávez, many people are hoping, will increase this likelihood.

Notes

1   Chávez Wants 68% of Venezuelans to Live in Communes, Eluniversal.com, Junio 13, 2012

2   Morales convoca al mundo a nacionalizar riqueza de los estados, Hoybolivia.com, Mayo 17, 2012

3   Mas:versión de que el Estado es mal administrador es invento del imperialismo, Hoybolivia.com, Marzo 14, 2012

4   Venezuela: Judge Afiuni Before the United Nations Human Rights Council, hrw.org, March 8, 2011

5   Jesús Casique, Crecimiento, gasto público y libre mercado, Analitica.com, Diciembre 24, 2009

6   Andrés Volpe, Defendiendo el capitalismo y el libre mercado, Analitica.com, Diciembre 12, 2011

7   Trino Márquez, Venezuela ante a la crisis financiera internacional, Analitica.com, Diciembre 16, 2011

8   Ibid.

9   La inflación golpea con más fuerza a las familias pobres, Eluniversal.com, Julio 9, 2011

10 Calcula que escasez de aceite y leche en polvo alcanza a 42.3%, Eluniversal.com, Agosto 14, 2011

11 Mary Anastasia Ogrady, How to Break the Tyranny of Oil Wealth, The Wall Street Journal, January 27, 2013

12 Guillemo García, Colombia bate record de inversión, Analitica.com, Diciembre 19, 2011

13 Pinera en el G20: "No sigamos el camino irresponsable que llevó a muchos países a una crisis", Lanacion.cl, June 18, 2012

14   Yossi Greenstein, Fisher: gironot matmidim mitztabrim mashpiim leraa al zthmichat arucat tevah, nrg.co.il, April 19, 2012

15   Alexander Guerrero, Inflación 2011: Hecha en el socialismo, Analitica.com, Diciembre 26, 2011

16   El presupuesto de 2011 se ha incrementado en 67%, Eluniversal.com, Diciembre 21, 2011

17   El capitalismo agrava desigualdades sociales, pero es la mejor alternativa, Eluniversal.com, Enero 25, 2012

18   Bret Stephens, Europe's Brain-Dead Right, The Wall Street Journal, May 15, 2012

19   Crece dependencia económica de los venezolanos con el estado, Eluniversal.com, Enero 25, 2012

20   Piñera en el G20: "No sigamos el camino irresponsable que llevó a muchos países a una crisis," Op-cit

21   Ernesto Ottone, Chile: El problema es político, Analitica.com, Abril 4, 2012

22   Ilan Evyatar and Steve Linde, Economics: Reason to Be Cheerful, The Jerusalem Post, April 26, 2012

23   Sharon Udasin, US Expert: 'Israel Is Model for the World,' The Jerusalem Post, May 6, 2012

24   English.farsne.com, May 20, 2012

25   Sharon Udasin, Israel Should Be 'Test Bed' For Renewable Energy, The Jerusalem Post, February 24, 2012

26   Sharon Udasin, Top US Tour Israel's Renewable Energy Sites, The Jerusalem Post, June 21, 2012

27   El ambientalismo de la 'economía verde' es el nuevo colonialismo de sometimiento a nuestros pueblos y a los gobiernos anticapitalistas, Cambio, Bolivia, Junio 22, 2012

28   Asamblea Nacional aprobó acuerdo que respalda retiro de Venezuela de la CIDH, Agencia Bolivariana de Noticias, Mayo 9, 2012

29   John Lyons, Cocaine: The New Front Lines, The Wall Street Journal, January 14, 2012

30   En Bolivia hay carteles del narcotráfico colombianos, Hoybolivia.com, Junio 5, 2012

31   Sanbaria dice que encubren a funcionarios públicos narcos, Eldeber.co.bo, Mayo 21, 2012

32   Andrea Espinoza, Célula industria narcotráfico se expande en Ecuador, Elpais.com.es, Mayo 31, 2012

33   Opinión de HOY, Mas señales de creciente penetración del narcotráfico, Hoy.com.ec, Junio 28, 2012

34   Thalia Flores y Flores, Ecuador es una bodega de cocaína, Hoy.com.ec, Agosto 5, 2012

35   Luis Fleishman and Nancy Monges, Silence on Fraudulent Rule in Nicaragua- Detrimental to Latin America and U.S Interest, The American Report, December 1, 2011

36   Martha Vásquez, Celula narco en Nicaragua, Laprensa.com.ni, Junio 2, 2012

37   Roberto Mora, Periodista de la prensa acusado, Laprensa.com.ni, Enero 23, 2012

38   Los derechos humanos amenaza dividir a la OEA, Hoybolivia.com, Junio 4, 2012

39   Israel acusa a Chávez de financiar programa nuclear iraní, Hoybolivia.com, Junio 27, 2012

40   Irán retoma el papel de la DEA en Bolivia, Hoybolivia.com, Junio 20, 2012

41   Kenya: investigan tráfico de drogas en asesinato de diplomática, Hoy Bolivia.com, Agosto 7, 2012

42   Narcotráfico detrás de la muerte de Fonseca, Hoy.com.ec, Agosto 20, 2012

43   Uribe asegura que Chávez convirtió a Venezuela en paraíso del narcotráfico, Eluniversal.com, May 18, 2012

44   Bolivia no sale de lista de países observados por el GAFI, Los tiempos.com, Junio 26, 2012

45   Venezuela prohíbe la venta de armas a particulares, Elpais.com.es, Junio 1, 2012
46   Fernando Mires, Barack Obama y las elecciones en Venezuela, Analitica.com, Julio 16, 2012
47   Alfredo Michelena, Chavismo democrático, Analitica.com, Noviembre 10, 2011
48   Kejal Vyas and José De Córdoba, Venezuela (and Investors) Ponder Life Without Chávez, The Wall Street Journal, December 10, 2012
49   Gabriela Turzi Vegas, Dietrich: Chávezism without Chávez is actually possible, Eluniversal, December 31, 2012
50   Ibid.
51   Pierpaolo Barbieri, Pierpaolo Barbieri: A Lesson in Crony Capitalism, The Wall Street Journal, August 8, 2012
52   Fernández imita a Correa y pide ley de ética periodística, Hoybolivia.com, Agosto 10, 2012
53   Mary Anastasia O'grady, Venezuela After Chávez, The Wall Street Journal, March 6, 2013
54   Jorge G. Alvear Macías, Chavismo sin Chávez, Eluniverso.ec, Marzo 8, 2013
55   Proponen declarar al narcotráfico y corrupción delitos de lesa humanidad, Hoybolivia.com, Junio 5, 2012
56   Sara Schaefer Muñoz and Keith Johnson, With Chávez's Death Comes Grief for His Socialist Allies, The Wall Street Journal, March 7, 2013
57   José De Córdoba and Sara Schaefer Muñoz, Victory Tightens Chávez Grip on Power, The Wall Street Journal, October 8, 2012
58   Carlos Alberto Montaner, El triunfo de Chávez, Analitica.com, Octubre 9, 2012

Index